BURN
THE
SEA

BURN
THE
SEA

FLAME WARFARE, BLACK PROPAGANDA AND THE NAZI PLAN TO INVADE ENGLAND

JAMES HAYWARD

The
History
Press

First published 2016

The History Press
The Mill, Brimscombe Port
Stroud, Gloucestershire, GL5 2QG
www.thehistorypress.co.uk

British Library Cataloguing in Publication Data.
A catalogue record for this book is available from the British Library.

ISBN 978 0 7509 6598 9

Typesetting and origination by The History Press
Printed and bound in Great Britain by TJ International

CONTENTS

FOREWORD

In December 1968, the Soviet news agency Tass revealed to foreign correspondents in Moscow that Soviet newspapers would expose the intimate connection between the Secret Intelligence Service, MI6, and British editors and journalists. Sure enough, a series of articles appeared in *Izvestia* alleging that collaboration existed across a swathe of news organisations.

'Secret Service men are to be found in the sedate *Sunday Times* and the brash *People*,' the piece proclaimed. 'They control scientific publications in London, as well as provincial newspapers.' The supposed links between the spooks and the scribblers were trumpeted by Moscow as 'evidence not of the strength but of the weakness of the ideological concept of imperialism'.

Fleet Street's response to the article was derision. However this theory of collusion between military intelligence and the Fourth Estate is no more evident than in the reporting of a strange case which began on the coast of Suffolk and Norfolk in the autumn of 1940. Now James Hayward provides us with a textbook view of the still secret clandestine channels by which British intelligence agencies waged a psychological war across occupied Europe in 1940 and 1941. It is also a study of the fine art of the 'Big Lie' and people's willingness in wartime to believe almost anything they see in print.

As Senator Hiram Johnson famously said: 'The first casualty when war comes is truth.' Our attitudes to history are moulded by what we read in wartime, and what we read too often bears little resemblance to reality. Myths are shaped, facts suppressed.

One fact we can be sure of, however, is that Operation Sealion, the planned invasion of the British Isles in September 1940, never set sail, and by the close of

October had been indefinitely postponed. We might well ask, then, what was the truth behind the rumours of large numbers of bodies washed ashore on the eastern and then southern coasts of England that autumn? How did it come to pass that the *New York Times* – a paper of record – reported that as many as 80,000 German troops had drowned or burned to death while attempting an invasion? And why did a version of the story surface again as recently as 1992, leading to questions in the House of Commons and fresh allegations of conspiracy and cover-up.

Izvestia, no doubt, might have delivered a scornful opinion, had the Soviet Union not dissolved a year earlier. We will probably never know the whole truth about events in 1940. Strange things were happening within British intelligence during the early part of the Second World War. Once it was over, most people were keen for normal life to resume as quickly as possible, and were prepared to give the official version the benefit of the doubt. Few had the stomach for a long investigation. Fortunately James Hayward has continued to dig away at this fascinating mystery for more than two decades, and in doing so has uncovered a great deal more than it was ever intended the general public should see.

Phillip Knightley

INTRODUCTION:
THE SMOKE AND THE FIRE

At the beginning of September 1940, civilians in the small village of Crostwick, a few miles north of Norwich, were astonished by the sudden appearance of a seemingly endless convoy of army trucks and ambulances. The vehicles moved very slowly, their drivers sporting grim expressions. One let slip to Mrs Barnes, the wife of a local poultry farmer, that they were carrying the bodies of German soldiers washed up on the Norfolk coast, the grisly aftermath of a failed invasion attempt.

Later that same month, Gunner William Robinson, stationed at Herne Bay with 333 Coastal Artillery Battery, was sent south to Folkestone to take part in a macabre fatigue. Together with half a dozen other men, Robinson was instructed to search the beach between Hythe and St Mary's Bay for dead Germans. On the first day two such bodies were located, along with seven or eight more over the next two days. All were taken by truck to an isolated field west of New Romney, where they were discreetly unloaded behind a canvas screen. An NCO checked the corpses for identity discs and paybooks, which were then handed over to an officer. Robinson recognised the dead men as German soldiers, rather than Luftwaffe airmen or naval personnel, on account of their field-grey uniforms. Some appeared to be slightly burned from the waist down; all looked to have been in the water for some time.

By way of reward for discharging this unpleasant duty, Robinson and his colleagues drew a daily ration of twenty Woodbine cigarettes and additional pay of 2 shillings.

The bodies kept on coming. On 21 October the decaying corpse of a German infantry soldier, identified as Heinrich Poncke, was recovered from the broad shingle beach at Littlestone-on-Sea. His remains, like the bodies recovered by Gunner Robinson's party, were removed to New Romney for burial. Unlike the others, Poncke's posthumous arrival was widely reported by British newspapers and the BBC.

Were these casualties connected to the several long hospital trains observed in Berlin by American broadcaster William L. Shirer? On two consecutive days, 18 and 19 September, the future bestselling author of *The Rise and Fall of the Third Reich* spied large numbers of wounded German servicemen being unloaded at the Potsdamer and Charlottenburg yards. 'I picked up a conversation with a railway workman,' Shirer recorded in his earlier *Berlin Diary*. 'He said most of the men taken from the train were suffering from burns. I wondered where so many wounded could have come from, as the armies in the west had stopped fighting three months ago.'

But burned how? According to the *New York Times*, while attempting nothing less than a full-scale invasion of England. On 15 December 1940, the paper reported that there had already been two such attempts, and that in both instances 'the Nazis were literally consumed by fire'. French civilians in the occupied Channel ports estimated that as many as 80,000 German troops had perished. 'Hospitals in occupied France are filled with Nazi soldiers, all of them suffering from severe burns. Thousands of dead Germans have been washed ashore.' A wave of mutinies apparently followed in September, when many troops refused to face the 'burning sea' again on learning that a third attempt at invasion was planned.

Little wonder, then, that the chief press censor in Britain, Rear Admiral George Thomson, was eventually forced to concede: 'In the whole course of the war there was no story which gave me so much trouble as that of the attempted German invasion, flaming oil on the water and 30,000 burned Germans.'

It is established historical fact that Operation Sealion, the planned German invasion of the British Isles in September 1940, never set sail, and by the close of October had been postponed until the following spring. What, then, was the truth behind the rumours of large numbers of bodies washed ashore along the southern and eastern coasts of England that autumn? Had a German landing force met with disaster in the Channel? Could it really be true that the sea itself had been set on fire? Was Hitler's villainous scheme really derailed by a secret weapon still confined to the drawing board?

The myths and legends of the Second World War are legion, and often surprisingly durable. Indeed, conjecture that a German raiding force was thwarted by flame would again spark a small media firestorm in 1992, this time focused on the tiny Suffolk fishing hamlet of Shingle Street, a few miles north of Felixstowe.

Soon, what began as a minor local story exploded across national print and television media, with questions raised in the House of Commons, the early release of classified wartime files and robust denials of a conspiracy and cover-up by the Ministry of Defence.

In truth, the Shingle Street legend was nothing more than an echo of unavowable black propaganda from 1940, concocted and spread by MI6 and the Foreign Office at a time when Britain's 'finest hour' was fast becoming her darkest. 'The burning sea story was our first large-scale attempt at a "Big Lie" and it proved amazingly successful,' observed its creator, Major John Baker White of the Directorate of Military Intelligence. 'It was produced by people who were still amateurs at the game, and projected through a machine still far from complete. But it worked.'

Burn the Sea provides the first comprehensive account of the origin, circulation and astonishing longevity of the myth of the 'invasion that failed' in 1940, as well as its remarkable revival in 1992. It is also the story of the oddball Petroleum Warfare Department, the rusted death trap fireships of Operation Lucid, mysterious foreign bodies, adroit double-cross by MI5 and MI6, and the still secret clandestine channels by which British intelligence agencies waged expert psychological warfare across occupied Europe and the United States in 1940.

Finally, it is a study of a textbook exercise in the deceptive art of the Big Lie, and of boundless credulity undimmed by the passage of fifty years.

James Hayward
2016

I

SUBTERRANEAN ACTIVITIES

Attempts by the Petroleum Warfare Department and other agencies to 'set the sea on fire' are generally regarded as typical of the hurried improvisations of mid-1940, at a time when Britain expected to be invaded at any moment. In reality, however, the notion of combining the disparate elements of fire and water as a weapon of war is rooted in deep antiquity.

Dating from 500 BC, the earliest known military manual, *The Art of War*, written by the great Chinese general Sun Tzu, described the use of incendiary arrows (known as *Huo Chien*), while the Athenian philosopher-historian Thucydides detailed how the Spartans constructed great bellows to project flames derived from sulphur and pitch during the Peloponnesian War. An early form of flamethrower, the siphon was reputedly fixed to the prows of fighting ships in Ancient Greece. Legend also credits a miraculous compound called Greek Fire with the preservation of Constantinople through two Arab sieges. In his classical text *The Decline and Fall of the Roman Empire*, first published in 1776, Edward Gibbon described this Byzantine super-weapon thus: 'The principal ingredient was naphtha, or liquid bitumen, a light, tenacious and inflammatory oil, which springs from the earth and catches fire as soon as it comes in contact with the air.' Instead of being extinguished, naphtha was said to be nourished and quickened by the addition of water. 'Sand, wine or vinegar were the only remedies that could damp the fry of this powerful agent, which was employed with equal effect by sea or land, in battles or in sieges.'

By 1200, Greek Fire had fallen out of favour with naval tacticians and its chemical secret lost forever. Thereafter, the legend of liquid or maritime fire lay dormant, to resurface periodically like some exotic strain of malaria. The most celebrated resurrection came in 1588, when Sir Francis Drake launched fireships against the Spanish Armada off Gravelines, once again 'singeing the beard' of troublesome King Philip II. On land, during the American Civil War, a Major-General Quincy Gillmore besieged Confederate troops at Charleston with artillery shells charged with so-called Greek Fire, although the destructive effect of his 'villainous compound' was dwarfed by its value as propaganda.

The psychology of flame warfare is rooted in an elemental fear common to all humankind. Flame differs from most types of modern weaponry in that it is highly visible, whereas bullets, bombs and shrapnel make their presence known only by their sound – or sudden impact. 'On the first sight of flame in an attack the choice of two alternatives – to stand or to run – is vividly presented to a man,' offered a blunt appraisal issued by the War Office after the end of the Second World War. 'His deep-rooted fear of fire, combined with a feeling of helplessness to counter its searching effect, is more likely to induce him to run than would be the case if he were attacked with normal weapons, whose capabilities and limitations are known.'

No race or national grouping was immune. 'It was at one time contended that the Japanese stood up better to flame than did the Hun, but this was disproved. They liked flame no better than the Germans.'

In the twentieth century, the idea of unleashing blazing oil against a seaborne invasion of the British Isles was first mooted by Maurice Hankey as early as 1914. A key player in the British political establishment, and one who would go on to make the rare transition from civil servant to Cabinet minister, Hankey's interest in flame warfare stemmed from a classical education, and a well-thumbed copy of Gibbon's *Decline and Fall*. Following the outbreak of the First World War, Hankey, then an assistant secretary to the Committee of Imperial Defence, took it upon himself to commission a series of incendiary experiments using several of the 'best petroleum experts of the day'. Attempts to reformulate Greek Fire on an Admiralty pond near Sheerness met with abject failure ('Gibbon's prescription was quite useless'), but a fuel mixture capable of burning on the surface of open water was perfected by specialists at Chatham Dockyard, and tested successfully on the River Ore in Suffolk in December. Hankey had hoped to strike at the large German naval base on Heligoland, but found his lengthy report all but ignored by the powers that be. His biographer suggests that these imaginative proposals were dropped due to French fears over possible German reprisals. Within a year, however, Germany would introduce the flamethrower (*flammenwerfer*) to the gruesome arsenal of trench warfare, and unleash the first chlorine gas attacks on the Western Front.

Ultimately, the Admiralty concluded that burning oil was of little practical use as a maritime weapon, not least because the quantities required were too great, and its transport and delivery too problematic. Undeterred, Hankey continued to ponder several rudimentary mechanicals. On 9 October 1915, at the height of the disastrous Gallipoli Campaign, his diary records a letter to Commodore Roger Keyes conveying a suggestion that 'submarines should carry barrels of my Greek Fire lashed on, and let it go to burn up lighters etc. in the Dardanelles'.

At the end of the Great War in 1918, most armies consigned portable flame-throwers to the scrapheap, the War Office conceding some 'anti-morale' value, but judging them to be of little significance as a casualty producer. Poison gas was demonstrably far more effective, although in any event both these inhumane forms of killing would be prohibited under the Geneva Protocol of 1925. Nevertheless, the dream of firing the sea itself was not entirely extinguished. On 5 May 1937, Colonel C.E. Colbeck of the Royal Engineer and Signals Board addressed a memorandum to a Dr Wright of the Admiralty's Department of Scientific Research. Colbeck's idea was to 'block or burn' hostile landing craft by distributing petrol over the surface of the water at vulnerable beaches:

> Depending on the amount of petroleum used and, if necessary, continuity of supply from a controlled source, I believe that it would be possible to render beaches quite unapproachable over prolonged periods. Alternatively, wholesale and decisive casualties could be inflicted upon a landing force if they were caught at a really propitious moment.

Colonel Colbeck mooted several different delivery systems, including an underwater pipeline, as well as floating fuel tanks moored offshore. Evidently his memo aroused a degree of interest, for in December the director of Armament Development minuted that consideration was being given to the use of burning fuel on water at defended beaches, as well as ports and congested anchorages. In August 1938, the War Office asked the Admiralty to lend a helping hand to the Royal Engineers, who for reasons of 'secrecy and safety' were by then unable to continue work at Christchurch: 'They are trying to carry out experiments, mainly with the idea of keeping a minimum of men actually on the beaches while the bulk are in reserve. What they now want is to carry out a small experiment at sea, preferably off Weymouth.'

Sadly, nothing more is known of Colonel Colbeck's exploits. Nevertheless, as we shall see, a series of more or less identical proposals would be more thoroughly investigated following the establishment of the Petroleum Warfare Department in July 1940.

A separate scheme to attack enemy harbours with burning oil was investigated by the Admiralty off Shoeburyness in May 1939. Seventeen tons of petrol were discharged, and found to burn for five minutes after spreading over an area of 1,100 square yards. From this and other experiments, the Admiralty calculated that at least 80 tons of fuel were required to fire 10,000 square yards of open water for the same period. These discouraging statistics conspired to put the project on hold.

In Britain, as abroad, the outbreak of the Second World War in September 1939 brought about the rejuvenation of countless vivid, ingenious and often desperate schemes. During the Phoney War period, the Admiralty circulated a hopeful paper evaluating several methods of firing enemy waterways. The given target was the Rhine in the Ruhr industrial zone, with the stated object of destroying wharves, barges and goods in transit. Three different means of delivery were considered: aircraft, fuel-laden barges and pipelines leading from bulk tanks concealed in French territory. None held much promise. Air-delivered means, the report found, were impractical, since sufficient oil could not be lifted, while the other options underline all too clearly how unlikely the rapid conquest of France and the Low Countries by Germany was considered – just eight weeks before the unthinkable occurred.

If simple flotation seemed the method most likely to succeed, the tactics put forward bordered on farce. Having drifted downstream for three or four days, some 18,000 tons of fuel would be ignited in the target area by air-dropped incendiaries – assuming that no one in Germany happened to notice such a vast slick of oil. This was Phoney War indeed. 'Our action might be considered akin to unrestricted aerial bombing,' warned a tremulous marginal note. 'Before using oil, therefore, we should most carefully consider the effect on neutral opinion and possible retaliatory measures by the enemy.'

In the event, this unlikely plan was superseded by a more conventional scheme code-named Operation Royal Marine, in which fluvial mines were streamed into the Rhine. In the first week following the German assault in May, nearly 1,700 mines were released, causing some damage, although this minor Allied victory was swept away in a deluge of wider defeat. Nevertheless, the notion of floating flammable fuel down the Rhine was not entirely abandoned, and would be resurrected by the US Army as late as 1945.

Already, in November 1939, German seaplanes had set about seeding British ports and anchorages with state-of-the-art magnetic mines, resulting in the surprise loss of the destroyer HMS *Gypsy* outside Harwich harbour. Thirty of her crew, including the captain, were killed; some said the mine had been dropped by the same three-man Luftwaffe crew rescued by *Gypsy* earlier that day. Altogether, more than 200,000 tons of British shipping was lost to magnetic mines in November alone. The following month, a minute circulated by the Naval Intelligence Division offered a novel spin on Maurice Hankey's proposal for Greek Fire at Gallipoli in 1915:

> The American navy had been considering for some years the possibility of the Japanese using seaplanes to lay mines, as is now being done by the Germans. They had studied the best method of attack, and had reached the conclusion that neither bombs nor machine gun fire would be really effective. In consequence, they had carried out trials with a small submarine, into one of whose blowing tanks 20 to 30 tons of petrol had been placed. When the wind was onshore and favourable, the submarine blew her petrol tanks, and very shortly afterwards ignited the petrol by port fires or rockets. He assured me that in a very short time a very large area of the sea was on fire, and that it was a physical impossibility to put it out. No seaplane could possibly exist under such conditions.

Evidently some credibility attached to these generous American claims, for the following year similar trials were conducted with a training submarine, *L26*, operating from Gosport. Regrettably, the first trial, which took place on 16 April, yielded discouraging results. After diving to periscope depth, the submarine blew approximately 2 tons of petrol from her main ballast tanks, which was seen to spread rapidly on the surface. From this point onwards, however, failure was total. Two attempts at firing the slick using the underwater signal gun failed, one after the other. In desperation, the crew brought *L26* to the surface and tried to ignite the slick – by now over 100 yards long and 20 yards wide – with a bundle of burning rags tossed overboard from the conning tower. Once again, the oil refused to burn.

A second experiment, on 22 April, met with greater success. Chief amongst several modifications were four special incendiary candles manufactured at Woolwich Arsenal, while a submarine tender, HMS *Dwarf*, proceeded to sea towing a motley assortment of scrap seaplane debris in lieu of a real target. Eighteen tons of petrol were successfully released and ignited, producing a blaze measuring 800 square yards. Unfortunately, this conflagration was judged to be too brief to inflict anything more than superficial damage to metal-skinned seaplanes, such as the Heinkel 115. There was also the inconvenient fact that Luftwaffe pilots could hardly be relied upon to wait patiently for several hours until a British submarine arrived on the scene and released its flammable cargo.

Had the silent service managed to bag a German seaplane, the deliberate roasting of enemy aircrew might well have gifted Berlin a potent propaganda opportunity. Due to the appalling human toll inflicted by the 'frightfulness' of chlorine, phosgene and mustard gas on the Western Front between 1915 and 1918, chemical weapons had eclipsed incendiaries in post-war treaties. While gas accounted for some 5 per cent of hospital admissions on the Western Front in 1918, burns and scalds from all causes totalled only a tenth of that figure. Flamethrowers were specifically outlawed by the Treaty of Versailles and therefore vanished from most peacetime arsenals. Yet it was not until 1925 that incendiary weapons came under close international scrutiny via the Geneva Protocol, by which thirty-eight signatories – Britain and Germany included – concurred that the use in war of 'asphyxiating, poisonous or other gases, and of all analogous liquids, materials or devices' stood condemned in the 'general opinion of the civilized world'.

Deemed to be 'analogous' with chemical weapons under the terms of the Protocol, incendiary devices were proscribed by association alone – a sanction so vague as to negate any practical effect. The League of Nations Disarmament Conference of 1933 might conceivably have resolved these ambiguities, but the deteriorating political situation in Europe eroded faith in the new treaty, so the inadequate Geneva Protocol of 1925 would remain the most powerful restraint on chemical and biological warfare for several decades to come.

Flawed as the Protocol was, Britain understood as well as any other major power that flame warfare – like gas and unrestricted area bombing – amounted to an ungentlemanly act, and one likely to prompt retaliation in kind.

Two years after initiating chemical warfare in 1915, Germany launched a concerted effort to raze London using incendiaries (*brandbomben*) delivered by the world's first strategic bomber force, operating Gotha and Gigant aircraft from forward bases in Belgium. What the British military mind may have lacked in technical ingenuity, however, it more than made up for in psychological guile. During the First World War, imaginative British propaganda agencies proved masters of the Big Lie, graduating from romantic tales of protective bowmen and angels at Mons in 1914, and 80,000 Russian reinforcements passing through England 'with snow on their boots', to more lurid depictions of Hunnish depravity, such as the gory legend of the Crucified Canadian in 1915 and grisly reports of a corpse factory, where dead German soldiers were rendered down to produce domestic products such as glycerine and soap. Their opposite numbers were never able to match this mendacious dexterity, besides which, Germany regularly queered its own pitch by causing the deaths of innocent civilians, whether during the brutal march of the Kaiser's army through Belgium, the naval bombardment of east coast resort towns such as Hartlepool and Scarborough, the sinking of the passenger liner *Lusitania* or raining bombs on London from Zeppelins and Gothas. Each successive outrage served to cement the reputation of Germany as a barbarous nation populated by 'baby killers' and bestial Huns.

Berlin responded by sending warships to shell the country home of Lord Northcliffe, owner of *The Times* and the *Daily Mail*, and chief propagandist for the Allied cause. Besides killing the wife of his gardener, this 'desperate, disgraceful and criminal' bombardment also did for a mother and baby in nearby Broadstairs. Thus a misconceived attempt at assassination by shell served only to deliver another grisly own goal for the German side.

Following the Armistice in November 1918, the dark art of political warfare was left in the hands of the Foreign Office, along with the Secret Intelligence Service, MI6. Only in 1938 did the Committee of Imperial Defence, chaired by flame enthusiast Maurice Hankey, draw up plans for a dedicated Propaganda to the Enemy Department. Its first director was Sir Campbell Stuart, a veteran of First World War propaganda operations at Crewe House under Lord Northcliffe and subsequently employed as managing editor of both his flagship dailies. Funded through the Foreign Office, the skeleton section was allocated office space at Electra House on Victoria Embankment, and thus became known as Department EH.

The Munich Crisis in September 1938 saw the hasty preparation of several anti-Hitlerist leaflets, approximately 10 million of which were to have been dropped over Germany from lumbering Whitley bombers and small balloons. It was even envisaged that civilians in key target areas such as the Ruhr should receive twenty-four hours' written notice of actual air raids with actual bombs – a kindness that would also alert German anti-aircraft defences. In the event, no paper bombardment of the Reich took place, yet this dry-run was not without value, for on 4 October Department EH dispatched a note to the Air Ministry, where it crossed the desk of a seasoned permanent secretary named Sir Donald Banks.

Like Hankey, Banks was a career civil servant. As the first director-general of the Post Office several years earlier, he could claim credit for the introduction of the 999 emergency service, along with the speaking clock. According to the memo from Electra House, the 'sharpest and most urgent lesson' taught by the Munich dress rehearsal was the need for 'properly co-ordinated arrangements for the conveyance of information [propaganda] into enemy countries'. Evidently Sir Donald took careful note. Indeed, in July 1940 he would find himself appointed as the first director-general of yet another hush-hush organisation set up by Hankey: the Petroleum Warfare Department.

On 1 September 1939, two days before war was declared, Britain's several military intelligence services were mobilised alongside the rest of the armed forces.

The Ministry of Information was also activated, growing in four weeks from a staff of just twelve to a notorious 999. Fearing immediate destruction from the air, Department EH was hastily relocated from Central London to the rural surrounds of Woburn Abbey in Bedfordshire, known thereafter as Country Headquarters, with planning, editorial and other staff housed in the large riding school. There they were joined by a smaller team from Section IX, an MI6 subsection charged with 'unavowable' activities on foreign soil, chiefly sabotage, subversion and propaganda. Much of the latter was 'black' in character – misleading information, impossible to trace, and released in such a way that it appeared to originate within enemy countries or occupied territory. In order to engage the enemy more closely, EH also opened a European office in Paris, run by the celebrated actor and playwright Noël Coward.

Unfortunately, during the Phoney War period, work in Woburn and France appeared as moribund as the conflict itself. 'If the policy of His Majesty's government is to bore the Germans to death,' warned Coward from Paris, 'I don't think we have time.' The first nine months of the conflict saw EH concerned almost exclusively with the creation of ordinary 'white' material, aimed at 'good Germans' and delivered via air-dropped leaflets nicknamed 'bomphs' – 20 million of them in September 1939 alone. One such alleged that Göring had smuggled abroad a personal fortune of more than 30 million marks, and Himmler another 10 million. Meanwhile, obedient British newspapers ran insipid reports that the Siegfried Line had been constructed in haste from inferior concrete and that Luftwaffe aviation spirit was of a very low grade. Another early effort held that U-boat losses were far greater than Berlin cared to admit, with only two out of every three boats returning from patrols. German bombers, it was rumoured, were flown by women, as well as effeminate airmen with 'painted lips and enamelled nails'. One fantastical scheme put up in March 1940 proposed the projection of enormous magic lantern images over opposing German lines, conveying discouraging messages to reduce morale. None of these squibs seemed likely to end the war by Christmas.

Far more effective was the canard that many German tanks were merely dummies constructed from wood and canvas, although this fiction would be exposed in dramatic fashion on 10 May 1940, when a dozen all too real Panzer divisions punched an iron fist through the Allied front line. At Eben-Emael, a supposedly impregnable fortress guarding the Albert Canal in Belgium, German glider-borne troops used flamethrowers and shaped-charges to knock out hardened defences, quickly forcing the surrender of the enormous complex to just fifty-six men. Regrettably, this dazzling *coup de main* set the tone for the entire campaign, with Hitler's armoured spearhead reaching the Channel coast in less than a fortnight.

June saw the chaotic evacuation of the British Expeditionary Force from Dunkirk, followed in short order by the capitulation of France, the occupation of the Channel Islands and the ousting of the ageing Sir Campbell Stuart as head of Department EH. His successor, Hugh Dalton, was a senior Labour politician appointed minister of economic warfare by Winston Churchill after the formation of the coalition government. A month later, on 16 July, Dalton also took charge of another new body, the Special Operations Executive (SOE), a clandestine organisation tasked with co-ordinating acts of sabotage and subversion in territory now under Nazi occupation, thereby 'setting Europe ablaze'.

With this incendiary mission in mind, it seems only fitting that two of those present at the original SOE summit meeting on 1 July were Lord Hankey, veteran advocate of flame, and Geoffrey Lloyd, lately appointed to the post of petroleum secretary. Prior to the outbreak of war, Hankey had retired from government service after twenty-six years of faithful service and briefly served as a director of the Suez Canal Company. In 1939, with a new conflict looming in Europe, this supremely competent and trustworthy administrator was recalled to Whitehall by Neville Chamberlain, hastily ennobled, and as minister without portfolio tasked with undertaking an unprecedented review of the secret service, including MI5, MI6 and GCHQ. Within the crepuscular world of military intelligence, therefore, Lord Hankey became once more an omnipresent mandarin, whose broad purview ranged from propaganda to signals interception and the double-agent system, and even the foundation of the Special Operations Executive. Not for nothing would his three-part biography be titled *Man of Secrets*.

Less conveniently, Hankey harboured grave reservations about the new prime minister, who returned the compliment by excluding him from the inner War Cabinet formed in May. 'Lord Hankey had been, and still was, a remarkable man,' wrote John Cairncross, his private secretary in 1940:

> He was highly regarded for his quiet and modest manner, and for his ability in military matters, since he was almost alone in the Cabinet in having the experience needed to stand up to Churchill in this field. His real ability lay in running the various Cabinet committees with tact and efficiency.

Unfortunately, it later transpired that John Cairncross was a Soviet mole, and may have leaked details of the Western atomic bomb programme, code-named the Manhattan Project. Fortunately, Hankey enjoyed a firmer friendship with Major Desmond Morton, Churchill's personal intelligence advisor, and Geoffrey Lloyd, the new petroleum secretary. A poised Old Harrovian blessed with 'volcanic' levels of energy, according to Hankey, Lloyd had entered Parliament in 1931 as the Conservative member for Birmingham Ladywood, and for several years acted as private secretary to Stanley Baldwin. A lifelong bachelor, noted for his dapper dress sense, it was said that on first taking office in Whitehall, Lloyd insisted on new carpets to match his wallpaper. The two men quickly found a common purpose, as Hankey later recalled:

> I learned from Lloyd that we had very large quantities of petroleum products. All the oil that would have gone to Norway, Sweden, Denmark, Holland, Belgium and France had been coming to this country and our storage was so full that ships have had to be kept waiting, both at home and abroad. Talking it over together, we came to the conclusion that some means should be found for using our surplus oil for defensive purposes.

By the end of May 1940, as the BEF was plucked from the beaches of Dunkirk, the prospect of a German invasion of the British Isles appeared suddenly all too real. In correspondence with the Home Secretary, Sir John Anderson, Hankey advocated a literal scorched earth policy, urging that Britain's 'vast' stocks of petroleum should not only be denied to the enemy, but used as an obstacle. On dry land, he proposed, petrol stores in wayside garages could be emptied to flood roads as enemy vehicles approached. Other bold ideas included fireships, aerial spray from bomber aircraft, petrol in submerged barrels moored off likely landing beaches and arrangements for 'rough storage' on the coast, with 'runnels or gutters leading to the sea by which massive quantities could be released on to the water and ignited.'

Concurrently, Geoffrey Lloyd invited the several oil companies which made up the Pool Board to consider ways and means of pitting burning fuel against enemy armour. Indeed, so dire were the straits that Hankey even looked into the possibility of disabling marauding Panzer tanks with great belches of flammable town gas. Curiously, in their haste to discover ways of roasting the enemy with surplus fuel, no one thought to revisit the research undertaken by Colonel C.E. Colbeck and his Sapper team at Christchurch between 1937 and 1938, whose object in burning oil on water had been to block or burn landing craft at vulnerable beaches. More surprising still, Colbeck's experiments were ignored even after the foundation of the Petroleum Warfare Department on 9 July, an unofficial development steered by Hankey, Lloyd and Desmond Morton. It would be Colbeck's fate instead to sit out the war on a series of obscure Royal Engineer and Signals Board committees.

Hankey referred to subversive operations, dirty tricks and other forms of clandestine warfare as 'subterranean activities'. In reviewing arrangements within the Secret Intelligence Service (MI6), Hankey favoured leaving propaganda to Department EH and the Foreign Office. In the event, EH soon found itself folded into the Special Operations Executive, with elements of EH becoming SO1, and rival Section IX of MI6 absorbed into SO2 – albeit with considerable overlap, and no little friction. The following year EH and SO1 would be reorganised yet again as the Political Warfare Executive (aka the Political Intelligence Department), while the unreliable commander of IX, Major Lawrence Grand, was quietly sidelined. Hankey's wide-ranging review had already flushed out that the maverick major was spending the astronomic sum of £11,000 a month on subversion and propaganda, chiefly in Eastern Europe. Closer to home, an attempt by Section IX to sabotage Swedish iron ore supplies to Germany ended in embarrassing fiasco and eight years' hard labour for the agent concerned. 'To pit such a man against the German General Staff and the German military intelligence service,' declared one observer of Grand, 'is like arranging an attack on a Panzer division by an actor mounted on a donkey.'

Fortunately, the production of propaganda material at Woburn in due course became every bit as streamlined and efficient as it had been at Crewe House during the First World War. Set up in July 1940, the Underground Propaganda Committee (UPC) gathered on Friday evenings to consider ideas put forward by various interested bodies, including individual service departments as well as MI6, the FO and the Directorate of Military Intelligence. 'Black' rumours came to be known as sibs, a term derived from the Latin verb *sibilare*, meaning to whisper or hiss. Final approval for political sibs lay with the Foreign Office, while military whispers were placed before the Joint Intelligence Committee (JIC). Those which stood approved were then returned to the UPC before being passed on to MI6 and SOE for circulation abroad, for the most part by word of mouth.

One of the few detailed UPC documents to be declassified and released to The National Archives at Kew confirms:

The object of [black] propaganda rumours is to induce alarm, despondency and bewilderment among the enemies, and hope and confidence among the friends. It should be emphasised that the method of dissemination is essentially oral, and this is the most difficult form of propaganda for enemy security services to deal with … Rumours are therefore the most covert of all forms of propaganda. Although the enemy may suspect that a certain rumour has been started by the British government, they can never prove it.

Departments and individuals whose sibs were taken up were expected to monitor their effectiveness once released, and in due course report back to the Committee. A set of 'important rules' soon emerged:

1   A good rumour should never be traceable to its source.
2   A rumour should be of the kind which is likely to gain in the telling.
3   Particular rumours should be designed to appeal to particular groups.
4   A particular rumour should have a particular purpose. The objectives of rumour-spreading may be many, but a single rumour cannot be expected to serve more than one of them.
5   Rumours are most effective if they can be originated in several different places simultaneously and in such a way that they shuttle back and forth, with each new report apparently confirming previous ones.

One of those charged with hoodwinking the enemy during the tense, confused summer of 1940 was Major John Baker White. A veteran of the British radical Right, and a Conservative MP post-war, White claimed to have worked in a circus as a youth in order to gain a wider knowledge of human nature. Whatever insights he may have gained among the clowns and acrobats were subsequently applied to very different ends as a director of the Economic League, a shadowy private bureau funded by British industry to monitor communist and trade union activity during the 1930s. Together with a cabal of like-minded anti-communists, White also founded a self-styled counter-subversion cell known as Section D, although this volunteer group should not to be confused with the MI6 unit of the same name. Before war broke out, White openly expressed admiration for Hitler on a number of occasions, an error of judgement which would nevertheless provide a useful *entré* into Nazi Germany, where he apparently acted as an amateur spy before being obliged to quit the Reich in April 1939 – in something of a hurry. 'A somewhat varied career in the underworld of international politics,' as White himself put it. 'The job was political warfare, and I had been in the game since 1923.'

Never a member of MI6 or MI5, White began the war as a territorial officer in the London Rifle Brigade, only then being transferred to a small subsection of the Directorate of Military Intelligence charged with the delivery of disinformation to enemy troops. Their task became all the more urgent after Dunkirk and the Fall of France. 'Our task was not to stop the Germans finding out about the real state of our defences,' he wrote in *The Big Lie*, a fascinating memoir published in 1955:

That was the job of the security agencies. What we had to do was to create in the minds of the German High Command, and of Hitler himself, a completely fictitious picture of what they would have to face if they launched an invasion attempt. A picture of a powerfully armed Britain, and above all armed with new weapons of terrible destructive power. We had to put over the Big Lie.

The Big Lie proposed by Major John Baker White, and subsequently approved by the JIC, would be the brazen fiction that a new generation of British boffins had triumphed where Hankey had failed in 1914, and were now able to burn the sea with modern Greek Fire.

2

ROASTING THE NAZIS

On 4 June 1940, Winston Churchill rose to his feet in the House of Commons to deliver one of the most memorable speeches of the entire war. 'There has,' he pronounced gravely, 'never been a period in all these long centuries when an absolute guarantee against invasion could have been given to our people.' In the wake of the hasty Dunkirk evacuation, Britain possessed just 333 anti-tank guns, and even fewer modern tanks capable of meeting German panzers on equal terms. Nevertheless, the new prime minister chose to close his speech with a stirring call to arms: 'We shall defend our island, whatever the cost may be. We shall fight on the beaches, we shall fight on the landing grounds, we shall fight in the fields and in the streets, we shall fight in the hills. We shall never surrender.'

As Churchill sat down, he is said to have muttered to James Stuart, the chief whip: 'God knows what with. Broken bottles, I suppose.'

Or flame traps, and burning oil. Following the fall of France, petroleum warfare rapidly became a *strategie du jour* in certain quarters. That same month, the Petroleum Secretary, Geoffrey Lloyd, circulated a paper, *Use of Oil for Offensive and Defensive Purposes*, summarising methods of deployment on land and water. 'There is no doubt that use might be made of burning oil in defence against invading troops,' urged Lloyd. 'Barrels containing oil mixture and an igniting device might be used with advantage in defiles to roll down a hill at approaching tanks, or to be fired electrically as the tanks near the barrels.'

Presenting his findings to Lord Hankey on 12 June, Lloyd urged that an experimental programme be undertaken by suitably qualified experts, with technical assistance from the Pool Board. Coincidentally, the popular thriller writer Dennis Wheatley also proposed several forms of flame warfare in a 12,000-word essay on Resistance to Invasion, written late in May. Encouraged by his wife, Joan, who worked at MI5, Wheatley submitted his unsolicited paper to the War Office. Among several recommendations were the removal of signposts, an idea that was soon adopted, and a 230-mile barrier of fishing nets to foul the propellers of German landing craft, which was not. Wheatley also predicted that in the battle to come, Britain's 'most important ally' would be fire, by virtue of fireships moored a mile or so offshore, and the spread of flaming oil to ignite enemy craft.

These proposals evidently made waves, for soon after the author of *They Found Atlantis* and *The Devil Rides Out* was given a place on the Joint Planning Staff. Since Lord Hankey had been dropped from the new War Cabinet, it was left to Major Desmond Morton to address a note on flame to Churchill, who had by then been prime minister for six eventful weeks. An SIS officer since 1919, Morton had acted as his personal intelligence advisor for more than a decade and was now rewarded with a seat on the Security Executive. 'Mr Geoffrey Lloyd told me today that he has so much petroleum in the country or held in store in tankers in America that he did not know what to do with it,' Morton told Churchill on 27 June. '[He is] very anxious to try and get some of it used offensively against the enemy. He has collected two or three Sapper officers and they are considering ways and means.'

Morton favoured sailing fireships into ports under German control, to be detonated in situ with 'most pleasing' results. Somewhat sceptical, the prime minister demurred until Professor Frederick Lindemann, his quixotic chief scientific adviser, felt ready to deliver an opinion. On land, it was pointed out, large volumes of smoke might seriously hamper the defence. Churchill also declined to authorise the establishment of a dedicated 'petroleum warfare executive', as Hankey proposed, fearing duplication of effort.

In any event, the PM considered poison gas more expedient than Greek Fire. 'I do not understand this squeamishness about poison gas,' Churchill had written as far back as 1919, when permission was granted for the RAF to use chemical weapons against 'recalcitrant Arabs' in Iraq. 'It is sheer affectation to lacerate a man with the poisonous fragment of a bursting shell and to boggle at making his eyes water by means of lachrymatory gas.' Then the Secretary of State for Air, Churchill declared himself strongly in favour of using gas in order to spread 'a lively terror' amongst 'uncivilised tribes'. The Italian air force followed this sorry colonial example in Abyssinia; during the Allied intervention in Russia, British DH9 bombers also dropped arsenical smoke generators on Bolshevik positions at Archangel. Although the feeble Geneva Protocol of 1925 barred signatories from initiating chemical attacks, aggressed nations reserved the right to reply in kind. Hence, in 1939 Britain still held reserves of mustard and phosgene amounting to several hundred tons.

Had Hitler launched an invasion attempt during the summer of 1940, liquid mustard would have been sprayed over beaches from Broadstairs to Dungeness by a variety of aircraft types from Bomber Command. 'Enemy forces, crowded on the beaches, with the confusion inevitable on first landing, would make a splendid target,' offered General Sir John Dill, chief of the Imperial General Staff. 'Besides gas spray, contamination of beaches and defiles by liquid mustard would have a great delaying effect.' Unfortunately – or fortunately – Plan Y raised many practical difficulties. According to one estimate, the opening hours of Operation Sealion might have seen approximately 3,000 aircraft enter an area above the Dover Strait just 30 miles square and 15,000ft high. Given this mighty collision of air power, in which the Luftwaffe could maintain local superiority, losses among the vulnerable Lysanders, Hampdens, Blenheims and Wellingtons attempting low-spray operations would have been grievous. As for the chances of RAF pilots holding course to discharge sustained and accurate clouds of gas, these would have increased only in inverse proportion to their chances of survival. As T.E.A. Spong, a Lysander pilot with 225 Squadron, later recalled: 'It was death or glory stuff – and not much of the latter.'

In the meantime, Geoffrey Lloyd gathered together a small team consisting of several Sapper officers borrowed from the Army Petroleum Division, as well as Colonel Henry Medlicott, lately of the British Expeditionary Force and now seconded to advise on security at oil installations. 'I obtained the services of two young cadets just returned from France and started work at once,' Medlicott wrote later. 'It seems farcical now to look back at our plans, but it must be remembered that about one division – and that a Territorial division – stood between the Channel coast and the City of London.'

Neither of the officer cadets, Henry-Hodges and Sinclair, boasted much in the way of relevant know-how. Both were public school educated linguists fresh from an ill-starred foray into occupied France organised by MI(R), a subsection of the Directorate of Military Intelligence, whose brief also extended to irregular warfare. In June the pair were put ashore near Étaples with Colonel Alan Warren of the Royal Marines, hoping to locate and rally stragglers from the BEF, large numbers of whom were believed still to be at large in France. Churchill later described this early commando mission as a 'silly fiasco', and with good reason. After three weeks behind enemy lines not a single British soldier had been located, and once radio contact was lost the party was obliged to row home in a stolen dinghy, to be rescued in a state of disarray by the Dungeness lightship. Whether the two cadets were assigned to what would soon become the Petroleum Warfare Department as tyro intelligence officers, or merely under a cloud, is hard to determine.

The first flame warfare conference was held on the Kent coast at Deal on 29 June, with Lord Hankey presiding. Besides Geoffrey Lloyd and Colonel Medlicott, delegates included representatives from the military, Home Office and Petroleum Board, whose discussions ranged from exploding fuel drums to the flaming of roads and 'defiles' from concealed tanks, and setting the sea on fire off Shoeburyness using 'hulks and barrels'. On 1 July, the group met again, this time learning that the Petroleum Board possessed some hundreds of surplus bulk storage tanks which could be mounted on trucks to create 'mobile land barrages'. It was also agreed that new mixtures should be developed which gave off a minimum of smoke and burned more slowly.

'It is not a question of manufacturing apparatus,' Hankey wrote enthusiastically to Churchill, 'only of organising means. Give us the word, and we believe that something substantial can be done to develop a weapon to supplement the means of defence at present available.'

One such existing apparatus was the fearsome Livens Projector. In 1917, Colonel William Howard Livens, a Royal Engineer and chemical warfare specialist, had devised a large mortar-like weapon capable of discharging a drum of liquid phosgene over enemy positions. This, its inventor calculated, would reduce the cost of killing Germans to just 16 shillings apiece. The colonel also developed the Livens Large Gallery Flame Projector for use on the opening day of the Somme offensive, albeit with limited effect. Long retired by 1940, Livens now turned his hand to adapting his deadliest device to launch 5-gallon drums of petrol instead of poison gas. Field trials near Hythe were nothing if not eventful. 'While Livens was explaining how it was intended to deposit these flaming comets upon a beach some 200 yards away,' an observer noted, 'something established contact between two bare wires and the most remarkable display of projection fireworks took place.' By a stroke of luck there was faulty connection to the battery of drums in the middle of which the observers stood. 'The consensus was that it was safer to stand on the drums themselves than anywhere else in the neighbourhood.'

The flame mortar scheme was not pursued, although a Home Guard unit attached to the London Midland and Scottish Railway constructed a large catapult capable of hurling 4-gallon drums over a short distance. Drums also featured in an Admiralty scheme to foil enemy seaplane landings, still a high priority so far as the Senior Service was concerned. On the Norfolk Broads, an RNVR sub-lieutenant named Friggens developed the 'Wroxham Roaster', designed around a chain of submerged barrels that a vigilant operator detonated by remote control. While functional, however, the device was of little practical value, the blaze produced being brief and highly localised.

Conventional incendiary bombs aside, the Royal Air Force displayed little interest in flame prior to the development of gelled-fuel weapons such as napalm. Fortunately, there was no shortage on initiative at unit level. Early in June 1940, Pilot Officer Malders of 13 Squadron (operating Lysanders from Hooton Park in Cheshire) submitted several suggestions for 'flame-throwing aeroplanes' to the Air Ministry. The proposed weapon, tail-mounted and dual-purpose, was meant to provide a means of escape for aircraft bounced from behind, and could also be used against ground targets in low-level attacks. After some discussion, the idea was rejected on the grounds that 'the flamethrower would be a most uneconomic weapon, and not be easy or pleasant to handle'.

In Britain the development of man-pack flamethrowers (a German innovation) had lapsed after 1918, and research was begun again only in December 1938, when the General Staff formulated a requirement for a tank-mounted projector. Such records of 1914–18 development as could be unearthed were of little use, with the result that technicians were faced more or less with a blank page. By June 1940, both the Marsden and Harvey models had been favourably evaluated, and later the Lifebuoy model came to be widely adopted. Limited numbers of a wheeled Home Guard flamethrower were also issued to eager platoons, as well as other devices of dubious local origin. One, produced by an eager unit in Durham, discharged flammable dry-cleaning fluid through a stirrup pump. Another, the Nuttall, consisted of a 45-gallon drum perched on the chassis of an Austin 7 car, and was said to be capable of throwing a flame 75ft for three minutes. Had these contraptions been trundled into combat, it is not difficult to predict on which side casualties would have been heaviest.

After due consideration of these and other schemes, on 1 July the deputy chiefs of staff cautiously concluded that blazing oil might have some limited military application. It was agreed that the War Office would evaluate operations on land and in defence of beaches, while the Admiralty scrutinised ships and ports. The following day, 2 July, Hitler issued preliminary orders for a possible invasion of the British Isles. 'A landing in England is possible,' it was stated, 'providing that air superiority can be attained and certain other necessary conditions fulfilled.' Crucially, these preparations would be made on the basis that invasion was merely an option, rather than a declaration of intent. Thanks to the Enigma codebreakers at Bletchley Park, this worrisome development was known to British intelligence within hours, although as yet there was no indication of where or when landings might occur. With the Channel Islands already occupied, some guessed wildly that Iceland or the Shetlands would be next to fall.

During this period, German deception activity was remarkably effective. 'Secret Service reports from Norway make it clear that invasion is being prepared from there as well as other quarters,' Churchill's secretary, John Colville, noted in his diary. 'A feint will be made against the east coast, but the real attack will be from the West.' Reports published in American newspapers claimed that Germany now possessed 25,000 combat aircraft ready to support an invasion, backed up by new guns with a range of 40 miles. 'Troop-carrying aeroplanes, trailing long tails of troop-carrying gliders, will also be used.' Mentions of the German invasion fleet were fewer in number, not least because Hitler did not yet have one. Instead, the Nazi leadership hoped to intimidate Britain into suing for peace. Churchill, conversely, maintained that the 'great invasion scare' served a useful purpose, in that it kept 'every man and woman tuned to a high pitch of readiness'.

On 3 July, as the Royal Navy pummelled the Vichy French Fleet at Oran, Geoffrey Lloyd and Colonel Medlicott staged an interim firework display at Dumpton Gap, a secluded cove near Broadstairs. Flanked by low chalk cliffs, the site seems to have been chosen on account of the access point, a narrow defile some 12ft wide – a feature perfect for flooding with petrol, though sadly absent from most landing beaches. Several devices were tested, including a rudimentary road flame trap, an exploding steel barrel containing 50 gallons of a petrol–gas-oil mixture and a catapult. Smaller 2-gallon drums fitted with time fuses were rolled over the cliff edge and an old car filled with cans of petrol and explosives before being driven across the sand towards a dummy tank. Besides keeping the local fire brigade busy, however, the festival of fire served only to demonstrate the effectiveness of flooding small areas of dry land from bulk supplies.

The extemporised trial at Dumpton also excited 'some inquisitiveness' on the part of German aircraft, and Lloyd would later claim to have been dive-bombed. Indeed the catastrophic fates which befell fresh endeavours to revive Greek Fire in east Kent seem almost biblical. 'An attempt to flood the sea with a mixture and set fire to it was abortive owing to the interruption of the tests by bombing, a heavy thunderstorm, and the receding tide.'

Medlicott's team conducted fresh trials at Dymchurch on 6 July, this time in full (and no doubt deliberate) view of the enemy-occupied Channel coast. It was here that Colonel Livens almost roasted several observers, in doing so confirming the utility of piped fuel to stop Nazi tanks. 'A street is, of course, a defile,' reasoned Hankey. 'In some places, particularly seaside places, it might be worth it to risk some loss [of property] by fire to destroy enemy AFVs.' Should the invader penetrate as far as the suburbs, it was suggested that garden lawn sprinklers could be charged with petrol. Meanwhile, the Joint Intelligence Committee circulated a memorandum on 'Action designed to disconcert the Enemy in relation to the Invasion of the United Kingdom'.

Four days later, an interim report confirmed that 'very large' quantities of fuel were required to produce effective results. Delivery by aircraft was therefore impractical, while fireships required a highly concentrated target. Flame barrages on landing beaches presented difficulties in terms of bulk storage and continuous supply, while an 'offshore mine-field of oil drums' was judged impractical by reason of blaze scale and timely ignition. On land, only Static Flame Traps and Molotov cocktails could be pressed into service immediately. 'In conclusion we have not yet got any satisfactory method of burning oil effectively on a grand scale. We can make use of it in various ways to produce powerful local effects. The War Office should continue to press on with experiments.'

The War Office also pressed ahead with Plan Y. Overruling objections from some quarters that Britain would throw away an 'incalculable moral advantage' by initiating chemical warfare, Churchill continued to press for the 'prompt drenching' of Nazi invaders with poison gas as soon as they landed. By the end of the first week in July, existing stockpiles of mustard – some 450 tons – had been dispersed around the country, including 6,000 Livens drums and a quantity of artillery shells. The main effort, however, would be delivered from the air. Come *Der Tag*, Lysanders, Wellingtons, Battles and Blenheims operating from a dozen airfields between Grangemouth in Scotland and West Malling in Kent would press home repeated low-level attacks with spray tanks and gas bombs, almost certainly with crippling losses. In theory, Bomber Command possessed sufficient stocks to spray a strip '60 yards wide and some 4,000 miles long'. In practice, during the summer of 1940 supplies of mustard and phosgene would have been exhausted after a single day of drenching.

At least one senior RAF commander showed an interest in flame as well as chemical agents. Described as a 'pretty shrewd Rhodesian' in a letter sent to Hankey at the end of July, Air Vice Marshal Arthur Harris was then in charge of 5 Group – a dozen squadrons of vulnerable Handley Page Hampden bombers, for the most part relegated to mine-laying operations, known obliquely as 'gardening'. As well as using redundant ships charged with pressurised liquid oxygen against the invader, the man later infamous as 'Bomber' Harris also declared himself in favour of 'dropping light containers of petrol in quantity' into the sea, thus putting up 'a concentration on the surface of the water which would present an effective barrier to small craft coming in to beach'.

Trials were put in hand during August and a 45lb incendiary device developed to ignite patches of oil on water. This was essentially a 5-gallon fuel can holding

4½ gallons of petrol and 2 pints of a special ignition mixture, fitted with a fabric streamer to provide stability before impact. At the end of the war, Harris would claim that Hitler was warned off invasion only by the 'wholesale destruction' of landing barges in the Channel ports by Bomber Command – a claim as controversial as the man himself. However, there is no evidence that the 45lb petrol bomb was used operationally in 1940 and development seems to have been abandoned the following year.

At the urging of Hankey and Lloyd, the task of integrating flame weapons into a conventional defensive plan was now entrusted to an entirely new organisation: the Petroleum Warfare Department, or PWD. Initially the core team consisted of the keen band of arsonists gathered together by Colonel Henry Medlicott, although at the beginning of July Sir Donald Banks took over as director-general. A First World War veteran and career civil servant, Banks had been the first director-general of the Post Office in 1934, then a permanent undersecretary at the Air Ministry. After rejoining the army in 1939, Banks served again with the BEF in France, this time as deputy adjutant general, and had attained the rank of brigadier by the time he was nudged sideways into flame warfare.

Despite early opposition from Churchill, by the end of the year the staff of the Petroleum Warfare Department had swollen to sixteen, occupying office space within Westminster House on Dean Stanley Street. Its personnel included representatives from all three armed services, as well as a trio of electrical engineers from the Post Office and specialists seconded from every major commercial oil company, including Esso, Agwi, Shell, Shell-Mex, BP, Scottish Oils and Anglo-Iranian. The PWD initially trialled fuels and mixtures at the premises of Burt, Boulton & Haywood at Belvedere, on the Thames near Erith, but soon relocated to Moody's Down Farm near Sutton Scotney in Hampshire. Lord Hankey had envisaged a dynamic petroleum equivalent of the chemical warfare companies, flaming the Hun on the beaches and landing grounds, filling every last ditch with fire and brimstone. Alas, during the fevered invasion summer of 1940 the department's brief was rather more limited, being largely restricted to the provision of advice on different combustible mixtures. Responsibility for developing flame-throwing hardware remained with the three fighting services, along with the armament research section of the Ministry of Supply.

On 16 July, just a week after the PWD officially came into being, Hitler issued Directive No. 16, instructing his army, navy and air force to prepare a cross-Channel invasion of the British Isles. The initial order proposed surprise seaborne landings on a broad front between Ramsgate and the Isle of Wight, supported by paratroops, with the Luftwaffe acting as flying artillery. Preparations were to be completed by the middle of August, mastery of the skies having first been wrested from the RAF by more than a thousand modern fighter aircraft. This absurdly ambitious plan was freighted with a curiously flabby code name: Operation Sealion. Hitler stated: 'Since England, in spite of her hopeless military situation, shows no signs of being ready to come to an understanding, I have decided to prepare a landing operation and, if necessary, to carry it out.'

Three days later, to members of the Reichstag gathered at the Kroll Opera House in Berlin, Hitler broadcast a grandiloquent final peace offer, underpinned by the wishful prediction that Churchill would soon up sticks and flee to Canada. *Das Engellandlied*, a campaign song specially composed by Nazi bandleader Herms Niel, found rapid popular success, in particular the ominous premonitory lines '*denn wir fahren, denn wir fahren, denn wir fahren gegen Engelland*'.

The Führer himself was more circumspect. The caveat 'if necessary' in Directive No. 16 again tends to confirm that Operation Sealion was in large part an exercise in brinkmanship, intended to force Britain to sue for peace long before Hitler's as yet non-existent invasion armada put to sea. A Big Lie, in fact. 'The whole German machine seems to have concentrated on defeating us through propaganda,' observed Guy Liddell, the counter-espionage director of MI5, having correctly deduced that Berlin was flying a kite. Within days, the German Embassy in Washington made it known that draft terms were available for inspection. In a paper on The Continuation of the War Against England, Hitler's chief of staff, General Alfred Jodl, confirmed that 'political measures' were to be preferred over blockades, bombers and a jerry-built fleet of invasion barges. 'A landing in England should not have as its objective the military conquest of the island, an objective which can be obtained by the Luftwaffe and the German Navy. Its sole purpose should be to provide the *coup de grace*.'

Hitler also believed that a diplomatic solution would avoid the disintegration of the British Empire, an eventuality likely to benefit Japan and the United States far more than the Reich. Many of his senior military commanders certainly saw through Sealion as an 'imaginary enterprise', in the words of General Günther Blumentritt, chief operations officer for Army Group A. Blumentritt also confirmed that Field Marshal Gerd von Rundstedt, the senior German Army commander in France, understood that the invasion plan was essentially an elaborate bluff. 'Rundstedt did not take Operation Sealion seriously, nor did the rest of his staff. This is borne out by the fact that he never attended seaborne exercises by either of the two army groups. Even Hitler himself never asked Rundstedt about work in progress.' Nor would the Führer travel west to watch a single practice landing on the Channel coast. 'When the Field Marshal returned from Berlin in July he informed us that Hitler had told him in private that he did not intend to carry out Sealion.'

Much the same was confirmed by General Erich von Manstein, chief architect of the blitzkreig campaign which defeated France with lightning speed, and one of Hitler's most able commanders. 'Hitler did not want to land in Britain. His hope was that Britain would give in. However this political concept was at odds with the strategic requirements which followed from victory in the west. The disastrous part of it was that his concept encountered no sympathy in Britain.' Tens of thousands of printed copies of a grandiose 'last appeal to reason' aired on 19 July were subsequently dropped over Britain by the Luftwaffe. Most would be pressed into service as firelighters, or toilet paper.

Regardless of whether Operation Sealion was a blind, there was no time to lose. For all concerned, an immediate priority was to develop effective weapons against enemy armour. The fall of France had left anti-tank guns in desperately short supply, with 500 2-pounders and 50 Hotchkiss weapons lost on the road to Dunkirk. Blazing oil promised to disable a tank by starving both engine and crew of oxygen, it being calculated that an engulfing fire might stop a tank in six seconds. Hence, flame traps came to consume the bulk of the PWD's energies throughout July and August.

Vulnerable fuel bowsers were quickly superseded by two far more practical delivery systems: the Static Flame Trap and the Flame Fougasse. The former usually took the form of a sunken road lined with perforated pipes, in turn connected to a 600-gallon tank concealed on top of an embankment. The release of the fuel was triggered from a manned observation point, with gravity providing sufficient force to spray a 25 per cent petrol/75 per cent gas-oil mixture over advancing Nazis at a temperature of 500°F. Eight or nine Static Flame Traps were listed as operational as early as 20 July. In all, some 200 would eventually be installed, primarily on routes leading inland from likely landing beaches between Kent and Cornwall. At a few sites, such as the long hill leading from Dover to Canterbury, power pumps enabled a greater area of road to be flooded. No little ingenuity was displayed in camouflaging feed pipes. Across the stone bridge at Kingstone in Devon, for example, the sprays emerged from the gutters; at other sites they were made to resemble handrails. Most civilians assumed, or were told, that these works were improvements to the sewerage system.

In *Flame Over Britain*, Sir Donald Banks recalled fears that fires raised by flame traps might wreak untold havoc across the countryside. These concerns were dispelled during tests conducted by XII Corps at a farmhouse near Steyning on 3 August. 'Apart from a door post being badly charred and some blistering of paint, the house was virtually undamaged,' wrote Banks:

An even more spectacular affair was staged in a sunken woodland lane where the flames licked up from the depths … But although one tree trunk was badly damaged, and undergrowth was burned away, there was no general conflagration, and the fire brigade which had turned out in force had disappointment writ large upon their faces.

Several larger flame barrages were constructed to defend key beaches. At Hastings, bulk fuel reservoirs were disguised to resemble Martello towers of Napoleonic vintage, one on the site of a children's boating lake in the fish market and another beneath the east cliff. Another substantial beach barrage was installed at St Margaret's Bay in Kent. Situated midway between Dover and Deal, the gently-sloping shingle beach there was sheltered by tall chalk cliffs, behind which sat a battery of huge 14in naval guns nicknamed 'Winnie' and 'Pooh'. Being the closest point on the English coastline to France, St Margaret's seemed to be an obvious jumping-off point for a German raid. The flame barrage ran from Ness Point as far as the first of the houses, whose residents had already been evacuated, and was fed from bulk storage tanks on top of Bay Hill.

Major John Baker White, a deception specialist attached to the Directorate of Military Intelligence, visited the site sometime in late July or early August:

> The burning beach defence was an unobtrusive and unexciting piece of mechanism stuck into the bank just where the road took its last turn to run down to the beach and the trans-Channel cable hut. We were assured that it could cover the whole of the beach with a sheet of all-destroying flame.

Presumably, the barrage at St Margaret's had already been tested. Driving back to London, White's imagination was inflamed by vivid pictures of fire spurting from the rocks where he had bathed and netted prawns as a child …

Less complex, and more numerous, was the Flame Fougasse, developed by the redoubtable Colonel Livens. Named after a type of medieval mine, the Fougasse typically took the form of a 40-gallon drum buried in the ground at a suitable location and primed with guncotton. When activated, the weapon shot out a fearsome tongue of fire 10ft wide and 30 yards long; for optimal effect, drums were sited to catch enemy vehicles at points where they were forced to slow down, such as corners, hills and road blocks. Dug into a roadside bank and well camouflaged, a Fougasse remained more or less safe until it was armed. Each was charged with a mixture of 40 per cent petrol and 60 per cent gas-oil, later replaced by an adhesive tar/lime/petrol gel known as 5B. Most were installed and manned by the Home Guard, and promised to kill so many Germans that by June 1941 some 12,000 drums and 7,000 flame traps had been deployed, chiefly on roadsides in southern England.

Meanwhile, Hitler's armies gave every appearance of standing poised across the Channel. While flame might hamper the invader inland, Britain's best chance was still reckoned to lie in firing landing beaches, or better still the sea itself. Experiments on Haslar Creek near Portsmouth succeeded in producing a 'fine blaze' on calm water, but even under ideal conditions consumed daunting quantities of fuel. 'We are struggling with the problem and are still full of hope,' the navy informed Hankey, 'though perhaps not very confident of success.' Churchill himself continued to pour scorn on oil warfare research, and let it be known that he was 'not at all confident that this is a very useful line of development. Several generals I have met seem unimpressed by it. Projectiles and explosives are far more deadly, and less cumbrous.'

It hardly helped that the prime minister had not been informed of the creation of the Petroleum Warfare Department a month earlier. Indeed, it was not until 24 August that Sir Donald Banks and his beleagured team finally managed to set a blaze on the surface of the sea itself, choosing a stretch of open water on the Solent at Titchfield, a few miles west of Fareham. Pipes from ten Scammel fuel tankers were rigged from the top of a low cliff and fed down to the sea below the high water mark, a crude but effective system capable of delivering oil at a rate of 12 tons an hour. 'Admiralty flares and a system of sodium and petrol pellets were used for ignition,' Banks wrote. 'Within a few seconds of the pumps being started a wall of flame of such intensity raged up from the sea surface that it was impossible to remain on the edge of the cliff, and the sea itself began to boil.'

The Titchfield blaze lasted thirty-five minutes and stretched fully 300 yards, reaching a temperature in excess of 1,800°F. Surviving footage of later tests demonstrate clearly that blazing inshore waters presented no small hazard to the enemy, with any living thing not incinerated likely to be asphyxiated by dense clouds of choking black smoke. Bernard Kimpton, who served as an electrical engineer with the PWD throughout the war, recalled the sea-fire spectacle:

The psychological effect of a flame barrage was tremendous. The smoke was the thing you saw from the sea, with flames shooting out underneath it. I occasionally had to go out in a boat and check for gaps during tests, and I can tell you it was a horrible thing to watch. The combination of fire and water instilled an instantaneous fear.

Indeed the black velvet pall darkening the sky above Titchfield on the afternoon of 24 August did not go unnoticed. By now the Battle of Britain was being fought in earnest, the Luftwaffe having launched 'Eagle Day' on 13 August, striking at airfields and radar stations in a concerted effort to write-down Fighter Command. 'It was a glorious calm summer day and the smoke was billowing thousands of feet into a blue sky when "raiders overhead" was reported from Portsmouth,' Banks recalled in *Flame Over Britain.* 'It was too late for concealment, so the show went on and "all clear" was duly reported. Next day, however, in the German communique it was stated that south coast towns had been attacked with excellent results, very large scale fires having been observed in the vicinity of Portsmouth.'

The 'vast fires' reported by the official German news also apparently extended to Bristol, yet here we encounter an enigma. For despite such opportunistic claims, wartime records indicate that the enemy was aware of the true nature of British sea-fire research as early as 10 August. Unsurprisingly, the revelation that Britain might use burning oil for coastal defence was a matter of some concern to the German High Command, and spurred prompt investigation of viable countermeasures. German naval historian Peter Schenk records that the *Kriegsmarine* conducted trials at the *Chemisch-Physikalischen Versuchsanstalt* in Wilhelmshaven on 18 August. Using 100 tons of a petrol-oil mixture, certain obvious dangers were demonstrated, for in calm conditions oil was found to burn for almost twenty minutes, producing a great deal of smoke and heat.

If both sets of records are accurate, we are faced with a curious paradox, in that German technicians succeeded in simulating this sinister secret weapon fully six days before the PWD achieved the first notable success at Titchfield. Banks, writing in 1946, and thus constrained by official secrecy, infers that this forewarning was due to 'some inquisitiveness on the part of enemy aeroplanes' overflying Dumpton Gap a few weeks earlier. Be that as it may, at precisely the same time German military intelligence was being fed disinformation about flame defences as part of a shrewd deception operation mounted by 'black' propaganda specialists in Britain.

Soon after his first visit to St Margaret's Bay, John Baker White of the DMI had hit on a novel opportunity to hoodwink the enemy. 'I do not claim complete authorship,' the modest major wrote later:

As in the case of so many successful rumours, it was not any one man's invention but was born from conversation between two or three people devoting their thoughts and discussion to the same question. I think we all saw the same sort of picture. The fleet of invasion barges approaching the coast suddenly engulfed in a sheet of flame.

Undoubtedly, Hankey and Lloyd both deserve praise, yet the official history of the Political Warfare Executive credits Baker White alone with the creation of 'the most widely reported sib of the whole war' at a time when a German invasion of Britain seemed imminent: 'That the British have a new weapon which spreads an inflammable surface over the sea for an enormous area and sets fire to it.'

First, however, the novel sib proposed by the DMI had to be passed by the UPC, as well as the PWD. 'Before the rumour was fed into the "pipeline" it had to get over certain hurdles,' Baker White wrote in *The Big Lie*. 'It had to be technically watertight, so that the German chemical warfare specialists could not shoot it down as impossible. Our experts told us that to set the sea on fire with a mixture of petrol and oil was a perfectly feasible but extravagant and expensive operation. Extravagance and expense did not bother us.'

The Underground Propaganda Committee was less enthusiastic. According to Baker White, the burning sea rumour came back from Woburn approved, but endorsed with the pungent remark: 'No objection, but we think it a pretty poor effort.' The sib then passed out of his hands. Several weeks went by, during which nothing more was heard. 'All of us who looked upon the burning sea as our own particular baby started to get very despondent. No come-backs from neutral capitals, no traces from postal censorship, no gossip from prisoners of war, not a word from that hive of rumour, the Café Bavaria in Geneva.' As well as Switzerland, the veteran political warfare specialist also identified the rumour 'pipeline' laid by the Foreign Office and MI6 as running from 'the bar of the Grand Hotel in Stockholm, the Avenida in Lisbon, the Ritz in Madrid, and other places in Cairo, Istanbul, Ankara and elsewhere, not forgetting New York'.

The major need not have worried. By 18 August, the German Navy were already busy conducting trials of their own at Wilhelmshaven, followed six days later by the large-scale PWD burn at Titchfield on the Solent, overflown by the Luftwaffe, and all too appropriately described by Sir Donald Banks as a 'show'. Then, on 27 August, a remarkable cipher telegram reached London from Berne, sent by David Kelly, the newly appointed british minister to Switzerland. A former intelligence officer himself, Kelly had already fielded peace offers mediated by a senior Red Cross official. Now the ambassador had cause to report:

A story which seems to have obtained some currency among German troops is that the English have discovered new weapon for defeating attacks by sea. Story is, that we spread oil on the sea and by lighting it when boats approach have already defeated several attempted landings.

According to Kelly, this surprising information had reached him from occupied Vichy France, where Luftwaffe airmen in Lyons spoke of the Wehrmacht having 'suffered heavy losses in attempting to attack Dover by this method'. Writing in *The Big Lie*, Baker White was obliged to gloss over this top secret intelligence conduit, claiming instead that confirmation came via a German flyer shot down over Kent, and held at the Combined Services Interrogation Centre on the Trent Park estate near Cockfosters.

The mere suggestion of flame barrages was also of genuine material value for Britain. As German naval historian Peter Schenk records, the search for practical countermeasures at Wilhelmshaven caused Sealion planners considerable logistical headaches: 'One early solution involved the use of depth charges, but it was soon discovered that water jets were quite sufficient to counter oil slick fires.' Pumping and fire-fighting vessels were assigned to protect the first assault wave, and in addition 150 small fire-fighting pumps from the *Reichsluftschutzverband* (Reich Air Defence Organisation) were earmarked for installation on individual craft, including tugs. This figure soon rose to 200, and finally 800. 'These were to be distributed as evenly as possible amongst the assault harbours, mainly for use by the advance detachments.'

A further assessment of the extent of the German effort is provided by American naval historian Walter Ansel in *Hitler Confronts England*, an academic study published in 1960 and based on primary research with surviving participants:

> The *Kriegsmarine* reached a generally negative conclusion about extensive fires off an open coast. A five-mile stretch took a prohibitive amount of oil, boosted by gasoline and fitted with specialised ignition. In isolated localities, such as marshland behind beaches, it was held that oil fires might be made to burn. The German army went after this angle as a combat problem, while the Navy pursued the seagoing fire hazard. Both reached workable countermeasures. In the case of the Navy, special fire-fighting tugs, each towing a long chain of logs, were to accompany advance detachments. When an oil slick or burning water was encountered off a beach, the tug was to encircle the danger and enclose it in a log chain. So enclosed, the fire could be towed to sea and extinguished by materials on the tug.

Tugs and log chains were unlikely to counter a large sea-flame barrage fed from bulk supply, although as yet none existed. Interestingly, Ansel also records that Sealion planners expected to encounter 'oil fires' on the waters of Romney Marsh, where one such barrage was eventually installed. The German officer tasked with research into countermeasures was Rear Admiral Karl Witzell, chief of the *Marinewaffenhauptamt*, or naval weapons directorate. 'The novel idea enjoyed wide popular appeal, and the many burning water tales led to extra investigation of the subject,' Ansel concluded. 'Neither Navy nor Army suffered noteworthy casualties in the experiments.'

Myth would soon credit the new Greek Fire scheme with 80,000 casualties. 'I am convinced that one rumour, one deception above all others discouraged the Germans from launching their invasion attempt in 1940,' averred John Baker White of his greatest invention. 'It consisted of eight words – *the British can set the sea on fire.*' Despite being judged a 'poor effort' by the UPC, the sib was undoubtedly successful in breeding 'nervousness, reluctance, uncertainty and even real fear' on the far side of the English Channel. Certainly it beat any number of rival fictions that were patently absurd, such as those which held that the rivets on Messerschmitt fighters were made of wood, and that 200 man-eating sharks had been imported from Australia and released into the Channel.

'The vast majority of sibs were feeble and often childish,' admitted David Garnett, author of the official history of the Political Warfare Executive. 'That suggested by Major Baker White spread like wildfire over the Continent … It was successful because it satisfied the longing of conquered peoples of Europe.'

The conquerors understood this too. 'The art of propaganda consists of being able to awaken the imagination of the public through an appeal to their feelings, in finding the appropriate psychological form that will grab the attention and appeal to the hearts of the national masses.' The author of this uncharacteristically pithy quote was none other than Adolf Hitler, writing on the subject of war propaganda in *Mein Kampf.*

The art of strategic deception would come on in leaps and bounds during the decisive summer of 1940, as did the double-agent system run by MI5. However, as the Battle of Britain raged overhead it became increasingly clear that subterranean whispering campaigns might not be enough. Thus the steady trickle of subtle sibs was soon joined by a gushing torrent of overt anti-invasion propaganda, such as the arrival of many thousands of lethal Thompson sub-machine guns from America, along with the deployment of barge-busting 'super mines' at sea, capable of destroying three shallow-draft landing craft at once. Both these fictions were transmitted to Germany during July and August by Arthur Owens, the double-cross agent code-named SNOW by MI5, and Johnny by the Abwehr. Other double-cross assets, including two captured spies known as SUMMER and TATE, agreed to feed back false reports of a coastline bristling with troops, anti-tank guns and machine-gun nests, backed up by mobile reserves and a million eager Home Guards.

Several of these 'black' puffs turned 'white' after being released to British papers by the Ministry of Information, notably the purchase of large numbers of Tommy guns from the States, whose rate of fire now miraculously increased from 750 to

1,500 rounds a minute. When reporting that 'all British troops' were being issued with automatic weapons, Owens also warned of draconian orders 'not to evacuate invaded areas. Orders given to bomb English civilians if necessary.' Unsurprisingly, this brutal embellishment was not passed on to the press. Nevertheless, several of SNOW's transmissions must surely have taxed the credulity of his Abwehr controllers in Hamburg. 'Home defence staff anxious for invasion,' the treacherous Welshman buzzed on 14 August. 'Defence measures terrific. Large forces ready attack if you invaded here.'

Moreover, sibs had a habit of surfacing inconveniently like moles on a well-tended garden lawn. In *The Black Game*, a memoir by PWE print specialist Ellic Howe, the author confirms that dissemination of rumours which stood approved by the Underground Propaganda Committee was 'typically from selected bars in Lisbon, Stockholm, Ankara' and New York, as well as unoccupied Vichy France. 'Thus a rumour invented at Woburn and launched at Zurich could find its way back to London and be published in a slightly different form in the *Daily Mirror*.' Indeed, Britain's chief press censor, Rear Admiral George Thomson, afterwards admitted that the burning sea rumour turned into the most troublesome story of the entire war.

As yet, however, the sib devised by John Baker White appeared nowhere in newspapers at home or abroad, nor did it figure in any of the carefully controlled wireless transmissions by tame double-cross agents such as SNOW. Undoubtedly this owed much to the clandestine nature of the secret intelligence pipeline running to Switzerland and elsewhere. In addition, this absence may have owed something to a revival of the bold fireship scheme first mooted by the Admiralty at the end of June, and now set in motion under a menacing – if slightly obvious – code name.

Operation Lucifer.

3

OPERATION LUCID

In the wake of an enthusiastic memorandum sent by Desmond Morton to Winston Churchill on 27 June, predicting 'most pleasing results' if enemy-held ports and harbours were attacked with fireships, the viability of such a scheme was addressed seriously for the first time in July. An annex attached to a report prepared by the deputy chiefs of staff on 10 July estimated that at least 7,000 tons of fuel would be required to inflict significant damage:

> The difficulty of sending a fireship to a harbour is similar to that of sending in a block ship. To be successful an attack of this kind must be carried out during dark hours otherwise she is likely to be sunk by aircraft. The harbour would need to be near the sea and the ship patrols would have to be avoided. In these circumstances the chances of using oil are confined to ports such as Ostend, Calais and Boulogne. And when the operation is carried out the tide would have to be making ...
>
> The chances of passing the patrols that may be expected are small and one torpedo would stop the attack. Similarly the chances of getting into the harbour are slender when past experience is recollected with ships far handier than a 7,000-ton tanker. It is for decision whether these chances justify the loss of the tanker, or whether several small 1,000-ton tankers might be used for this purpose.

Evidently spare tonnage was found, for on 8 August a surplus Thames petroleum barge named *Suffolk* was loaded with 50 tons of fuel and blown up in shallow water off Maplin Sands. According to Banks in *Flame Over Britain*, a fierce fire was produced, burning briefly before 'consuming itself by its own violence'. Although his unofficial history of the PWD makes no mention of the Admiralty fireship scheme, in some respects the spectacular destruction of the *Suffolk* served as a dry run for what would shortly become Operation Lucifer, and finally Operation Lucid.

An audacious yet simple plan, Lucifer was envisaged as a contemporary sequel to the fireships launched by Sir Francis Drake against the Spanish Armada off Calais four centuries earlier. Under cover of darkness, several aged tankers, their holds filled with a highly combustible fuel mixture, would shape course across the Channel for the enemy-occupied invasion ports of Dunkirk, Calais and Boulogne. At the entrance to each target harbour, the tankers would be abandoned by their skeleton crews and then detonated, the flood tide carrying in the blazing fuel to wreak havoc amongst the wharves, tugs and landing barges.

Given Operation Lucid's illustrious ancestry, it was only fitting that another bona fide naval hero, Captain Augustus Agar, was given command. In 1919, Agar had led a daring motor torpedo boat raid on the Russian fleet anchored at Kronstadt during the Allied anti-Bolshevik intervention. A cruiser, the *Oleg*, weighing 6,645 tons, was sent to the bottom, and two dreadnoughts damaged. In order to maintain the fiction that the Royal Navy were in no way involved, his men dressed in ordinary civilian clothes. For this exploit Agar was awarded the Victoria Cross, in the process becoming known as the 'mystery VC' on account of the delay in revealing precisely why he had won Britain's highest military honour. Had Operation Lucid achieved its purpose two decades later, Agar's fireship operation might well have assumed as prominent a place in the annals of naval history. In reality, Lucid would end in abject failure. Nevertheless, in his autobiography *Footprints in the Sea*, published in 1959, Agar included a detailed account of this remarkable operation. While there exist several discrepancies between Agar's published version and the facts set out in official records opened in 1972, none tend to suggest that the operational history of Lucifer/Lucid differed significantly from the following account.

After being assigned to the fireship project towards the end of August 1940, Agar expected the Ministry of Shipping to allot him several 'small and handy' tankers, each capable of around 15 knots. With serviceable tankers in short supply, however, Lucid was instead saddled with four highly unreliable tramp oilers: *War Nawab*, *War Nizam*, *Mytilus* and *Oakfield*. Each had been laid up for a number of years and drew more than 30ft of water. From the outset, therefore, the chances of coaxing them across the Channel seemed doubtful, even under tow.

Agar, ever an optimist, elected to press ahead. Early in September, the naval dockyards at Plymouth, Portsmouth and Chatham were each allotted one tramp oiler for hurried engine and boiler overhauls. Unfortunately, in the limited time available the repairs were far from adequate, as Agar recalled:

Every effort was made to obtain the quickest preparation for the expedition. One ship was taken in hand in the dockyard on September 15th, after having been in disuse for a considerable time. She had to be docked and scraped, and as soon as she was scraped repairs had to be made to her bottom. The engines and boilers worked all right, but the age of the ship rendered it impossible to produce more than 6 knots. Another ship taken in hand at a different dockyard only reached the dockyard four days before the operation.

With a German invasion expected daily, delay was never an option. Working flat out, the oilers were made ready in just one week; in an effort to maintain secrecy, rumours were allowed to spread that the aged tankers were to be used as blockships. The Lucid operational plan was finalised by the Admiralty simultaneously with the repairs. With Dover out of bounds to most shipping, thanks to German long-range shelling, the motley flotilla would instead sail from Sheerness, escorted by destroyers and minesweepers from Nore Command. Bombers would also strike at the target ports shortly before the fireships were due to arrive.

Each Lucid crew numbered a dozen or so volunteers, lured by the promise – later broken – of extra pay. Once the time fuses were set, the men would make good their escape in motor launches. To many it smacked of a suicide mission. According to Richard Greenland, a newly-commissioned RNVR sub-lieutenant who was 'asked to volunteer' for a three-day job, only to find himself skippering *Mytilus*, the scheme quickly became known as Operation Stupid.

A further week was required for loading each tanker with between 2,000 and 3,000 tons of 'Agar's Special Mixture', a lethal concoction prepared by the PWD and consisting of 50 per cent heavy fuel oil, 25 per cent diesel oil and 25 per cent petrol. Bundles of loose cordite were added to nourish the flames, with depth charges and guncotton placed in the holds for added explosive effect. Thus charged, it was reckoned that each tanker packed sufficient punch to disable its allotted target harbour, even if only on a temporary basis. Any delay was worthwhile, since worsening autumn weather would render a seaborne invasion more or less impossible.

Unsurprisingly, on-board smoking was subject to strict controls. 'We did so by adopting the old tanker rule by which every match, after use, had to be put back in the box and never thrown away,' wrote Agar. 'Besides this, two special places only were set aside for smoking. The matchbox rule soon became a habit which it was to the interest of each member of the crew to enforce.' The fact that air battles were raging overhead day and night was not lost on anyone attached to Lucid, as a chief petty officer named Ronald Apps recalled:

Those four weeks were a bit hairy because the tanker was full up with fuel oil when it came to us and it was primed and ready to explode and there were air raids at night. When you're in a tanker, sitting on all this explosive material and the Germans are coming over and dropping bombs, it's not [a] very ... shall I say 'sleep inspiring' experience. I got round to the idea that I had to sleep or I wouldn't be able to walk around the next day.

From the outset, certain senior figures at the Admiralty viewed Operation Lucid with ill-concealed scepticism, notably the First Sea Lord, Admiral Sir Dudley Pound. Churchill had been appraised of the fireship plan in June, yet it was not until 18 September that he would demand specific 'Action This Day', ordering his chief staff officer, General Hastings Ismay, to:

> Make enquiries whether there is no way in which a sheet of flaming oil cannot be spread over one or more of the invasion harbours. This is no more than the old fireship story with modern improvements that was tried at Dunkirk in the days of the Armada. The Admiralty can surely think of something.

Given that Major Desmond Morton had informed the prime minister of the fireship proposal fully three months earlier, this eleventh-hour fillip was almost certainly a light torpedo directed at Pound and other doubters.

The choice of target ports was limited both by the length of passage from the available home ports and the accessibility of enemy shipping. Meteorological and tidal factors served to restrict sailings to a just few days during each lunar month, so that the earliest suitable date on which the fireships would be fit for use was identified as the night of 25–26 September. Shortly before the Lucid flotilla put to sea, Agar was summoned to Downing Street to give Churchill a personal briefing, raising a chuckle when he referred to Lucid as 'roasting the Nazis'.

'I explained the difficulties and also my doubts about getting the old oilers across the Channel,' Agar recalled. 'He understood but said there was no time to change that now, and if we went, it must be "at once". He then went on to talk about the chances of invasion, and I remember so well his saying, "It is not so much I don't want them to come. Nobody does. I want them to be beaten before they come, Agar. I don't want one single German soldier to set foot on English soil."'

In parting, Churchill advised Agar not to hesitate in aborting the operation if the onerous task of coaxing the 'cranky' oilers across the Channel became too hopeless. Indeed, only the perceived urgency of launching an attack on the growing enemy barge concentrations justified ordering Lucid to sea without further repairs to its unworthy vessels. In the event, just three were ready in time for the first sailing, the force being further disadvantaged by having to depart from separate ports. *War Nizam* and *Oakfield*, both assigned to Calais, set out from Sheerness, while *War Nawab*, tasked with Boulogne, sailed from Portsmouth. A diversionary bombardment was also ordered against Ostend.

The Sheerness flotilla weighed anchor late in the afternoon of 25 September – coincidently, the same day that Berlin dismissed as 'silly lies' newspaper reports that the English Channel was choked with German corpses. Agar directed the operation from the bridge of one of the escort destroyers, HMS *Campbell*, but Lucid's first shining was damned from the outset. A strong wind and unfavourable weather soon forced the motor torpedo boat escort to turn back, and as darkness fell the 'very dicky' *Oakfield* was also forced drop out. *War Nizam* plodded stoicly on, but before long a red glow from her funnel indicated boiler problems. Since the success of Lucid was wholly dependent upon surprise, to squander the 'new' weapon by deploying a single doubtful ship (*War Nawab*) in unfavourable conditions was deemed inexpedient. Reluctantly, Agar called off the attack at 10.30 p.m.

By the time the abort signal reached *War Nawab*, the ageing tanker had crept to a position just 7 miles off Boulogne, from which her crew could observe the havoc wreaked by Bomber Command. Their uncomfortable return journey was later recalled by her captain, Lieutenant Commander William Fell:

> By this time there was big trouble in the engine room, which was common to the boiler room. The coffer-dams between the fuel tanks and engine and boiler room bulkheads had filled with light petrol, which was now squirting through rivet holes into the engine and boiler rooms, where it vaporised. The two men below passed out with the fumes. The Stoker Petty Officer and another Stoker kept the steam for another 20 minutes while we hauled up the other two, who were unconscious and vomiting badly.

With the highly volatile mixture leaking dangerously, Fell elected to shut off steam. *War Nawab* finally crept into Sheerness the following morning, the harbourmaster concluding as he climbed aboard that her reeling crew were blind drunk.

Despite this inauspicious start, the Admiralty granted Agar permission to try again. Following a more thorough overhaul of the boilers Agar was able to inform Churchill that four ships capable of 9 knots would be available by 2 October. However, while three tankers sailed from Sheerness on the night of 3–4 October, *Mytilus* soon developed a heavy list, and owing to adverse weather conditions the whole force was recalled by Admiral Drax. A third attempt on the night of the

4–5 October was pencilled in, this time taking only two tankers for the shorter run to Calais and Dunkirk. But again the operation was cancelled, this time because a diversion operation by the RAF was grounded by more bad weather.

The need for further running repairs, and rest for long-suffering crews, all conspired to delay another sailing. The fourth and final Lucid attempt shaped course on the night of 7–8 October, with the force now pared down to *War Nizam* and *Oakfield*. Yet again, disaster struck in mid-Channel when the destroyer *Hambledon*, with Agar on board, triggered an acoustic mine. The convoy promptly scattered and was unable to regroup in the limited time available. Once more, Operation Lucid was reluctantly aborted. As if to add insult to injury, the return leg saw one oiler break down and the other develop additional faults.

Agar and Drax were keen to press ahead, and provisional plans were made to sail four seaworthy tankers on the night of 1–2 November. Alas, it was not to be. On 12 October, Hitler postponed Operation Sealion until the following spring, a decision quickly confirmed to British intelligence via ULTRA decrypts from Bletchley Park. The reduced threat of invasion meant that the considerable resources needed for each fireship sailing could no longer be justified and, in the face of deteriorating weather conditions, Lucid – like Sealion – was called off indefinitely.

Churchill remained enthusiastic, urging fireship 'Action This Day' in memos as late February 1941. Indeed, records indicate that a Lucid II was planned for that same month, a minute from Agar dated 17 February informing the prime minister that two fireships were at seven days' notice for offensive operations. Whether the operation sailed, and against what target, is unclear. Curiously, Agar states in *Footprints in the Sea* that by the end of 1940 he had already left the fireship project for good, having lost his place in the queue of captains waiting for regular sea commands, and being 'again available for odd jobs that came along'. Quite why he omitted to mention that one such job was Lucid II remains a minor mystery.

Faint echoes of Lucid – and likely losses – may be detected in the execution of the daring St Nazaire raid in March 1942, when an obsolete destroyer packed with delayed action explosives rammed a dry dock used by large German warships. Two decades later, Agar summed up the ill-starred fireship adventure thus:

> Looking back on Lucid I suppose we should be glad that it never came off, which is a mild way of saying it failed. First, because we might – and probably would – have lost half the crews of the fireships; and secondly because many German soldiers were spared the dreadful fate of perishing in flames.
>
> I know there were several sighs of relief when it was finally cancelled and the plan put into cold storage, lest it should be used against us. Imagine thousands of

tons of burning oil floating up the Thames on a strong flood tide in the middle of heavy air raids on London! Such a feat was not impossible if resolute men volunteered to carry it out.

On the other hand, the morale effect of a bold offensive stroke like Lucid would have helped a great deal to convince the United States and other neutrals that Britain was no 'quitter', and was determined at all costs to see the war out to the bitter end. From this we would have gained immeasurable prestige.

Regrettably, fate conspired to submerge immeasurable prestige in heroic failure. Despite the fact that the Petroleum Warfare Department had provided the combustible mixtures for Lucifer/Lucid, the fireship operation is nowhere mentioned in *Flame Over Britain*, nor by John Baker White in *The Big Lie*. One reason (among several) is that the PWD and the Admiralty never really rubbed along. 'Much of their technique is at variance with Naval experience,' carped one haughty memo of attempts to perfect a sea flame barrage at Studland Bay in Dorset. Soon after, the senior service took delight in a recommendation by General Alan Brooke, Commander-in-Chief, Home Forces, that no further marine barrages should be installed. Like Churchill, Brooke favoured spraying the enemy with mustard gas rather than flame should the field-grey horde attempt to cross the Channel.

The Admiralty even preferred to set up their own experimental establishment. At Langstone Harbour, adjacent to Hayling Island in Hampshire, 'various fiery forms of harbour defence and flame bombs' were tested, including laying a trail of flaming oil behind a tanker and uncoiling a gigantic wick of coconut matting steeped in oil over the stern. Best of all, in a scheme to rival the apocalypse, certain areas of open water between Beachy Head and Weymouth would be flooded with fuel from existing bulk storage facilities, then ignited by air-dropped incendiaries as the enemy invasion force grounded.

The latter task was assigned to Pilot Officer D.H. Clarke, a Fleet Air Arm pilot flying Blackburn Skua dive bombers from Gosport. By way of training, Clarke was allowed just one practice ignition, diving to release his bombs at 1,500ft. 'The sea erupted with an unheard woomph! which made the aircraft quiver,' he later recollected. 'Almost instantaneously visibility was cut to zero by a black cloud of oily smoke which stunk like hell. Anyone afloat in that inferno would certainly have recognised the similarity.'

Come *Der Tag*, Clarke was instructed to fly at low-level from east to west, lighting all points at the critical moment, before escaping under cover of the smoke pall. Armed with a single .303 Vickers K gun, his rear gunner would let fly at any surviving invaders, while simultaneously fighting off swarms of Messerschmitt fighters. In all probability the plan was an application of a scheme first mooted in the DCS report on oil warfare of 10 July. Certainly it involved death or glory: by September 1940, the obsolete Blackburn Skua had been largely relegated to the role of target-tug and stood no chance in a dogfight. Nevertheless, on the evening of 7 September, at the height of the celebrated 'Cromwell' invasion alarm, Pilot Officer Clarke found himself hauled from a local cinema and scrambled west towards Littlehampton. No less abruptly, the mission was scrubbed.

Before turning back, Clarke stared out across the grey evening waters of the English Channel for signs of the long-awaited invasion armada. 'There was nothing,' he recalled, with more than a hint of regret. 'Only the sea, grey after sunset, and the white surf stark in the fading light.'

Instead, a very different false alarm raised by the Admiralty would provide a fillip to the myth of a failed German invasion attempt in the autumn of 1940.

4

'BEACHES BLACK WITH BODIES'

In September 1940, Mrs Pat Barnes was a schoolgirl living on a poultry farm off Crostwick Lane in Spixworth, a small village some 5 miles north of Norwich. In a letter to Anglia Television news in 1992, she recalled:

> For two days a convoy of army ambulances occupied this lane travelling slowly from North Walsham Road to Buxton Road, the drivers very grim-faced. We used to get a lot of army traffic through the lane, but nothing like this. Occasionally an army lorry would stop for eggs and also apples, and so the next time my mother asked what was going on two weeks before. She was told they had contained dead bodies of Germans washed up on the beach, as an invasion had been attempted. But that was all we were told. This picture has remained vivid in my memory. It seemed as though there were hundreds of trucks, going from nowhere to nowhere at walking pace.

This intriguing story from Norfolk is a key piece in the jigsaw picture of the invasion that failed, for the vehicles seen moving westward along obscure roads north of Norwich were indeed loaded with the survivors of a catastrophic North Sea disaster. Moreover, the incident had left several hundred dead and was deliberately hushed up by the British authorities. 'A convoy of ambulances arriving in the dead of night at a hospital outside Norwich,' wrote John Baker White in *The Big Lie*, 'and an SOS sent to other hospitals in the area for anti-burn dressings … There are plenty of people in Britain who to this day remain convinced that there was an invasion attempt in 1940.'

Unfortunately, these dozens of casualties being driven inland were not the forlorn survivors of a calamitous German landing. Rather, they were injured Royal Navy personnel from the 20th Destroyer Flotilla, a fast minelaying unit based at Immingham. Something of the truth was revealed by Stephen Roskill in his authoritative account *The War at Sea*. On the night of 31 August 1940, while the entire flotilla was engaged in laying mines in German-controlled waters, air reconnaissance reported an enemy force off the Dutch coast, steering westwards towards the British coast. Fearing an invasion spearhead, the 20th Flotilla was ordered to intercept and 'not to lack daring'. In fact, the German force was nothing more dangerous than a minelaying unit en route from Cuxhaven to Rotterdam, but in their rush to engage the enemy the British destroyers ran into an uncharted minefield 40 miles north-west of the Dutch island of Texel. The *Esk* and the *Ivanhoe* were sunk, *Express* seriously damaged, and the Flotilla commander, Lieutenant-Commander R.J.H. Couch, fatally injured.

That the loss of three priceless Royal Navy destroyers was the result of an abortive anti-invasion dash is confirmed by Sir John Colville, then private secretary to Winston Churchill. In his wartime journal, published as *The Fringes of Power*, Colville noted on 31 August that 'after dinner the First Lord rang up to say that enemy ships were steering westwards from Terschelling. The invasion may be pending (though I'll lay 10–1 against!) and all HM Forces are taking up their positions. If these German ships come on they would reach the coast of Norfolk tomorrow morning.'

Neither account reveals the true scale of the Texel disaster. The *Esk* sank immediately with the loss of Couch and all but one of her 150-strong crew, while the mine struck by *Express* blew her bows off, killing Captain J.G. Bickford together with ninety other personnel on board. While taking off wounded from *Express*, *Ivanhoe* was herself mined, leaving fifty-three dead and the bulk of her crew injured. After several attempts to scuttle *Ivanhoe* failed, she was finally sunk by a British motor torpedo boat on 1 September. Several liferafts from the stricken ships drifted into the Dutch coast, where their occupants were taken prisoner. The combined death toll amounted to almost 300, with 100 more injured or missing. Only during the Dunkirk evacuation had the Nore Command suffered worse casualties in a single day. The long list of names, released to the press on 13 September, made for harrowing reading.

The fate of certain survivors of this ill-starred North Sea dash is related by Don Tate, then a young naval rating based at Great Yarmouth. On the evening of 2 September, a Monday, Tate paid a visit to a local cinema, and on his return to barracks at 10.30 p.m.:

I was asked to assist with Royal Navy survivors who were soon to be landed. Others were being rounded up around the town in similar fashion. I went immediately to the harbour and waited with the others, excitedly wondering what it was all about. After an hour or more the first ship came alongside with survivors – all of them RN personnel. The last ship in I recall was in the early hours of the 3rd. We dealt with the survivors how and wherever we could help – carrying a few wounded ashore, supplying blankets to those without clothing, passing around food and cigarettes, as well as listing names and numbers.

All the while we helped we talked to them, and I naturally asked many what had happened at sea that night. Repeatedly the answer came that they had been 'attacking barges' when, in the confusion, the ship struck a mine. A second ship, moving in to help the first, had also become mined. A few of the survivors that night also said that the RAF had been dropping oil bombs. Those who said that were in the minority, but all were emphatic that they had attacked barges.

What happened next is not difficult to piece together, and corresponds with reports of 'mysterious' ambulance convoys near Norwich mentioned by John Baker White, and observed at first hand by the Barnes family in Spixworth. Survivors from the 20th Flotilla were landed not by one vessel but by several, over an extended period. Whether because facilities in Yarmouth were inadequate, or for reasons of secrecy, some casualties were transferred to hospitals inland. Also for reasons of military secrecy or civilian morale, obscure roads such as Crostwick Lane were favoured.

No word appeared in the press. The Admiralty admitted something of the Texel disaster only on 5 September, announcing that survivors from all three ships had been landed 'at an East Coast port' and 'admitted to hospital'. Unusual movements and convoys inevitably excited the curiosity of the public, but rather than reveal the unvarnished truth, the loss of three precious British destroyers was artfully spun as a secret victory. Thus on 8 September an air raid warden and diarist in Ipswich named Richard Brown recorded rumours that the *Esk* and *Ivanhoe* had been 'part of a task force of 160 ships sent to Holland where concentrations of troops were reported'. At the same time, the Ministry of Information put out – incorrectly – that the submarine HMS *Sturgeon* had torpedoed a large German transport off the Swedish coast, drowning 4,000 troops after the ship exploded and sank.

Within a matter of days, the Texel incident would become confused in the public mind with the celebrated 'Cromwell' invasion alarm. At precisely 8.07 p.m. on Saturday 7 September, with a steady stream of Luftwaffe bombers overhead, GHQ Home Forces in London flashed the code word 'Cromwell' to all units in Eastern and Southern Commands, intending to bring troops to a 'state of readiness'. A number of factors combined to trigger this major alert, including tidal conditions, the movement of large numbers of barges to forward ports across the Channel, the onset of the first mass air raid on London during the afternoon and overseas intelligence gathered through diplomatic contacts and MI6. Moreover, four days earlier, several ill-prepared German invasion spies had landed on the Kent coast. 'Rather falsely alarming in its local magnitude,' declared MI5 of this curious episode. All four agents had paddled ashore between Dymchurch and Dungeness under cover of darkness; one even managed to transmit a few brief reports on local defences and landmarks prior to being captured. A report on their interrogations circulated on 6 September noted:

> The general German plan is to take London simultaneously from Rye/Hythe and Aldeburgh/The Wash … By reason of the fact that they had been given provisions for only 14 days, and from everything they gleaned from their contacts on the other side, the spies were convinced that invasion would take place before the middle of September.

Some within British intelligence suspected that the bungling Abwehr quartet were a blind. Others, including Guy Liddell of MI5, were prepared to believe that these agents had been entrusted with genuine details of the Sealion plan of attack, not least because the information disclosed under interrogation appeared to chime with intelligence gleaned through other channels. 'This made it difficult to believe that the spies had been sent over here to mislead us,' Liddell confided in his war diary. General Alan Brooke, in charge of Home Forces, tended to agree, judging Kent and East Anglia to be the 'two main threatened points'. In truth, German planners never considered crossing the North Sea to land on the east coast of England except as a feint. Landings between Aldeburgh and the Wash were simply a deception, as was Operation Sealion itself.

In any event, the Cromwell flash issued by GHQ triggered widespread panic and alarm across much of the country. The Home Guard found itself called out alongside regular troops and church bells were rung in Lincolnshire, Scotland and the West Country, all in the mistaken belief that a German invasion was actually under way. Five hundred German parachutists were said to have dropped on Newport, where all but one were shot on the wing; a similar rumour set tongues wagging in Dover. That night, Bomber Command dispatched ninety-two aircraft across the Channel, with most of the effort directed at the growing fleet of improvised invasion barges. Churchill wound up the tension further still on 11 September, delivering a sober broadcast to the nation as a whole: 'No-one should blind himself to the fact that a heavy, full-scale invasion of this island is being prepared with all the usual German thoroughness and method.' The coming assault, the prime minister warned gravely, could not be long delayed:

> We must regard the next week or so as a very important period in our history. It ranks with the days when the Spanish Armada was approaching the Channel, and Drake was finishing his game of bowls; or when Nelson stood between us and Napoleon's Grand Army at Boulogne.

Unfounded speculation that 'crack German troops' had already tested Britain's coastal defences appeared in the *Daily Mirror* as early as 3 September. An even taller tale held that the Isle of Wight had been overrun, leaving 5,000 islanders killed or injured. Columnists observed that the conquest of France and the Low Countries clearly demonstrated that nominal 'troop raids' and 'propaganda landings' were part of modern German tactical thinking. 'The landing of a platoon on some isolated Welsh rock would be enough to justify Germany proclaiming to the world that Britain was invaded.' In fact German propaganda tropes were seldom so effective. Moreover, the arrival and capture of the four Dungeness spies was kept from the public until the beginning of December, when three were convicted under the newly passed Treachery Act and hanged at Pentonville prison.

In reality, by the middle of September, Operation Sealion was more or less dead in the water. Repeated raids on the Channel invasion ports by Bomber Command, known as the 'battle of the barges', continued to inflict significant damage on the makeshift armada, while 10 September brought autumnal rain and cloud that persisted for fully four days. On 11 September, and then again on the 14th, Hitler stalled on ordering his fleet to sea. In London this spell of inclement weather was seen as both fortuitous and decisive. Regardless of conditions in the Channel, however, Hitler knew that his invasion fleet was likely to be defeated at sea by the Royal Navy. The inferior German *Kriegsmarine* had sustained heavy losses during the Scandinavian campaign six months earlier; now the Nazi leadership could only hope that an aerial blitz on London would force Churchill from office and persuade less resolute men to seek terms. Regrettably, codebreakers at Bletchley Park were only able to read Luftwaffe signals traffic, which revealed nothing of Hitler's elaborate intransigence. Britain, therefore, continued to expect a full-scale invasion any day, and the Cromwell alert remained in force.

In the midst of this tense information vacuum, an American tabloid, the *New York Sun*, dropped tantalising hints about a disastrous German thrust on the west of England. An influential – if populist – evening title, the *Sun* had achieved early notoriety for promoting the Great Moon Hoax of 1835, a fabricated account of lunar civilization falsely attributed to British astronomer Sir John Herschel. A decade later, the paper published a story by Edgar Allan Poe telling of an imagined Atlantic crossing by hot-air balloon in just three days. This, too, was pure invention, just as allegations of a Channel crossing in 1940 were so much hot air fanned by British intelligence.

The sources cited by the *New York Sun* in their report on 11 September were typically vague, being letters supposedly received from France and shown to a staff writer named William Bird, until recently the paper's correspondent in Paris:

> Revelation of an attempt by Nazi forces to land in England which failed disastrously is contained in letters received by French residents here, and from independent sources in Paris and in unoccupied France. The German invading fleet is stated to have started from St Malo in the expectation of landing on the west coast of England, but the reports received here indicate that in the result it proved to be 'nothing short of suicide'.
>
> Why news of the frustration of this attempted debarkation has not been released by the British can only be surmised … It sometimes happens that particularly in operations of a secret nature, each side waits to see what the enemy has to say before releasing its own version.

The letter from Paris, written by a French official acting in liaison with the German Army of Occupation, said: 'Paris is full of German officers who are having a wonderful time. They are only hoping they will be allowed to stay here. Especially they hope and pray that they will not be chosen to participate in another disastrous attempt to debark troops in England.'

The story bore more than a whiff of Woburn. Next day, several British papers quoted from the *Sun* report, much to the chagrin of Rear Admiral Thomson, chief press censor at the Ministry of Information. 'Nazi Invasion Attempt Was Foiled' trumpeted the *Western Morning News*, while the *Eastern Daily Press* exercised a greater degree of caution toward 'An Invasion Story Via America'. Nella Last, a diarist who also reported for Mass Observation, a volunteer social research organisation founded in 1937, noted on the 12 September: 'I wonder if the reputed invasion of Britain – at Southend and district – is true, and why we have not been told.' The government, she felt sure, had their reasons. 'But somehow I like to know the worst and find the "silver lining" for myself. If things are kept from me, I always fear the worst.'

Anecdotal stories of bodies washed ashore were recorded by British diarists as early as 12 September, just five days after the Cromwell alert. 'Tales begin to come through about an attempted invasion last Saturday evening,' noted John Allpress of Bury St Edmunds. 'Tales of how the enemy got to within 6 miles of our coast and were then sunk. Dead bodies on the beaches reported.'

For the moment, no mention was made of setting the sea on fire. The potent sib devised by John Baker White had already been in underground circulation for at least two weeks, as was clear from the cipher telegram sent by David Kelly from the British Embassy in Berne. Indeed, behind the scenes Churchill's attitude toward flame and Greek Fire was finally beginning to thaw. Kelly's message from Switzerland, reporting rumours of landings already attempted, and foiled by burning oil on the surface of the sea, was judged a 'favourable' development by the prime minister. 'I think by that he means that it is a good mark for the petroleum warfare idea in general,' explained Major Desmond Morton, corresponding with Lord Hankey on 4 September. Five days later, broadcasting to the nation – as well as to Hitler – Churchill adopted flame as a recurring motif:

> What he has done is to kindle a fire in British hearts, here and all over the world, which will glow long after all traces of the conflagrations he has caused in London have been removed. He has lighted a fire which will burn with a steady and consuming flame until the last vestiges of Nazi tyranny have been *burnt* out of Europe.

Listening to recordings of this speech today, the firm emphasis Churchill placed on the word 'burnt' and nine other combustible synonyms is striking. Soon after, Captain Augustus Agar was summoned to Downing Street to deliver a personal briefing on Operation Lucid. Kelly made no mention of intelligence work in his own post-war memoir, *The Ruling Few*. Nevertheless, some months later, while still in Berne, he would receive an appreciative personal note from Churchill: 'All your work excellent and messages deeply informative.'

In order to achieve optimum effect, British propagandists preferred rumours to appear to originate from several different places. Whereas the burning sea sib emerged first in Switzerland, reports of corpses on beaches and floating in the Channel were initially routed via the United States. Hence on 14 September papers such as the *New York Times* and *Brooklyn Daily Eagle* ran a fresh invasion story, this time quoting a respectable doctor named Charles F. Bove, formerly a senior surgeon at the famous American Hospital in Paris. Bove was a recent arrival in Jersey City on board the American Export Lines vessel *Excambion*, having returned to the States from war-torn Europe via Lisbon. Since Germany's lightning victory in the west, the capital of neutral Portugal had become a lively hub for intelligence and espionage activity virtually overnight.

'The Germans have already tried to invade England at different points and failed,' Bove averred, finding a ready audience in a press corps eager to report the adventures of one of the first American escapees from occupied Europe. The doctor went on to state that he had seen with his own eyes 'hundreds' of German bodies in the water near Cherbourg, presumed to be troops taking part in an attempted invasion of England. 'All along the French coast the Germans are constantly practising for invasion,' he added. 'They set out on ships and are made to leap overboard and swim considerable distances with all their equipment.'

Bove omitted these extraordinary details from a memoir published in 1956, when he wrote of fleeing from Paris direct to Biarritz, with no detour to Cherbourg or the Channel coast. Nevertheless, in September 1940 his story was immediately picked up by British editors, despite concerns that such coverage might spread alarm and despondency. Indeed, the ambivalent effect on morale these lively American reports had on anxious civilians in Britain is clear from diaries such as that kept by Vere Hodgson, a Londoner. 'Invasion is expected this weekend,' she wrote fretfully on 14 September. 'Apparently they tried last weekend; but this news has only come to us via America. Let us hope this tension does not go on for long – it is most unnerving.'

Sensational Stateside reporting also tweaked the interest of Ipswich air raid warden Richard Brown. Pausing to reflect on the Cromwell alert a week later, Brown wondered: 'What is the secret of last Saturday's affair? New York now has rumours that Jerry corpses were being washed up on the Yarmouth beaches in quantities. Green says 30,000 of them, but I should have thought they'd be too weighty with equipment to do anything but sink.'

Regrettably, the only corpses likely to have been washed up in the vicinity of Great Yarmouth were British casualties from the 20th Destroyer Flotilla. The grim aftermath of the Texel disaster does much to explain why some of the earliest rumours of bodies on beaches emerged from Norfolk and Suffolk. On 14 September, the diary of a London schoolboy named Colin Perry, later published as *Boy in the Blitz*, recorded more loose talk from East Anglia. 'I hear from Lancaster in the flats, who has just been to Wickham Market in Suffolk, that on Saturday night and again on Tuesday invasion was attempted. Not one Nazi returned. Their bodies are still being washed up along our shores. That is the end of all Nazis who seek to molest our freedom – death.'

Alarm and despondency might have been alien concepts to Perry, yet Sunday 15 September saw a singularly ferocious assault on Britain by the Luftwaffe, which mustered 1,500 aircraft and dropped several hundred tons of bombs. To many in the United Kingdom, this climactic event indicated that an invasion was imminent far more clearly than the muddled Cromwell alarm eight days earlier. Summaries prepared by Mass Observation confirm that landing rumours were ubiquitous by the middle of the month. 'Most people anticipate an invasion within a few days, and are very confident it will be a failure,' noted the central MO log. 'Rumours that it has already been attempted and has failed are reported from many quarters.' In Nottinghamshire, word of mouth told of enemy landings in Lincolnshire as well as on the south coast, leaving hundreds of bodies floating in the Channel. 'From the Northern Region it is stated that there are many requests for a public denial or an explanatory statement.' In Northampton, meanwhile, wagging tongues maintained that the enemy had instead come to grief in the Irish Sea, while observers in Edinburgh noted 'vigorous rumours' of a landing in north-east Scotland. A regional diary kept by the Home Guard in Cornwall likewise identified 15 September as the first occasion on which 'we heard reports of bodies washed ashore all along the south coast'.

In reality, reluctant German naval chiefs had insisted on a narrow front landing between Rottingdean and Hythe. The loose talk recorded by diarists and Mass Observation, as well as widespread coverage of American reports, prompted the Ministry of Information to issue the first of several firm denials from its towering headquarters at Senate House in Bloomsbury. 'There is no foundation for the stories in circulation to the effect that an actual attempt at invading this country has been made by the Germans,' a communiqué assured on 15 September. 'These stories have been of a circumstantial kind. In one the enemy was supposed to have landed a force which was immediately overcome. Another made the suggestion that large numbers of dead invaders had been picked up off the Goodwin Sands.'

Paradoxically, on the far side of the Channel these same stories were still being vigorously promoted by agents and embassies in neutral territories. William H. Shirer, a leading American radio correspondent with Columbia Broadcasting, and then based in Berlin, had been visiting his wife and children in Switzerland on 15 September. While in Geneva he noted: 'The news coming over the near-by border of France is that the Germans have attempted a landing in Britain, but that it has been repulsed with heavy German losses. Must take this report with a grain of salt.'

With delicious irony, on the very same day the Air Ministry put up one of the biggest lies of the entire war, announcing triumphantly that 185 German aircraft had been destroyed in combat. In fact the tally for 15 September, subsequently commemorated as Battle of Britain Day, was just a third of that number. This exaggerated record bag also played well in America, defeating determined German attempts to correct it, and triggering excited correspondence in the *New York Times*, calling for a military alliance between Britain, the Commonwealth and the United States. Not for nothing would Department EH soon be reconfigured as the Political Warfare Executive.

The *New York Times* was a prestigious – and usually measured – paper of record. Next day, however, its pages carried an equally dramatic story, this time based on an Associated Press wire sent from Lisbon:

> British informants arriving here [Lisbon] by plane from London declared today that a small-scale German attempt at a landing somewhere along the English coast last week was beaten off with heavy losses to the would-be invaders. They were unable to give the exact time and place, but asserted that they were convinced of the accuracy of their information.
>
> 'British coastal artillery and small patrol craft played havoc with German barges,' one of the British informants said here, 'and not a single German reached land alive. Scores of bodies are reported still being washed up on our shores.' The informant agreed the landing attempt – if it had been made – was not a full-dress attempt at invasion but perhaps designed to test British defences.

For British informants, read British agents. Another New York paper, the *Daily News*, appeared to corroborate the story in *The Times*, informing readers that a member of its own staff had received a letter from a 'well-informed person' in bomb-drenched London, promising that 'great things are happening about which I cannot write, and of which no German remains alive to tell'. The truth was a good deal less sensational. 'Still no invasion,' noted General Alan Brooke, the Commander-in-Chief, Home Forces, in his diary on 16 September. 'Rumour has it that tonight is to be the night.'

It was not to be. With Fighter Command still undefeated, and Bomber Command still pounding the Channel ports, on 17 September Hitler finally issued a directive ordering the postponement of Sealion until further notice. *Das Engellandlied* faded swiftly from the airwaves, along with other short-lived campaign songs such as 'Infantry to England' and 'England, We're On Our Way'. While news of Hitler's decision was not immediately known in London, later in the day, Bletchley Park learned that invasion-specific loading equipment at certain Dutch airfields was to be dismantled. This nugget was passed directly to Churchill by Group Captain Frederick Winterbotham, the MI6 officer charged with the distribution of precious ULTRA material. Winterbotham promptly found himself summoned to address the chiefs of staff at half past seven that evening. 'I was struck by the extraordinary change that had come over these men in the last few hours,' he recalled of this briefing in *The Ultra Secret*. 'There was a very broad smile on Churchill's face now as he lit up his massive cigar and suggested we should all take a little fresh air.'

Alas, the sky above them was again full of Heinkels and Dorniers. Göring, if not perhaps Hitler, still clung to the belief that Britain could be forced to capitulate through bombardment from the air. 'PM becoming less and less benevolent towards the Germans,' observed his secretary John Colville a few days later, after the Luftwaffe began to drop blockbusting landmines on London. 'He is doubtful whether invasion will be tried in the near future, but talks about castrating the lot.'

Even after Operation Sealion was postponed, the fiction of a failed invasion bid continued to grow in the telling. 'Thousands of German soldiers under tarpaulin in the barges may have been killed by British bombs,' trumpeted the *Daily Mirror*, quoting from the *Herald Tribune* in New York. A few stories originated closer to home, such as a variant of the corpse story run by the *Western Morning News* on 17 September, prompted by a 'mild hurricane' in the Channel. 'There was a rumour yesterday morning that a considerable number of bodies of German soldiers have been washed up on the sands at Bigbury-on-Sea, Challaborough and Cockleridge, and also on the South Cornish coast.' The paper sent staff from Plymouth to make enquiries on the spot, where it was noted that high tides and rough seas were likely to have swept away all detritus. 'Our reporters personally searched the sands and coves at the foot of the cliffs without finding any trace of bodies or clothing.'

A week later, on 24 September, Harold Cardozo, a reliably unreliable special correspondent for the *Daily Mail* in Spain, filed more sensational copy. 'Hitler lost between 50,000 and 60,000 picked troops in the disaster which scattered his invasion fleet a week ago today. They were victims of Channel storms and a merciless RAF bombardment.' Somewhat fancifully, Cardozo claimed that the Sealion armada had been deliberately dispersed to avoid being written down by Bomber Command. 'The invasion fleet, consisting of thousands of barges and small vessels, was taken out of the ports and moored along the lonely Flanders coast. Most of the vessels carried their full complement of troops, since the keynote of the Nazi plan has been readiness for instant action.'

By this account the long-awaited cross-Channel dash had been pencilled in for 15 September, but was called off after the Luftwaffe lost – so it was said – 185 aircraft in a single day. 'Then on Monday, south-west gales swept the Channel. The Flanders coast is notoriously dangerous at this season. It became a death trap. The German tugs tried desperately to get the barges to safety, but scores of them were overturned, drowning thousands of soldiers.'

Once again, official sources in London declined to comment. In Berlin, the Reich internal security service (*Sicherheitsdienst*) carped that the absurd figure of 60,000 dead was widely believed by German civilians, and deemed British propaganda an existential threat. In 1940, all German households were issued with a copy of a booklet, *Was tue ich im Ernstfall?* (*What Should I do in an Emergency?*), setting out what to do in various crisis situations, including air raids – and onslaughts by enemy propaganda. 'A new and sinister weapon is being used,' its authors warned:

> Enemy propaganda seeks to break the will to resist of the German people by slander and rumour, and by political and military lies. Germany lost the World War of 1914–18 because it did not recognise the danger of enemy propaganda. It collapsed spiritually. That cannot and will not happen again!

Readers were politely reminded that the death penalty applied to the German equivalent of spreading alarm and despondency through careless talk.

By the time the *Daily Express* got round to covering 'the story that is sweeping America' on 27 September, the facts had changed yet again, and now indicated a large-scale invasion rehearsal along the French coast. 'But the British, tipped off by their smooth-working espionage system in France, caught the embarked enemy off their base, smashing them down in a torrential bombing and machine-gunning attack.' Once again, the RAF was credited with destroying a large number of transports and barges, and exacting a 'huge toll of lives' before the enemy could reach the safety of dry land. 'German bodies were washed up for days along the shores of northern France and Belgium, particularly off Le Havre, Calais and Boulogne, where the largest forces were caught.'

Occasionally, both sides of this clandestine battle of wits might be played out in a single newspaper article. Reporting 'more American stories' on 21 September, the *Eastern Daily Press* even found itself printing propaganda generated by the Axis as well as the Allies. From New York, a Dutch refugee named Carl Ter Weele spoke of mutinous German troops in the Netherlands, many of whom were 'sent back to Germany with their hands tied behind their backs' after refusing to take part in hazardous invasion exercises. In Washington, conversely, German sources were clearly behind a letter from 'an unnamed Norwegian shipping magnate' declaring that hundreds of fishing smacks had been commandeered for the coming invasion. 'They have fitted wheels to the bows so that the boats running at full speed will roll right up to the shore.' Each was said to be capable of carrying at least thirty-five fully equipped storm troopers. 'Hitler is preparing to attack England from all sides simultaneously, and is willing to sacrifice 80 per cent of his army in order to gain a foothold.'

Fanning fears of widespread Fifth Column activity, the same piece also revealed that Wehrmacht quartermasters in Norway possessed a British uniform for each German soldier. This alarming claim mirrored an ill-conceived stunt staged in the middle of August, when Luftwaffe aircraft had scattered espionage paraphernalia across the Midlands, including rucksacks, target maps, wireless sets and parachutes stencilled with eagles and swastikas. In support of this elaborate charade, German radio broadcast that parachutists in British uniforms and civilian clothes had already linked up with a home grown Fifth Column. The story was squashed in Britain, and no panic ensued. The episode serves to illustrate that the blustering tone adopted by Nazi political warfare specialists was seldom as subtle – or credible – as their British counterparts. 'The attack will come as soon as the foggy season permits,' the anonymous Norwegian Quisling signed off by way of a grand finale. 'It will be accompanied by 11,000 aeroplanes and super gunfire from across the Channel.'

Inevitably, playback of American reports by British papers tested the patience of the press censor, Rear Admiral George Thomson:

> Each time I received a story about the 'invasion that failed' I rang up the editor
> of the paper concerned and assured him most emphatically that it was not true.
> In every case where this happened the editor took my word and did not publish
> the story. But nothing I could do prevented it from cropping up again and again
> … It was the most persistent legend of the war.

Tellingly, in *Blue Pencil Admiral* Thomson compared the invasion legend of 1940 to an equally tall tale from 1914: that of the Russians in England. 'That wonderful story,' the former submariner recalled, 'which had as its final touch of proof that they had snow on their boots.' Precisely the same comparison was drawn by John Baker White in *The Big Lie* and Sir Donald Banks in *Flame Over Britain*. In September 1914, during the opening weeks of the First World War, the Kaiser's Schlieffen Plan forced the Allied armies into headlong retreat. At one stage the French 6th Army edged so close to defeat that it was saved only by a fleet of Paris taxicabs, pressed into service to rush 6,000 reservists into the front line. On the far side of the Channel, British civilian morale was bolstered by rumours of a friendly foreign horde, said to be passing in secret from north to south en route to reinforce the crumbling Western Front. Russian troops shipped from icy Archangel were observed landing at Aberdeen, Leith and Glasgow; or being fed at York, Crewe and Colchester; or glimpsed smoking cigars in closed carriages; or stamping snow from their boots on station platforms. Invariably, the alleged eyewitness was a railway porter, never precisely identified. At Carlisle and Berwick-on-Tweed, the Russians called hoarsely for vodka, and at Durham managed to jam a penny-in-the-slot machine with a rouble. Cossack lances were spotted in guards' vans, and troop transports observed at Folkestone, destined for Le Havre. Numbers were variously estimated at between 30,000 and little short of a million.

In truth, the Russians in England was another Big Lie. Remarkably, however, this imaginary foreign legion also operated as a cunning double-cross sting. At the end of August 1914, the War Office dispatched 3,000 Royal Marines to Ostend in a desperate effort to stiffen the crumbling Allied line in Belgium. Their blue uniforms and round caps looked nothing like those worn by ordinary British troops. At the same time, MI5 was busy shadowing a German spy named Carl Lody, who posed as an American to travel around Scotland and note details of naval bases and coastal defences. Little did Lody know that his coded letters home were being intercepted and read. One such warned his handlers of the 'great masses of Russian soldiers' passing through Edinburgh 'on their way to London and France'. Lody put the number at 60,000, a fiction which MI5 saw no harm in allowing to slip through to Berlin. The German high command subsequently diverted precious reserves, and in consequence – some said – lost the Battle of the Marne.

When Thomson published *Blue Pencil Admiral* in 1946, he was still in post, and thus tightly constrained by official secrecy. Four years later, in writing the foreword to an early espionage history called *They Came to Spy*, he elected to speak a little more freely. 'Many things were known to me which I had to ensure were kept close secrets until the days of peace came again,' the erstwhile censor confirmed. 'It is well these things should now be revealed. For the lifting of the veil makes clear the nature of the battle of wits that was fought out ceaselessly, remorselessly and silently.'

The live Russians passing through England in 1914 and the dead Germans clogging the English Channel in 1940 share a surprising amount in common. Deception and double-cross aside, the sheer ubiquity of the Russians from Aberdeen to Folkestone and all points between prefigured guidance drawn up by Department EH in the Second World War, which recommended that all good rumours should appear to originate from several different places, and be likely to gain in the telling. Proof of the wildfire spread of the failed invasion story in September 1940 is provided by Naomi Royde-Smith, a prolific writer and diarist, and doyenne of the London literary scene:

> It began with a reported tocsin in Cornwall, spreading to Hampshire, heard by many … The Germans had landed somewhere in Dorset; in Kent; in Lincolnshire. This was officially denied. Then a whisper started that the corpses of German soldiers, in full battle dress, had been washed up all round the coast. Presently the horrid detail that each corpse had its hands tied behind its back was added. Then the tale grew into patent absurdity. The whole of the Channel from Weymouth to Devonport was covered with the corpses of stricken armies … The entire population of the Reich must have perished.

Another oft-repeated version told of a landing in Sandwich Bay, where the inshore waters were said to be black with German dead, later buried in secret among the sand dunes. In an account of 'authentic conversations' heard in Kent at the end of September, diarist James Hodson recorded the supposed remarks of an infantry officer. 'I suppose you've heard the tale about all the dead Germans washed up on the beach after their invasion which failed? The latest addition is they were tied up in bundles of three – they refused to go on board and were shot and disposed of in this way. Lots of funny stories go about.'

At Southend-on-Sea, it was whispered, enemy remains were collected in corporation dustcarts, while in Southampton the wreckage from barges was said to have solved a local fuel shortage. 'The fact is that the whole coastline is in the occupation of the military authorities,' one man told a reporter. 'If they thought it was necessary to conceal the dead bodies of Germans they would have no difficulty. For myself, it is enough that closed lorries going to and from the beach at one point and mysterious ambulances at another, are indications that out-of-the-ordinary things have been happening.'

The military, too, took note. On 25 September, a summary of 'rumours and indiscreet talk' prepared by II Corps noted that 15 Division 'report the currency in their area of a rumour that the bodies of thousands of German soldiers have been washed up on the beach at Clacton'. The source of the story could not be traced, although on the same date most units in Southern and Eastern Commands received a message offering to install 'an impenetrable barrage of flame on the sea' and soliciting suitable locations. From the same 15 Division sector in North Essex, an intelligence summary prepared by 45 Infantry Brigade reported:

It has been noticed, particularly during the last month, that rumours of a spectacular nature have been very widespread. The following were the principal ones noticed:

(i)   Nearly all troops in the Sub-Area have heard the rumour that thousands of bodies of German troops were washed up on the South Coast of England in the early part of the month.

(ii)   rumour, not so widespread, is that an invasion by sea was started but was destroyed before reaching this country.

There have also been scattered and diverse rumours, none of which have been treated seriously, to the effect that parachute troops had landed in different parts of the country and even that an invasion had taken place in the North of England. The origins of these rumours are difficult to trace but the majority of them are thought to have originated from civilian sources, ie correspondence from friends and relations.

Matters were further complicated when the bodies of actual German soldiers began to wash up along the south coast. Towards the end of September, William Robinson, a Royal Artillery gunner stationed at Herne Bay with the 333rd Coastal Battery, was sent to Folkstone to take part in a macabre detail. Together with half a dozen other servicemen, Robinson was instructed to search the beach between Hythe and St Mary's Bay for dead Germans. On the first day, two such bodies were located, together with seven or eight more over the next two days. All were taken by truck to a field west of New Romney and unloaded behind a canvas screen. There an NCO checked the corpses for identity discs and paybooks, which were in turn handed over to an officer. Robinson recognised the dead men as German soldiers, rather than Luftwaffe airmen or naval personnel, by virtue of their field-grey uniforms.

All appeared to have been in the water for some considerable time. By way of reward for discharging this highly unpleasant fatigue, Gunner Robinson and his colleagues were given a daily ration of twenty Woodbine cigarettes and promised additional daily pay of 2 shillings.

Robinson recounted his remarkable story on a BBC television programme, *First Hand*, broadcast in November 1957. Repeating his account for the *Daily Mail*, he added that the uniforms bore no insignia and that the dead men were assumed to have perished while taking part in an exercise. There is no reason to believe that Robinson was lying, not least because bodies continued to arrive on the Dungeness peninsula over the weeks that followed. Indeed, on 22 October, in a shining example of astute news management, the Ministry of Information encouraged British papers from *The Times* down to report that:

> The body of a German soldier was washed ashore yesterday at Littlestone on the Kent coast. He was wearing the uniform of a German infantry regiment and appeared to be about 28. The body had been in the sea for several weeks and death is believed to have been due to drowning.

The war diary of the 5th Battalion Somerset Light Infantry confirms that the body was actually found on 20 October. Over the same weekend, the remains of a Luftwaffe airman were recovered slightly further to the west. The discovery of a genuine dead German soldier at Littlestone was also announced by the BBC, with the *Folkestone, Hythe and District Herald* sketching in further detail a few days later:

> An examination of the body left no doubt as to its identity. The man, aged about 30, was wearing the field-grey uniform of a German infantry unit, and he was probably an NCO. The body, it was estimated, had been in the sea possibly as long as six weeks, and such a period fits in with the report recently published that the RAF inflicted severe losses on the German invasion troops on the other side of the Channel at about that time. There were no signs of injury externally.

Arrangements were made to bury the dead man at New Romney. Today, the grave of Heinrich Poncke, identified as belonging to Anti-Tank Reserve Company 19, can be visited at the *Deutsche Soldatenfriedhof* at Cannock Chase, Staffordshire. Poncke is unlikely to have perished during an attempt to invade Britain, nor was his corpse one of 30,000 or 50,000 more. Rather, Poncke drowned either while training for Operation Sealion, or – perhaps – during a 'cutting-out' operation mounted by the Royal Navy against German anti-aircraft trawlers in the Channel.

Several days earlier, on 11 October, three motor torpedo boats operating from Dover sank two such flak trawlers moored north of Calais. A total of thirty-four crewmen were captured, with several others drowned. Over the next few weeks, Poncke's body may have been carried by the tide to Littlestone; other corpses would arrive elsewhere, on both sides of the Channel. For British propagandists, the MTB operation was a great stroke of luck. 'Shortly before dawn the Royal Navy put ashore at Dover the trawler crew and ten rather bewildered German soldiers,' John Baker White explained in *The Big Lie*. 'As soon as he looked at their pay books and interrogated them, the Intelligence officer realised that the ten men were drawn from eight different units. Someone jumped to the significance of this fact from the point of view of political warfare and deception.'

That same evening, on the German Forces Programme, as well as in the ordinary German civilian programme from London, it was announced that ten soldiers had been landed at Dover, 'rescued from the sea'. These agreeably defeatist broadcasts also included the name, number and unit identification of each Wehrmacht prisoner. 'We know nothing of the fate of their comrades', the announcer intoned gravely, before concluding with mordant funeral music by Wagner.

No record exists of the discovery of the dozen or so bodies mentioned by Gunner Robinson, nor of any formal burial at New Romney. That said, according to John Baker White, there was some discussion of dropping German corpses back into the Channel in order to add verisimilitude to the rumours already in circulation:

> When we were engaged in building up the burning sea deception we considered a hundred and one ways of adding substance to it. One ingenious plan involved the use of human bodies. So far as I know, it was never put into operation, but it had a much more important counterpart later in the war. Our scheme was to take the charred bodies of Luftwaffe men shot down in the Battle of Britain, dress them in the burnt uniforms of German infantry soldiers and float them ashore on the tide at various points along the invasion coast.

The counterpart referred to was the masterful deception known as Operation Mincemeat. In April 1943, false documents were planted on the body of a dead Welsh tramp named Glyndwr Michael, whose mortal remains were artfully disguised as a major in the Royal Marines and floated ashore from a submarine off Spain. Accepted as genuine by the Abwehr, these carefully faked plans for landings in Greece and Sardinia paved the way for the successful Allied invasion of Sicily in July. Mincemeat only became public knowledge after a British diplomat named Duff Cooper published an unauthorised novel, *Operation Heartbreak*, which drew heavily on the hitherto secret wartime deception, and forced an official acknowledgement in 1953. The true identity of Glyndwr Michael – the so-called 'Man Who Never Was' – remained classified for more than half a century, finally being discovered in 1996.

Like double-cross stings, corpse deceptions had featured in British tactical planning since the First World War. Brigadier General John Charteris, chief intelligence officer for the British Expeditionary Force from 1915 to 1918, later revealed details of a plan to plant a forged diary on a dead German soldier on the Western Front – an unauthorised disclosure which was quickly suppressed. Bearing this episode in mind, and Operation Mincemeat, Major Baker White's corpse scheme from 1940 might not be as odd as it seems at first blush.

'A great many profound secrets are somewhere in print,' wrote Sir Lewis Namier, the diplomat and historian, himself a veteran of propaganda and political warfare operations during the Great War. 'But most are easily detected when one knows what to seek.'

5

'THE STORY THAT IS SWEEPING AMERICA' (AND SWITZERLAND)

The steady stream of disinformation flowing from New York concerning failed landings and floating bodies demonstrated the astonishing effectiveness of British Security Co-ordination, the Big Apple intelligence hub opened by MI6 in June 1940 under the tried and tested guise of a Passport Control Office. In time, BSC came to occupy two whole floors of the International Building at Rockefeller Center, an upscale development consisting of fourteen towering art deco buildings, occupying 22 acres of prime Manhattan real estate. The Secret Intelligence Service leased this valuable office space from the Rockefeller family for a penny rent, and chose a telex address which read as if plucked from a dime store spy thriller: INTREPID.

The elevated New York station was run by Sir William Stephenson, a wealthy Canadian entrepreneur who had served with the Royal Flying Corps during the Great War and won championship titles as a lightweight boxer. During the interwar years, his impressive business portfolio steadily expanded to include aeroplanes, automobiles, pressed steel and construction, as well as real estate, radios and phonographs. The diminutive tycoon even owned the patent on the first apparatus for transmitting photographic images by wireless, which alone generated royalties of £100,000 per annum. 'A man of few words and a magnetic personality and the quality of making anyone ready to follow him to the ends of the earth.' The author of this flattering thumbnail sketch was Ian Fleming, a wartime commander in the Naval Intelligence Division and a frequent visitor to BSC. 'James Bond is a highly romanticised version of the true spy. The real thing is William Stephenson.'

During the summer of 1940, British intelligence charged Stephenson with three main tasks in the United States: the procurement of vital war materials, the protection of convoy shipping from enemy sabotage and the distribution of Allied propaganda. Operating from its highly mechanised eyrie at Rockefeller Center, BSC would in due course take over responsibility for all MI5, SOE and Political Warfare Executive functions in North America, along with the supervision of each and every MI6 station from Mexico to Argentina. Members of Stephenson's largely Canadian staff even infiltrated Axis diplomatic missions as well as those of neutral powers. For the moment, however, a priority task for Stephenson was the rapid acquisition of American weaponry to beat off a likely German invasion, this in defiance of the several Neutrality Acts passed by Congress between 1935 and 1937. As the quiet Canadian spymaster revealed to his subordinate and biographer, Harford Montgomery Hyde:

> The procurement of certain supplies for Britain was high on the list. It was the burning urgency of the attempt to fulfil this requirement that made me instinctively concentrate on a single individual who, despite all my contacts in high places, might achieve more than any widespread effort on the official or sub-official levels which had so far been unproductive.

'Little Bill' Stephenson turned to 'Wild Bill' Donovan. A former classmate of President Franklin D. Roosevelt at Columbia Law School, of Irish immigrant stock, Colonel William Donovan had risen to become a successful public attorney in New York City and wielded considerable influence within Republican circles in Washington. Donovan also boasted impressive credentials as a soldier, having earned the nickname 'Wild Bill' during the Pancho Villa Expedition into Mexico in 1916, before going on to command the 'Fighting 69th' Infantry Regiment in France, winning the Congressional Medal of Honor and returning home as America's most decorated soldier of the First World War. During the inter-war years he travelled extensively in Europe, becoming personally acquainted with leaders such as the Italian dictator Benito Mussolini, and eventually concluding that a second major European war was inevitable. Donovan and Roosevelt may have belonged to opposing political parties, yet both men firmly opposed Hitler and his expansionist Nazi regime, and after war broke out were determined to resist the isolationism prevalent across much of America.

Inconveniently, one of the leading advocates of non-intervention in Europe was Joseph Kennedy, in post as the US ambassador in London since 1938, and a Roosevelt appointee. 'Democracy's all done,' ran one of Kennedy's gloomier predictions, once German bombers began pounding British towns and cities in earnest. 'Democracy's finished in England.' Worse still, a cipher clerk at the American Embassy named Tyler Kent had already been unmasked by MI5 as a hostile agent, having passed details of sensitive private correspondence between Churchill and Roosevelt to the Italian consulate.

With the German Army hardly two dozen miles across the Channel, and no time to lose, Stephenson arranged for Donovan to visit the British Isles to assess the situation at first hand. Given the abundant political sensitivities in play, Donovan travelled as a private emissary rather than as an official American observer. Chief among several open questions for his sponsor, President Roosevelt, were: could the RAF defeat Hitler's vaunted Luftwaffe, and was the shattered and demoralised British Army still capable of beating off a full-scale invasion? Joseph Kennedy, for one, viewed Britain as a lost cause. It was therefore imperative that London appear resourceful and resolute, and in so doing enable Stephenson to secure the release of 'surplus' American armaments and munitions, as well as obsolete warships to help protect the Atlantic convoy routes from marauding U-boats.

Donovan arrived in London on 16 July, the very same day that Hitler issued orders to prepare a cross-Channel invasion of the British Isles. During the course of a busy fortnight, the colonel was introduced to King George VI and Winston Churchill, as well as the respective heads of MI6, MI5 and the SOE. At the same time, British procurement agents in Washington held clandestine meetings with senior American industrial planners, from which emerged plans to significantly expand the US aircraft industry. Neither of the two Bills, Stephenson and Donovan, would be particularly well served by diligent biographers during their lifetimes. Nevertheless, Stephenson is said to have talked up the importance of flame and petroleum defences by the author of *A Man Called Intrepid*, while in *Donovan of OSS* writer Corey Ford asserts that:

> Because he was Bill Donovan, the British showed him things no American had seen before: their top secret invention of radar, their newest interceptor planes, their coastal defences. They unlocked their safes, and initiated him into the mysteries of the SIS and the techniques of unorthodox warfare. He was made privy to some of Britain's ingenious propaganda devices, including the carefully planted rumour that a system of underwater pipelines could turn every beach and cove into a sea of flaming oil in case of German landings.

Given that no working sea flame barrages existed in July 1940, it seems unlikely that Donovan can have witnessed one in operation. Nevertheless, the Petroleum Warfare Department had just been formed, numerous flame traps were under construction inland, along with a smaller number of beach installations, and Operation Lucifer was beginning to take shape. There is little reason to doubt that the colonel was briefed on petroleum warfare experiments, and none at all that he came to form a part of the covert pipeline by which Big Lies were circulated worldwide. 'Much of what Donovan saw was an elaborate deception to persuade him that Britain possessed the means to continue the fight,' confirms intelligence historian Nigel West. 'His dramatic visit to England will remain one of the greatest intelligence triumphs of the war.'

If much of what Donovan saw and heard in Britain was ultra top secret, his presence in the country was anything but. With his remarkable fact-finding mission completed, on 3 August the colonel returned to the States on board a flying boat from Poole. Within a week, newspapers on both sides of the Atlantic were openly reporting that Donovan was poised to tell FDR that 'a German invasion of England, if attempted, is not likely to succeed'. Already, on 4 August, General John J. Pershing had spoken out strongly in favour of arming Britain, broadcasting to the American people:

> With democracy and liberty overthrown on the continent of Europe, only the British are left to defend democracy and liberty in Europe. By sending help to the British, we can still hope with confidence to keep the war on the other side of the Atlantic, where the enemies of liberty, if possible should be defeated.

Roosevelt felt the same way. On the basis of the opinions Donovan expressed on his return, the President agreed to enter into negotiations with Britain which would result in the delivery of desperately needed equipment. During the summer and autumn of 1940, this took the form of munitions, automatic weapons and state-of-the-art Sperry bomb sights, as well as fifty mothballed destroyers. In return, Britain and Canada granted the US basing rights in the Caribbean and Newfoundland. This de facto Lend–Lease scheme hardly chimed with the stringent Neutrality Acts, an in addition a fiercely contested presidential election loomed ahead in November. In London, as in Washington, this delicate political game was finely balanced. 'If the picture was painted too darkly,' Churchill warned members of his War Cabinet, 'elements in the United States would say that it was useless to help us, for such help would be wasted and thrown away. If too bright a picture was painted, then there might be a tendency to withhold assistance.'

Donovan was soon followed by an official American Military Mission, whose three members spent a month in the United Kingdom during August and September, and in doing so witnessed something of the Battle of Britain at first hand. 'It was like a hawk coming down on chickens in a barnyard,' Brigadier General George Strong told reporters of a German attack broken up by Hurricanes on 15 September. 'The Germans scattered like a bat out of hell. I do not think that a single bomb was dropped.' On the subject of seaborne invasion, the future chief of the US Military Intelligence Corps judged that the 'odds on the attempted invasion are lengthening with each passing day', adding that the Germans could expect the 'surprise of their lives' on landing, the time having passed when a cross-Channel expedition might be attempted without 'appalling loss'.

Did this surprise involve burning oil? If Donovan was briefed on petroleum weapons, it seems safe to assume that General Strong would have been too. Beyond doubt is the fact that Bill Stephenson was extraordinarily well connected. Colonel Donovan aside, other high-level American contacts fostered by BSC included Colonel Frank Knox, then the US Navy secretary, who also happened to own the *Chicago Daily News*. 'I give Britain a better than even chance to defeat Germany,' Knox declared helpfully on 17 September. 'I feel quite cheerful about it. The chance of a successful invasion of Britain is getting weaker every day.'

Written in 1945, and a classified document until 1998, the official history of British Security Co-ordination confirms that the innocuously named intelligence hub was well placed to 'initiate internal propaganda' through an expanding network of 'undercover contacts with selected newspapers'. These were stated to include the *New York Times*, *New York Herald Tribune* and the *Baltimore Sun*, though the list was far longer, and took in the *New York Sun* and *Chicago Daily News*. Key syndicated columnists also played a part, as did radio. An independent American press agency was retained to place stories elsewhere, while advanced American wire service technology served to increase the speed at which British sibs and rumours could be spread abroad. 'This highly mechanised eyrie in Rockefeller Center,' wrote Ian Fleming, later the creator of super spy James Bond, 'was able to render innumerable services that could not have been asked for, let alone executed, through the normal channels.'

The official history of BSC goes on to acknowledge a debt to several named individuals who 'rendered service of particular value', including the *New York Times* publisher Arthur H. Sulzberger, as well as William L. Shirer of Columbia Broadcasting. Indeed, Shirer's bestselling *Berlin Diary*, published in June of the following year, would do much to ensure the longevity of the original Big Lie devised by John Baker White. As previously noted, sensational rumours of an invasion actually attempted began to feed back from America after the Cromwell alarm on 7 September, when the *New York Sun* reported a 'suicidal' thrust on the west of England. The helping hand of Colonel William Donovan is more explicitly revealed by an article run by the *New York Times* on 21 September, quoting a steel company executive named Robert Solberg, back in the States with his wife and daughter after living in France for two decades:

> Mr Solberg said the Germans were holding invasion practice off the French coast also. He asserted, as did other passengers, that the Dutch and the French were supplying the British with advance information of German exercises on self-propelled barges in the Channel, and that British bombers had taken a heavy toll. Mr Solberg added that he had definite information that the Germans have attempted no actual invasion of England. He said the British, tipped off by the Dutch and French, waited for the barges with planes and submarines and that 'thousands of Germans have been lost in this fashion'. Mr Solberg said he recently visited a French Channel port where bodies of German troops were being washed ashore daily.

Solberg's story appeared to confirm the account given a week earlier by Dr Charles Bove, a former surgeon at the American Hospital in Paris. Interviewed by journalists as he disembarked from the *Exeter*, Bove claimed to have seen hundreds of dead German soldiers in the sea around Cherbourg. A *Daily Mail* correspondent in New York teased further details from steel executive Solberg, who had escaped from Europe shortly after Bove, on 25 August:

> The British sent submarines and planes and sank the barges. It is estimated that at least 10,000 Germans lost their lives. Many of the German troops are refusing to continue the practice and hundreds are being transported back to Germany with their hands tied behind their backs. When these prison trains cross the border into Germany, air raid alarms are sounded to drive people underground so that they will not see Nazi soldiers in disgrace.

In truth, talkative Robert Solborg – the correct spelling of his surname – was no ordinary refugee, and like Dr Bove was reciting from a script prepared by British intelligence. Moreover, both men and their remarkable stories can be traced through the primitive deception networks extant in 1940 like a barium meal.

Solborg was in fact the son of a Polish Army general. Born in Warsaw, he had followed his father into the military and served as a cavalry officer in the Czar's army during the First World War. After suffering a serious wound in 1916, he joined the

Russian military purchasing commission in New York, only to find himself stranded by the Bolshevik revolution the following year. After taking American citizenship, Solborg was allowed to enlist in the US Army, serving briefly as a military attaché in Paris before taking up a position with the huge Armco Steel Corporation. By the time the Second World War broke out in 1939, Solborg had risen to become managing director of Armco in both Britain and France, and may have known Bill Stephenson through the steel industry. As a senior representative of the American parent company, Solborg was permitted to travel inside Germany during the spring of 1940 to observe industrial production. Being Polish by birth, Solborg naturally passed on his findings to MI6. He fled Paris with his family in June, and by the end of the year had joined – or more likely rejoined – the American military intelligence corps.

His commanding officer was none other than Colonel William Donovan. Indeed, in October 1941 Solborg would himself be sent on a mission to London as head of the Special Operations Branch of CO1, an organisation soon rebranded as the Office of Strategic Services (OSS) and later still the Central Intelligence Agency. Far from being just another displaced neutral fleeing war-torn Europe, Robert Solborg was a veteran secret soldier and spy who, within a year of returning to the States, was placed in charge of the American version of the Special Operations Executive.

Almost certainly, it was Solborg who briefed refugee surgeon Charles Bove on the story of the invasion that failed. In *A Surgeon in Paris*, a detailed memoir published in 1956, Bove records that in June 1940 he left the French capital after the German occupation forces confiscated most of his medical equipment. He spent a month in the luxurious resort town of Biarritz, on the Atlantic coast near the Spanish frontier, then retraced his steps to Paris, where he gathered together what remained of his money before heading south again, this time to Portugal via Spain, hoping to find a place on a ship bound for the United States.

Once his train crossed the frontier at Elvas, Bove took time out to stretch his legs. There, on the platform, he encountered an old friend from Paris: Robert Solborg. By his own account, the Armco executive had escaped Paris just ahead of the Germans, and now regularly drove up from Lisbon to the Spanish border to greet familiar faces on the train from Badajoz. More probably, Solborg was scouting for useful contacts on behalf of MI6 and offered Bove some kind of inducement – money, or guaranteed passage back to the States – in return for feeding a Big Lie or three to the press.

To secure a place on board the liner *Excambion* within days of arriving in Lisbon was certainly a remarkable achievement. 'I was surrounded by reporters on my arrival in New York,' Bove continued, 'since I was one of the first of my countrymen to bring personal experience of conditions in France under the Nazi occupation.' This interview, no doubt stage-managed by BSC, was widely reported across America, and thereafter the world. Charles Bove was hardly hostile to the Allied cause: during the previous war he had served with the American Expeditionary Force in France as a surgical major. His eyewitness account of 'hundreds' of dead German soldiers made for powerful propaganda in 1940, yet in his detailed memoir *A Surgeon In Paris*, published sixteen years later, the tale of a detour to Cherbourg and scores of bodies in the water was conspicuous only by its absence.

Reports carried by ostensibly neutral American media sources clearly packed far more propaganda punch than official statements released by the Ministry of Information in London. The following selection, taken from the *New York Times* and elsewhere, reflect the general tone of failed invasion rumours passed for circulation by the UPC at Woburn, doubtless with no little merriment. All conform to the 'important rules' laid down by EH/SOE and BSC, including multiplicity of origins, lack of traceability to a British source and potential for spontaneous exaggeration:

NAZI DEAD SAID TO HALT FISHING: A Scottish family received a letter today from a relative in Sweden reporting that Swedish fisherman were forced to abandon herring fisheries because the bodies of many German soldiers were floating in the waters off the southern coast of Sweden. The letter said the German authorities had offered a reward of about 75 cents for each body recovered with the uniform intact.

NAZI LOSSES SEEN IN INVASION DRILLS: The Germans have suffered severe losses in exercises and manoeuvres in the English Channel preparatory to an invasion attempt, according to passengers of the American Export Line. One estimate was that 10,000 men had been lost. 'The German soldiers,' said one passenger, who refused to give his name because he has relatives living in Holland, 'were heavily armed and weighted down with full equipment. They were taken a mile or so to sea off the Netherlands coast aboard flat-bottomed boats. The boats would come toward shore and the men were forced to leap out and swim. We people living near the sea saw thousands of floating bodies of officers and men floating in the water. Many soldiers rebelled and were chained and taken back to the interior of Germany to be punished for their insubordination.'

LETTER TO THE EDITOR FROM NORWAY: In Oslo truckloads of German soldiers – tied and bound – pass in the streets on their way to Fort Akershus, where they would rather be shot than drowned. The reason being that they refuse to invade England in the little boats much too small to cross the North Sea.

THOUSANDS OF NAZI TROOPS DIE IN BATTERED INVASION PORTS: There they have received a severe handling by the RAF. German losses in Cherbourg are estimated at between 40,000 and 50,000 killed and wounded. Almost every civil and military hospital from the Belgian to the Spanish frontier has been requisitioned. More than 12,000 wounded German soldiers occupy Bordeaux hospitals and approximately 7,000 are in Paris. The majority of the one-time fashionable hotels at Biarritz are now either convalescent homes or hospitals.

Predictably, the most sensational story by far came courtesy of the *New York Sun*. Citing an 'unofficial' British source, the tabloid informed readers that:

At dawn … from the fog and haze of the sea there emerged hundreds of flat-bottomed barges, each carrying about 200 German soldiers wearing full field equipment. The British were not taken by surprise because they had been expecting just such an assault for some time … While the British flyers battled the German air force the land batteries, protected by barrage balloons, raked the barges with fire. The carnage was terrific.

Meanwhile detachments of the British fleet, which had been hovering along the south coast of England, pushed in behind the barges and cut them off from France … The sun had risen meanwhile, dissipating the fog which had cloaked the Channel for the invaders and perfect visibility made the accuracy of the fire of the defenders even greater. When it was apparent that the barges could not reach the shore, the naval units withdrew to safety, leaving the Channel filled with bodies and wreckage.

Amusingly, the *Sun* portrayed crack German invasion troops as little more than Roman galley slaves:

The barges were very light wooden and metal affairs, hand propelled, and obviously intended for only a one-way trip … Levers along the sides connect with a drive shaft which is geared to a propeller, and the more men work the levers back and forth, the faster the craft will travel.

Despite the patent absurdity of the notion that Hitler had lost half his invasion force, or that troops were forced to swim ashore in full equipment, clothed in second-hand uniforms exchanged for miserly cash rewards, Berlin was obliged to issue the first of several formal denials:

CHANNEL LOSSES DENIED: Authorised German sources said today that there was no truth in reports that many thousands of bodies of German soldiers were being washed ashore along the English Channel. Such accounts were declared to be an indication of a situation that compels the British 'to put out such silly lies'.

Unfortunately for Nazi propaganda chief Joseph Goebbels, the BSC brief extended to counteracting equivalent German activity in North America. Thus on 20 September, their tamest paper, the *New York Herald Tribune*, ran a prominent report headlined 'Britannia Rules the Channel'.

That Britain and America enjoyed a special relationship was again demonstrated in fine style two days later. Shortly after midnight, Roosevelt dispatched an urgent telegram to Churchill, warning that the invasion would be set in motion at 3 a.m. The president's 'most reliable source' was Alexander Kirk, the American chargé d'affaires in Berlin, who enjoyed contacts with senior German figures opposed to the Nazi regime. In addition, Kirk had accurately predicted the German attack on France and the Low Countries in May. But it was not to be. 'Prospects do not look good for invasion,' John Colville noted at lunchtime. 'Pouring rain and a gale blowing up ... The PM, though slightly sceptical, kept himself busy telephoning to people about it all morning.'

***

When the British ambassador in Switzerland told London that 'queer stories about burning oil' were 'current everywhere' by the end of the first week in September, Churchill deemed the sib a 'favourable' development, then spoke to the nation of burning Nazi tyranny out of Europe with a 'steady and consuming flame'. Further evidence that Germany's southern neighbour was a major artery for the Big Lie devised by John Baker White in July would come via radio journalist William L. Shirer, thanked by name for rendering 'service of particular value' in the official history of British Security Co-ordination.

Shirer, a native of Chicago, had worked first as European correspondent for the *Tribune*, before becoming a wireless reporter for Universal, International News and finally CBS. His boss at Columbia, Ed Murrow, reported from London, while Shirer covered the Continent from Vienna, Paris and Berlin. Having heard rumours of a calamitous landing while visiting Geneva, Shirer recorded in his *Berlin Diary* for 18 September:

> The stories there were that either in attempted German raids with sizeable landing parties on the English coast, or in rehearsals with boats and barges off the French coast, the British had given the Germans a bad pummelling. The reports reaching Switzerland from France were that many German barges and ships had been destroyed and a considerable number of German troops drowned; also that the British used a new type of wireless-directed torpedo which spread ignited oil on the water and burned the barges.

Whereas a submarine scheme was technically feasible, as *L26* had demonstrated in April, oil torpedoes sounded more like a scheme inspired by Lord Hankey, who had suggested releasing barrels of Greek Fire from British submarines off Gallipoli in 1915. Certainly Major Desmond Morton fancied that highly conspicuous activity by the Petroleum Warfare Department on the south coast during August had played a part in capsizing Operation Sealion. After digesting the contents of Kelly's second coded telegram from Berne on 6 September, which told of a reluctance on the part of German troops to cross the Channel 'partly owing to stories such as that regarding oil', Churchill's trusted intelligence advisor fired off a congratulatory memo to Hankey, noting with pleasure that 'evidently your experiments have had a wholly unexpected success'.

In France and the Low Countries, the burning sea sib was reinforced by a witty propaganda leaflet dropped by the RAF over crowded invasion ports such as Calais, Boulogne and Antwerp. Mockingly titled *Wir Fahren Gegen Engelland* (the best-known line in the swaggering *Engellandlied*), this short invasion phrasebook was printed in French, Dutch and German, and plainly intended for consumption by friendly civilians as well as enemy troops. A complete facsimile is reproduced in Appendix 1, but of particular interest is section two, which made explicit reference to fire on the surface of the sea:

DURING THE INVASION:
1. The sea crossing – storm – fog – gale.
2. We feel seasick. Where is the bucket?

3. Is that a bomb – torpedo – grenade – mine?
4. Look out! English torpedo boats – destroyers – cruisers – battleships – bombers!
5. Our boat has capsized – sunk – BURNT – exploded!
6. Our squad – platoon – company – battalion – regiment is going under!
7. The others – the whole division – the entire army corps – too!
8. Another ship is beginning to sink.
9. Where is our fleet – our air force?
10. THE SEA SMELLS OF PETROL HERE!
11. THE SEA EVEN BURNS HERE!
12. SEE HOW WELL THE CAPTAIN BURNS!
13. Karl – Willi – Fritz – Johann – Abraham: CREMATED – drowned – minced by the propellers!
14. We must turn back!
15. *Wir fahren gegen Engelland!* (worse luck)

These same elements were adapted for wireless broadcast by Denis Sefton Delmer on the German service still maintained by the BBC. A British journalist of Australian heritage, Delmer was a fluent German speaker, having been born in Berlin, where he later represented the *Daily Express*, and even interviewed Hitler. During this period, Delmer found himself criticised for being a Nazi sympathiser and, for a time, the British government suspected that he was in the pay of the Nazis. Perversely, certain Nazi leaders thought he was an MI6 agent. In due course he would take over responsibility for all black propaganda activity undertaken by the Political Warfare Executive. In September 1940, however, Delmer's duties were largely confined to transmitting to the enemy 'cheerful little talks full of teasing and derision' two or three times a week. In his second volume of autobiography, *Black Boomerang*, he records the transmission in early October of a droll English lesson for would-be invaders. The mordant script ran thus:

We English, as you know, are notoriously bad at languages, and so it will be best, *meine Herren Engellandfahrer*, if you learn a few useful English phrases before visiting us.

For your first lesson we will take: *Die Kanaluberfahrt* ... the Channel crossing, the Chan-nel cros-sing. Now just repeat after me: *Das Boot sinkt* ... the boat is sinking, the boat is sin-king. *Das Wasser ist kalt* ... the water is cold. *Sehr kalt* ... very cold.

Now, I will give you a verb that should come in useful. Again please repeat after me:

Ich brenne ... I burn

Du brennst ... you burn

Er brennt ... he burns

Wir brennen ... we burn

Ihr brennt ... you are burning

Yes, *meine Herren*, in English, a rather practical language, we use the same word 'you' for both the singular and the plural:

Ihr brennt ... you are burning

Sie brennen ... they burn

And if I may be allowed to suggest a phrase: *Der SS SturmFührer brennt auch ganz schon* ... The SS captain is also burning quite nicely, the SS captain is al-so burning quite nice-ly!

Unsurprisingly, Delmer's name was added to the *Sonderfahndungsliste GB*, a 'black book' list of prominent persons to be arrested once Britain had fallen. In his memoirs, however, the veteran psychological warrior went on to make an even more extraordinary claim. Describing this inflammatory English lesson as 'crude stuff', Delmer also inferred that the broadcast was part of a wider scheme: 'The line about burning in the Channel fitted in perfectly, as of course it was intended to, with the information which our deception services had planted on Admiral Canaris, the head of Hitler's espionage.'

If true, this remarkable admission by a senior Allied propagandist may go some way towards explaining why the German Navy began to trial countermeasures against burning oil on water as early as 10 August. 'Our rumour agencies, too, had been busy spreading it everywhere,' Delmer continued, confirming the content of the several telegrams sent from Berne by Sir David Kelly:

> The mean murderous British, it was said, had apparatus in readiness with which they were going to set the Channel and the beaches on fire at such time as Hitler launched his boats. This was a lie. But it went over so well that it is believed by many Germans to this day.

The extent to which Admiral Wilhelm Canaris and the Abwehr actively collaborated with their counterparts in Allied intelligence during the Second World War is a subject still wrapped in mystery. Several senior Abwehr officers plotted against Hitler throughout the war, while Canaris would himself eventually be accused of treason and executed in brutal fashion in 1945. One of his section chiefs, Colonel Erwin von Lahousen, gave evidence against Hermann Göring and other leading Nazis at the Nuremburg war crimes tribunal. Another, Hans Oster, passed information to the Soviets via the Lucy spy ring, an anti-Hitler group based in Switzerland. The same covert network also included Hans Bernd Gisevius, the German vice consul in Zurich. Gisevius was also close to Canaris and regularly passed information to MI6. Indeed, between August 1940 and December 1942 no less than twenty-five reports based on information provided by Gisevius were dispatched from Geneva to London; after 1943, his contacts with the US Office of Strategic Services were even closer. Like Erwin von Lahousen, Gisevius would also survive the violent end of the Nazi regime and give evidence at the Nuremberg trial.

Astonishingly, MI6 maintained a top-secret channel of communication with Hitler's chief of intelligence, Wilhelm Canaris. This covert conduit consisted of his loyal subordinate Hans Bernd Gisevius, together with a Polish woman named Halina Szymanska, whom Canaris helped to escape to Switzerland in December 1939. Her husband, Antoni Szymanski, had been the last Polish military attaché in Berlin before the outbreak of war and was now a prisoner of the Soviets. His wife, 'a very attractive and formidable personality' according to one British intelligence officer, became mistress to Canaris. After reaching Switzerland with her three children, Szymanska was given a part-time cover job as a typist by the Polish legation in Berne – a position funded by MI6, who assigned her the code name Z-5/1.

However, secure communications with London were problematic. In Switzerland, as in other neutral territories, MI6 operated under cover of a Passport Control Office, located within the British Embassy in Berne. The diplomat in charge there was Sir David Kelly. A wireless set kept in Geneva by SIS could be used only as a receiver, since the Swiss authorities forbade foreign missions from sending encrypted messages abroad except through the Swiss Post Office. In reporting the spread of the burning oil rumour on 26 August, using this highly insecure official method, Kelly was obliged to describe the same kind of tortuous route then used by Bletchley Park to conceal the source of Enigma decrypts. Thus according to Kelly:

This tale first reached us via Vichy and French Embassy allegedly from American journalists talking to German soldiers in Holland. It is now repeated to Monsieur Bovet Grisel, brother of Federal Chancellor, Swiss Legation, Berlin … by Frenchmen who had it from German airmen at Lyons.

In the light of Sefton Delmer's remarks about Canaris, the route may have been simpler: Agent Z-5/1. Sealion intelligence was also being passed on to MI6 by another well-placed Abwehr officer named Paul Thümmell, designated A.54, who had volunteered his services to the Czechs before the outbreak of war. These reports, too, were routed through Switzerland. Delmer's candid admission, which might easily have attracted a D Notice ban in 1962, tends to support the idea that British intelligence fed disinformation about flame direct to the Abwehr, rather than relying only on sibs whispered across the bars of favoured Continental hotels.

Conceivably, the double-cross system run by MI5 was also involved. A colourful SNOW sub-agent code-named BISCUIT, in reality an unquiet Canadian named Sam McCarthy who had served jail time for drug-smuggling, was flown out to Lisbon at the end of July. Part of Biscuit's mission was to paint an 'extremely exaggerated and totally inaccurate' picture of British defences to Major Nikolaus Ritter, Arthur Owen's slippery Abwehr controller. Within two weeks of this meeting, the German Navy began their own trials with burning oil at Wilhelmshaven. 'His whole visit seems to have been a thorough success,' remarked Guy Liddell of MI5, after McCarthy returned to London in August.

***

In contrast to this flurry of subterranean activities in Europe, not a single word about oil torpedoes and burning seas would be circulated in America until the end of the year. Undoubtedly this coyness around the offensive use of flame owed much to the fact that Franklin D. Roosevelt desperately wanted to be re-elected for an historic third term on 5 November, when America went to the polls for the thirty-ninth quadrennial presidential election.

It is often overlooked that his Republican opponent, Wendell Willkie, was also a moderate, and like Roosevelt – and most of the American military establishment – favoured the continued supply of aid to Britain. However, the Republican Party itself was deeply divided between isolationists, adamant that the nation should avoid taking any steps which might drag America into a European war, and interventionists like Colonel Donovan, who held that America's survival depended on helping Allied democracies defeat totalitarian Axis powers. Established in September, the America First Committee rapidly gained ground as an anti-war pressure group, launching a petition aimed at strict enforcement of the 1939 Neutrality Act and accusing Roosevelt of lying to the American people. Charles Lindbergh, the famous aviator (and infamous anti-Semite), was already an outspoken advocate of non-intervention, and even went so far as to propose a neutrality pact with Nazi Germany.

Between August and October 1940 the presidential campaign played out against a background of fierce and frequently acrimonious debate. This period precisely coincided with the Battle of Britain and the Sealion invasion scare, and for much of it the popular vote in America was too close to call. Perhaps more than anyone else in the free world, Churchill understood the pressing need to return Roosevelt to the White House in order to secure the survival of Britain and of democracy itself. To reduce the risk of political blowback in Washington, the trial and conviction of Tyler Kent, the isolationist mole inside the US Embassy in London, who had leaked details of private correspondence between the British prime minister and the American president, was held back until 7 November, two days after FDR was safely returned to the White House. By the same token, banner headlines in the *New York Times* and *Chicago Tribune* asserting that Britain was ready, willing and able to roast German soldiers alive on a grand scale might have lost Roosevelt precious votes, if only by making the British seem every bit as bestial as the Nazis.

The first signs of change came in the middle of October. In London, a slender bulletin issued by the Air Ministry News Service on the evening of the 18th appeared to confirm that German assault troops had embarked for a landing on 16 September, only to be forced off their transports by pinpoint RAF bombing: 'The invasion plans were not adopted because of the sustained offensive by the Royal Air Force, whose extraordinary accuracy in bombing has incidently [*sic*] been much admired by the Dutch.' Many took this as gospel, including a Home Guard officer in Kent named Rodney Foster, who noted in his diary: 'There was evidently some truth in the American stories of an attempted invasion. We are now told that troops were embarked on 16 September, and some of the transports were sunk by the RAF when full of troops.'

Berlin responded by issuing another categorical denial, reported – albeit briefly – in the *New York Times* and elsewhere: 'Authorised German sources said today that "nothing is known" here about any foiling of a German invasion attempt to invade Great Britain by British air attacks on transports in the Channel harbours, as reported by British authorities.'

Reporting the gist of the Air Ministry bulletin the following day, along with fresh news of 'terrific' carnage and 'bodies and wreckage' from the *New York Sun*, *The Daily Telegraph* now suggested that the enemy invasion fleet gathered in the Channel ports had been 'burned' on the night of 15–16 September: 'In London it was stated that the destruction of these vessels was due to the effectiveness of the RAF bombardment, which, by setting fire to the petrol barges, automatically destroyed many of the ships.' As released, the Air Ministry bulletin made no mention of flame, although it may be significant that *The Telegraph* was a favoured title for deliberate leaks from Department EH at Woburn.

Other similar reports at the end of October repeated the canard of miserly cash rewards for uniforms recovered intact, at the same time adding the intriguing detail that '4,000 German patients are now in Paris hospitals suffering from burns'. *The War Illustrated*, a popular weekly magazine, then weighed in with a full-page summary of purple invasion rumours, pinning the same date on the failed attempt: 16 September. Bodies washed ashore figured prominently, as well as 'several thousand severely burned German soldiers' spied in French hospitals. Oil bombs, it was said, had been deployed by the RAF, bringing about 'a fitting end to the day which Hitler had chosen to be *Der Tag*'.

The first flame reports to appear in print scanned as if German personnel had been incinerated by accident, rather than deliberately burned to death. At this time, interested British parties including MI6, EH/SOE and the Foreign Office found themselves struggling to disseminate a glut of propaganda material, both black and white, as well as multiple shades of grey. In November, however, this bottleneck was eased when Colonel William Donovan set up a small London office, paid for by the White House from secret funds and located within the grand surrounds of Bush House, home to the BBC's foreign service. This covert bureau was run by William Whitney, an American lawyer and intelligence officer, whose main purpose (at least according to MI5) was to 'collect as much vital information as he can which has any bearing on the part being played by the United States and the possibility of her entering the war'.

In this way Donovan – and therefore Roosevelt – was able to bypass troublesome isolationist Joseph Kennedy, as well as suspect Embassy staff such as Tyler Kent. To some extent the Bush House office resembled British Security Co-ordination in Manhattan, not least because Whitney and his team were also engaged in 'press and propaganda' activities and are likely to have collaborated with BSC on a significant development of the burning sea story syndicated by the North American Newspaper Alliance. On 15 December, the *New York Times* ran a front page report attributed to one Boris Nikolaevsky, puffed as 'a distinguished Russian publicist and historian', but in truth a political refugee. Beneath the eye-catching headline 'Nazi Invaders Held "Consumed By Fire" – Dead Are Put At 80,000', the piece opened up a bold new chapter in British political warfare:

> There have been at least two attempts by the Germans to invade England from the French coast, and in both instances the Nazis were literally consumed by fire. This was the story told in France by workers from the occupied area along

the Channel coast and confirmed by nurses who worked in hospitals attending German soldiers who had escaped from the British flames.

The first invasion attempt was made in August, the second early in September. Both failed when British planes dropped incendiary bombs and set afire tanks of oil and gasoline in the Channel. As disclosed by Frenchmen in a position to know, the British sowed the Channel with oil tanks sufficiently beneath the surface to be hidden from view. Parallel with these the British anchored thousands of gasoline tanks. Then they waited for the Germans.

On the first occasion the Germans advanced in approximately 1,200 specially constructed aluminium barges, each bearing about 50 soldiers and equipment. They struck the oil and gasoline line about midway between the French and British coasts. At the same time British planes in the skies began raining incendiary bombs. In a few minutes the Channel was a mass of fire enveloping the Nazi barges.

CASUALTIES SAID TO BE HIGH: 'We were caught like fish in a frying pan' was the way a German soldier who escaped from the debacle described it to a French nurse. Only a few thousand Germans succeeded in reaching the French coast. The others perished in the sea or were burned to death. The Germans tried again in September, over another route, and suffered a similar fate.

People in the occupied French ports estimate that perhaps as many as 80,000 German troops perished in the two attempts. The fact is that hospitals in occupied France are filled with Nazi soldiers, all of them suffering from severe burns. Thousands of dead Germans have been washed ashore.

According to reports brought back by persons who succeeded in making their way to the unoccupied zone, there was a wave of mutinies in the German Army in September, many of the troops declaring that they would not face again the 'burning sea' when they learned that a third attempt at invasion of England was being planned.

Quite how a homeless Russian dissident had come by details of Britain's newest secret weapon was nowhere questioned. Indeed, given that the invasion threat had receded by December 1940, and that Roosevelt had won the election fully five weeks earlier, the timing of Nikolaevsky's extraordinary article begs a number of questions. No line of oil tanks were submerged in the Channel, just as no British submarines were equipped with a 'new type of wireless-directed torpedo' able to spread oil on the surface of open water. Or had the legend of deadly Greek Fire come full circle? In theory at least, both of these imaginary weapons could be deployed just about anywhere in the European theatre, and two days earlier, on 13 December, Hitler had issued orders for an invasion of Greece. Conceivably, the Nikolaevsky report was a shrewd ruse to bluff German planners that a seaborne landing in the Mediterranean might also be 'literally consumed' by flames.

From this point onwards the hitherto separate sub-plots of floating corpses and burning seas became a single narrative. Why Nikolaevsky should have become the catalyst can only be guessed at. Unlike Robert Solborg, who was a veteran of the Imperial Russian Army, Nikolaevsky boasted a colourful past as a leading Marxist revolutionary. Banished into Siberian exile no less than three times by the Tsarist regime, he was then denounced by the Soviets as a Menshevik and finally deported in 1922. The Leon Trotsky archive was later stolen from his office in Berlin, and after Hitler gained power in 1933 the dissident Russian socialist quit Germany for France. Like Dr Charles Bove, who arrived in New York three months earlier, Boris Nikolaevsky was another high-profile refugee in financial low-water, who probably agreed to promote this latest variation on the Big Lie in return for safe passage to the United States. His acquaintance with British intelligence could not have been more obvious if photographs had pictured him with snow on his boots.

Back in Britain, newspapers reliant on humdrum handouts from the Ministry of Information grew restless. 'All this stuff is at complete variance with the official statements,' complained the editor of the *Dover Express* after Nikolaevsky was quoted in several national titles. 'If it is true, Parliament ought to know why it was not made public.' The *Express* also rued that the foreign press corps seemed to enjoy greater freedom of movement in Britain than native journalists. Meanwhile the sinister weapon of Allied propaganda continued to score direct hits. Colonel Frank Knox, the US naval secretary and proprietor of the *Chicago Daily News*, now began dropping hints that Germany was 'contemplating in a big way' the use of poison gas if and when an invasion of Britain was finally launched.

Hokum such as the Nikolaevsky report belied the fact that the chemists and engineers of the Petroleum Warfare Department were still struggling to find a reliable means of firing the sea on command. By October 1940, the hush-hush team which frequently masqueraded as the Public Works Department had relocated all marine flame barrage research to a new Experimental School at Studland Bay, an isolated cove near Poole in Dorset. A separate sea barrage developed by the army at Shoeburyness was demonstrated successfully to Winston Churchill, but took several months to complete. The flagship barrage constructed by the PWD at Deal extended over a frontage of 520 yards yet also failed to deliver convincing results. 'We drove ahead there against many difficulties,' recalled Sir Donald Banks. 'Some of our sappers were blown up by beach mines. Occasionally we were bombed, and the long-range guns from Calais turned their attentions in our direction.'

Not long after it was completed, the barrage at Deal was wrecked by a violent north-easterly gale. Nonetheless, had Sealion beached there the unreliable installation might have provoked alarm of a different kind. Ignition was effected by a combination of electrical (Phoenix) and chemical (Eel) igniters, both of which proved susceptible to the vagaries of salt water and sand. A simple yet effective solution was suggested by the senior technician, a Mr H.J. Zass, who instructed his driver to tour around East Kent and buy up every available condom he could find, in the process earning the PWD an enviable – if slightly unsavoury – reputation.

6

FLAMING TO VICTORY

In December 1940, with President Franklin D. Roosevelt re-elected for a historic third term, Colonel William Donovan returned to London on a second mystery mission. Some guessed he would become the new US ambassador, stepping into the shoes of isolationist Joe Kennedy, who had lately tendered his resignation. Roosevelt's de facto intelligence chief was actually in town to gauge Britain's ability to withstand the Luftwaffe's aerial blitz, as well as the resolve of the Free French. Churchill gave Donovan a generous lunch at Downing Street, and as Christmas approached the colonel gifted his host another golden propaganda bullet. 'After my last visit here I said back at home that I found in this country determination, resolution and valour,' Donovan told an informal gathering of journalists. 'Now I would add "confidence" to that list.'

Back in New York, the political warfare effort being waged by British Security Co-ordination now graduated from quotidian newspapers to durable books. Like his Columbia Broadcasting colleague Ed Murrow, William L. Shirer was an enthusiastic promoter of the Allied cause long before the United States formally entered the war, and is one of several American journalists thanked by name in the official history of BSC. Indeed, Shirer was almost as famous as his boss, having delivered a memorable radio broadcast from the Forest of Compiègne in June, crouched outside the old railway coach in which the new Armistice was signed, chosen by Hitler and Göring to maximise the humiliation inflicted on Germany's old enemy, France. Fired by a 'deep burning hatred of all that Nazism stands for', Shirer elected to return to New York at the close of 1940 and wasted little time in writing up his *Berlin Diary: The Journal of a Foreign Correspondent*. Published by Knopf in June, this 'uncensored account' became an immediate bestseller in the

States, moving 600,000 copies in its first year and profoundly shaping American public opinion on Hitler and the Nazi regime.

As described in the previous chapter, while in Geneva on the night of 16 September, Shirer heard rumours from France that the Germans had attempted a landing in Britain, only to be 'repulsed with heavy losses'. The rumour seemed to refer to an attempt made that same day, scuppered by a new type of oil torpedo, about which Shirer rightly claimed to be sceptical: 'The stories were that either in attempted German raids with sizeable landing parties on the English coast, or in rehearsals with boats and barges off the French coast, the British had given the Germans a bad pummelling.'

Shirer would eventually conclude that reports of 'an actual full-fledged' invasion attempt, in line with the holocaust described by Boris Nikolaevsky, were without foundation. Nevertheless, Shirer's bestselling *Berlin Diary* served to provide the burning sea story with an even more significant fillip. For on returning to Berlin from Geneva, the American broadcaster bore witness to remarkable scenes that have never been satisfactorily explained:

18 September: We arrived at the Potsdamer Bahnhof right on time ... I noticed several lightly wounded soldiers, mostly airmen, getting off a special car which had been attached to our train. From their bandages their wounds looked like burns. I noticed also the longest Red Cross train I've ever seen. It stretched from the station for half a mile to beyond the bridge over the Landwehr Canal. Orderlies were swabbing it out, the wounded having been unloaded, probably, during the night. The Germans usually unload their hospital trains after dark so that the populace will not be unduly disturbed by one of the grimmer sides of glorious war. I wondered where so many wounded could have come from as the armies in the west stopped fighting three months ago. As there were only a few porters I had to wait some time on the platform and picked up a conversation with a railway workman. He said most of the men taken from the hospital train were suffering from burns.

Can it be that the tales I heard in Geneva had some truth in them after all? The reports reaching Switzerland from France were that many German barges and ships had been destroyed and a considerable number of German troops drowned; also that the British used a new type of wireless-directed torpedo which spread ignited oil on the water and burned the barges. Those cases of burns at the station this morning bear looking into.

Shirer also found room for a joke, adding that the newfangled wireless-directed torpedo was a Swiss invention – Switzerland, of course, being a land-locked nation with no coastline of its own. Deciding that the mysterious bandaged figures warranted further investigation, Shirer recorded the following day:

> **19 September**: Returning to town we noticed a large crowd standing on a bridge which spanned a railroad line. We thought there had been an accident. But we found the people staring silently at a long Red Cross train unloading wounded. This is getting interesting. Only during the fortnight in September [last year] when the Poles were being crushed and a month this spring when the West was being annihilated have we seen so many hospital trains in Berlin. A diplomat told me this morning his legation had checked two other big hospital trains unloading wounded in the Charlottenburg railroad yards yesterday. This makes four long trains of wounded in the last two days that I know have arrived here.

In his million-selling magnum opus *The Rise and Fall of the Third Reich*, published in 1960, Shirer would ultimately conclude that these wounded soldiers suffering mostly burns were casualties of an exercise caught by the RAF. Precisely what he saw in 1940, however, remains open to debate, since the entries in the *Berlin Diary* provide little by way of detail, while this seasoned observer turned a blind eye to the fact that on 15 September the Luftwaffe had launched a huge daylight attack on London, in doing so adding scores to the total number of airmen already killed and injured during the Battle of Britain.

Moreover, Shirer cannot be considered an altogether reliable witness. Close examination of the original typescript of the *Berlin Diary* by Swiss academic Michael Strobl reveals that many sections were substantially altered for publication, including an early entry from 1935 betraying a degree of admiration for Hitler as a national leader. Major revisions became less common after war broke out in 1939, yet the original journal entry for 16 September 1940 is missing from the Shirer archive held at the Steward Memorial Library in Iowa, while the entries covering 18 and 19 September were extensively revised. Tellingly, the original typescript for 18 September refers only to several airmen ('flyers') seen leaving the train at Potsdamer station, not soldiers, and Shirer makes no mention at all of any conversation with a railway workman. Unsurprisingly, the line 'those cases of burns at the station this morning bear looking into' is also conspicuous by its absence.

The original entry for the following day, 19 September, confirms his own sighting of a Red Cross train unloading wounded at a different station, as well as another train seen by an unidentified 'someone' the previous day. Two hospital trains, therefore, rather than four, and no diplomatic contacts, nor any sightings (or even gossip) about burned German soldiers. In short, all that Shirer actually saw in Berlin on 18 September were 'several wounded flyers' with bandaged heads and faces, who he guessed had suffered burns. Given that the Luftwaffe had just lost the Battle of Britain, none of this was terribly surprising.

Back in New York, Shirer obligingly wrote up the story of the special carriage and the Red Cross train to help promote the Allied cause, this at a time when the war was still going badly for Britain. Little wonder, then, that British Security Co-ordination would thank him by name as one who 'rendered service of particular value' during the Second World War.

Berlin Diary would not be published in Britain until October. Before then, the Big Lie devised by John Baker White more than a year earlier was periodically refreshed by occasional press articles meant to further demoralise German troops. A favoured outlet for propaganda puffs, *The Daily Telegraph* offered a new twist on the story headlined 'Invasion Test Horror – Germans Trapped in Sea of Fire'. According to Martin Moore, the paper's special correspondent in Lisbon, an unspecified number of Wehrmacht troops had been killed or injured while testing flame countermeasures near Moulins in the Auverne region:

> The Nazis sprayed petrol on a lonely reach of the River Allier outside the town. Then they set it alight. Troops in supposedly fireproof overalls were ordered to plunge into the resulting sea of flames. The test ended in disaster. The garments proved no protection. Some men were burned to death and others severely scarred.

At first glance, Moulins might seem a puzzling choice for a seaborne invasion rehearsal, given that it lies plumb in the centre of France, some 180 miles from the nearest coastline. However, in 1941 the town also sat on the border of the unoccupied *zone libre*, placed under the control of the puppet Vichy regime, from which information flowed more freely than the *zone occupée* in the north. Stating that his information came direct from a local French doctor, who had been asked to help some of the victims, Moore wrote it was impossible to know the exact number of casualties, or the scope of the experiment. The piece continued:

> It is firmly believed in France, among the occupation troops as well as the civilian population, that a German expedition set out across the Channel last autumn, but

was destroyed through British naval units spraying petrol on the sea and igniting it with incendiary bullets.

This story has never been confirmed or denied by official British quarters, but it had and still has a powerful effect on the morale of the German troops. They believe they are going to be sent on a suicidal expedition against Britain, and face the prospect with unconcealed dread. Invasion drill still forms part of their routine training.

In a radio programme broadcast by the BBC in February 1941, First Sea Lord A.V. Alexander memorably described Hitler's invasion troops as an army of the doomed: 'In his desperation he will not shrink from sending hundreds of thousands of the flower of German manhood to inevitable destruction ... We have repeatedly heard of the feelings of despair among the soldiers who know they may be fated to perish in this reckless folly.' In April, Berlin sought to redress the balance by claiming to have sunk large numbers of Allied transports off Greece, resulting in thousands of bodies being washed ashore in the Aegean. However, this borrowed counterclaim gained little media traction on either side of the Atlantic.

Decidedly tamer than Shirer's *Berlin Diary* was *The Battle of Britain 1940*, a book by James Spaight issued in Britain in July. A civil servant trained in law, Spaight was a highly respected writer on air power during the first half of the twentieth century, with over a dozen books to his name, although he was not a pilot and boasted no military experience. Instead, from 1918 until his retirement in 1937 Spaight had flown a desk at the Air Ministry, eventually rising to the rank of principal assistant secretary. While *The Battle of Britain 1940* is no way an official publication, his account of the 'mid-September mystery' was couched in terms acceptable to the Ministry of Information:

In mid-September something happened which is still a mystery. There were persistent rumours then that an invasion was attempted and was foiled by our naval forces. That was probably untrue, but it is fairly certain that some kind of disaster did overtake the 'invasion fleet' at that time. It is known that a large number of German soldiers had to be treated in hospital for burns, the result, it was reported, of a heavy raid by the Royal Air Force at that time.

The raid caught the troops just when they were engaged in a 'dress rehearsal' for embarkation; the boats in which they were carried were sunk and when they took to the water the oil, set alight by the incendiary bombs, burned them severely before they could be rescued. For days after this incident bodies of dead soldiers were being washed up on the French, Belgian and Dutch coasts.

A bad storm contributed to the German losses of boats and men at about the same date.

Spaight's polite prose spoke less of smoke and fire than smoke and mirrors, falling back on the surmise that the sea was fired by accident. Nevertheless, in his closing Summary and Conclusion the author drove his point home:

> One particular series of raids was especially damaging. It is believed to have caught the German soldiers and sailors just at the moment when a kind of 'dress rehearsal' was being staged and to have resulted in the killing and wounding of thousands of the troops embarked. There were certainly heavy demands on hospital accommodation in occupied France just about that time, in mid-September. Bodies of uniformed Germans continued to be washed up on our shores for some days after that date.

In *Blue Pencil Admiral*, Thomson records that by mid-1941 press and radio had been 'stopped' from repeating rumours of an enemy invasion attempt. However, censorship of books was not as stringent as for newspapers, and in Britain the burning sea story would again be revived in October with the British publication of Shirer's popular *Berlin Diary*, as well as a lesser-known book by Lars Moen, *Under the Iron Heel*. By his own account, this former newsman and movie screenwriter had been employed by a film manufacturer in Belgium and found himself overtaken by the rapid German advance in May 1940. Moen remained in Antwerp until late October, when he left to return to America. His book, sold with the tagline 'an American reports on occupied Europe', appeared first in the States, before being published – unabridged – in Britain in October 1941. Sales were brisk, for according to Moen:

> On or about 16 September, a considerable force of towed triple-barges set out from a point along the Belgian coast, constituting the first wave of the attack, which was to occupy a strip on the English coast at which liners could put in and disembark the invasion troops. At a point probably not far from the Belgian coast, they were spotted by the British. Destroyers of the Royal Navy then managed to cut them off, and forced them well out into the North Sea. Here planes of the RAF dropped oil drums with great quantities of oil on and near the barges, then followed with incendiary bombs which turned the whole into a blazing inferno.
>
> During the first weeks of October, the bodies of hundreds of German soldiers were being washed ashore along the Belgian coast, especially in the vicinity of

Ostend. Many of them were so badly burned as to be almost unrecognisable. Many of the invasion barges were missing, although the naval craft and merchant liners were still in the harbour, their number having been increased by fresh arrivals.

None of these facts, taken alone, could be taken as proof that an attempted invasion actually took place. Taken collectively, they all point in one direction. I believe these facts to be exact. I first learned of the burned patients from a Belgian nurse working in an Antwerp hospital; Americans living near Ostend confirmed reports of the bodies being washed ashore. Later, I heard these stories scores of times, which proves nothing – but it was extremely significant that reports from the most widely scattered sources were unanimous on one point: that a considerable number of German soldiers had been badly burned.

Moen freely admitted that his account had been pieced together from rumours heard first in Belgium and Lisbon, and again on board the liner *Exeter* during his return journey to the States. To this mixed bag we can probably add a news agency cuttings library, or else the offices of British Security Co-ordination at Rockefeller Center. Stringing together this 'corroborative' evidence – all of which was hearsay – Moen found an 'overwhelming probability' that an actual attempt at invasion had taken place.

In truth, the sole sight seen by Moen with his own eyes was the filming of fake landing footage in Antwerp, shot on a bathing beach on the far side of the River Schelde. Here, for two days, invasion barges beached and men leapt into the shallow water, firing as they advanced, while light tanks and motorcycles sped from the ramps and crossed the sands. This blatant forgery was excused on the basis that the real invasion would take place at dawn, when natural light was poor.

Moen's vivid account of the mid-September mystery contains nothing not already printed in the *New York Times*, *New York Sun* and a dozen other North American titles. It can safely be discounted, as can an imaginative piece in the *Essex Chronicle* by one Reg Thompson, marking the first anniversary of the Cromwell alarm, and describing 'hundreds of barges' attacked by Bomber Command, using 'incendiary missiles' filled with a substance that 'continued to burn on the surface of the water if it missed its mark'. Those Wehrmacht not drowned were forced to endure 'the agonies of burning from the blaze on the water'.

His virtual namesake was not amused. Rear Admiral Thomson singled out another friend of BSC, Ralph Ingersoll, as presenting the censor with particular difficulties, but so too did Harvey Klemmer. A career diplomat attached to the US Embassy in London, Klemmer professed to have little time for Joseph Kennedy's anti-interventionist stance and had lunched with a senior officer from MI5,

DAILY EXPRESS MONDAY JUNE 4 1945

FLAMING SEA BURNED GERMAN ARMY

1940 invasion secret out

REHEARSAL THAT WENT WRONG

Walls of flame guarded invasion coast

AN OPEN LETTER

And a postal order for 5/-

Germans escape to Dublin

From France

Leaflets tell Japs surrender

EDEN ILL | Canada buys

THE first details of Hitler's ill-fated attempt to invade Britain on September 16, 1940, can now be revealed. They are told by a special correspondent who has just returned from the Continent, and who confirmed the details in a recent visit to Brussels.

40,000 Died In Flaming Channel

OCTOBER 1, 1944

From JOHN PARRIS, British United Press Special Correspondent

THOUSANDS of German soldiers were maimed for life — burned to death when Hitler attempted to invade the British Isles on September 16, 1940.

Nazis Reported Losing 50,000

But London Won't Confirm Story of Disaster to Invasion Troops in Channel.

LONDON, Sept. 24 (A.P.).—Informed British military spokesmen refused to comment today on dispatches from the French-Spanish border, published here, that Germany lost "between 50,000 and 60,000 picked troops" in a disaster of September 16, when a channel gale scattered Adolf Hitler's "invasion fleet."

The assertions were made in the British bombing, the Nazi High Daily Mail by Harold Cardozo, special correspondent on the French-Spanish border.

Neutral military sources also were inclined to discount the report.

Mr. Cardozo's story, in full, said: "Hitler lost between 50,000 and 60,000 picked troops in a disaster which scattered his invasion fleet a week ago today, it is learned here. They were victims of channel storms and merciless RAF bombardment.

"Because the German troops had already suffered heavy losses from

Continued on Page 2.

British Fire Halted Invasion As Nazis Tried to Rush Coast

Sun's Informant Says Hand-propelled Barges Were Cut Off by Navy and Blasted by Land Batteries.

Further evidence to support the report published in The New York Sun on September 11 of an attempted invasion of England by the Germans from occupied French ports was obtained today from an unofficial British source

BRITISH DENY RUMORS OF INVASION ATTEMPT

No Evidence to Show Nazis Were Foiled by Raids on Ports

Special Cable to THE NEW YORK TIMES.
LONDON, Oct. 22 — A careful survey today showed that all the stories of an attempted invasion or the defeat of an invasion were made out of whole cloth, so far as the British know.

THAT 1940 RUMOUR

The gunner talks of the clues to a Hitler invasion

By Daily Mail Reporter

A FORMER Royal Artillery gunner makes a television appearance tonight to shed new light on a wartime invasion rumour.
Did Hitler try to invade England in September 1940?

NAZI INVASION LOSSES : 81,000

U.S. REPORT OF "SEA OF FIRE"

FROM OUR OWN CORRESPONDENT
NEW YORK, Sunday.

NAZI INVADERS HELD 'CONSUMED BY FIRE'

Blazing Oil on Channel Balked 2 Efforts to Reach Britain, Russian Historian Says

DEAD ARE PUT AT 80,000

Barges Ran Into Flames When R.A.F.'s Bombs Fired Tanks in Water, It Is Stated

This article is by a distinguished historian

NAZI LOSSES SEEN IN INVASION DRILLS

Passengers Arriving on Exeter Tell of Thousands Drowned in Channel Manoeuvres

BRITISH KEPT INFORMED

French and Dutch Are Said to Report German Moves—One Says French Guns Are Used

Lord Maurice Hankey first tried to set the sea on fire with burning oil on the Suffolk coast at Orford in December 1914. Famously a 'man of secrets', this painting of Hankey in Great War military uniform is by William Orpen.

Sir Donald Banks, director-general of the Petroleum Warfare Department.

Known for his dapper dress sense, career politician Geoffrey Lloyd had overall charge of the Petroleum Warfare Department until 1945. He is seen here in Berlin in 1938 examining German air raid precautions for the Home Office. (IWM)

War Nawab: One of several unreliable tramp oilers assigned to Operation Lucid, the bold fire ship scheme launched by the Admiralty in the autumn of 1940.

Ever since the days of Dunkirk rumours have spread about a mysterious attempt by Hitler to invade Britain—an attempt that failed. And a failure that, for some equally mysterious reason, was hushed up by the British. Rumour spoke of RAF planes wiping out invasion armadas in the Channel, and of charred Nazi corpses being washed up on our beaches. Now at last comes the truth from one of the few men in Britain who know the secret of the Big Lie. This is the first in a series of articles By JOHN BAKER WHITE

Above: Major John Baker White, attached to the Directorate of Military Intelligence in 1940 and credited with inventing the original burning sea rumour.

SPECIAL DISTRIBUTION AND WAR CABINET.

From: SWITZERLAND.

Decypher. Mr. Kelly (Berne).
27th August, 1940.

D.   1.02 a.m.   28th August, 1940.

R.   8.21 a.m.   28th August, 1940.

No. 790.

xxxxxxxx

According to Monsieur Bovet Grisel, [?brother of] Federal Chancellor, Swiss Legation, Berlin has reported to the Swiss Government that the invasion of England is not now to be expected as General Haldar has told Hitler that the army will not attempt to cross the sea.

Additional colour is lent to this report by rumours already reported from here of decline in German army morale.

A story which seems to have obtained some currency among German troops is that the English have discovered new weapon for defeating attacks by sea. Story is, that we spread oil on the sea and by lighting it when boats approach have already defeated several attempted landings. This tale first reached me via Vichy and French Embassy allegedly from American journalists talking to German soldiers in Holland. It is now repeated to Monsieur Bovet Grisel by Frenchman who had it from German airmen at Lyons. These airmen said Germans had suffered heavy losses in attempting to attack Dover defended by this method.

Please repeat to Service Departments.

Left: A cipher telegram from Sir David Kelly, British Minister in Switzerland, confirming widespread circulation of the burning sea rumour by 27 August 1940. (TNA)

Colonel William Donovan, Roosevelt's personal envoy to Britain in 1940 and founding father of the Office of Strategic Services (OSS), the American version of the Special Operations Executive.

Rockefeller Center in New York, the 'highly mechanised eyrie' occupied by British Security Coordination, the central hub for MI6, MI5, SOE and PWE activity in America.

Disaster off Texel: the destroyer *Express*, her bows blown off by an enemy mine, seen from the forecastle of HMS *Kelvin* on 1 September 1940. The loss of two destroyers and the landing of survivors at east coast ports fuelled rumours of a German invasion attempt. (IWM)

PWD flame barrage trials at Studland Bay, March 1941.

A still from the 1954 film *Canaris*. After the German chief of intelligence examines a reel of stolen film, he shows Sealion planners a model of a flame barrage at Hastings. Footage of 'bestial' British flame defences is then screened and the invasion plan dismissed as suicidal. Was the plot of the film less fantastical that it seemed? (Taurus Video)

A flame-throwing demonstration at Newhaven Harbour. (IWM)

Testing a beach flame barrage by the Petroleum Warfare Department. (IWM)

William Robinson (left) and Peter Fleming (right) discuss the bodies on the beach between Hythe and St Mary's on the BBC television programme *First Hand* in 1957. (BBC)

HEINRICH PONCKE

+20.10.40

EIN UNBEKANNTER
DEUTSCHER SOLDAT

Heinrich Poncke's headstone at Cannock Chase. Poncke, a German anti-tank gunner, was washed ashore at Littlestone-on-Sea in Kent on 20 October 1940.

Shingle Street pre-war, looking south, with the Lifeboat Inn directly above the civilian. (Michael Lucock)

The Lifeboat Inn, Shingle Street, c. 1930. In March 1943, the building was partially demolished when used as target for trials with an uncharged mustard gas bomb. (Ronald and Nina Harris)

A photo taken during the CDRE bombing trial at Shingle Street in March 1943, including police, fire brigade and RAF personnel. Percy Darvell (second right) stated in 1992 that the civilian scientist in the centre of the group is Sir Barnes Wallis. (Percy Darvell)

Guy Liddell. The brutal reality of the Nazi regime was brought home to the special attaché when he was machine-gunned by a Luftwaffe raider during a stay with wealthy American friends in Sussex, only narrowly escaping death. Early in 1941, Klemmer finished work on a lively book, *They'll Never Quit*, billed as 'an American tribute to the people of Britain', and eventually published in London in December. A chapter titled 'Will They Invade?' dutifully rehearsed the usual rumours of foiled landings in August and September, tanks of petrol below the surface of the Channel and the arrival of charred bodies and wreckage on the south coast.

So far, so familiar. Klemmer nevertheless managed to weave in a colourful strand which echoed the tale of the ten or so German soldiers snatched from a flak trawler off Calais in October, and landed alive – if bewildered – at Dover. 'One thing which kept the invasion stories going was the mysterious appearance, at a London railway station, of a contingent of captured Germans,' Klemmer wrote. 'Airmen are always being taken through London on their way to prison camps. These men were not airmen: they were soldiers, and they were obviously freshly captured soldiers. Had they been caught trying to land on the shores of Britain?'

Thanks to the censor, the British edition of *They'll Never Quit* left this loaded question unanswered. In the American original, published by Wilfred Funk a few months earlier, Klemmer suggested that the German troops were captured in France by a tyro commando unit, made up of fearsome Glasgow-Irish ('some of the toughest fighters in existence') cut with a sprinkling of Canadians and Australians, all led by a fearsome major 'with two cuts on his cheek' who had distinguished himself at Dunkirk. The men, it was said, were paid $60 a month for special raiding duties along the coastline of France and the Netherlands, where most practised – and enjoyed – silent killing with the knife:

> It seems that the boys got thirsty one night in France and went into an estaminet. They found that the place had been pre-empted by some Germans. They didn't want to kill the Germans in cold blood and they couldn't afford to turn them loose. The only solution was to bring them along. That is why German soldiers were seen on the streets of London.

The first British commando units had been raised as early as June 1940, when Churchill, fired up by the idea of 'setting Europe ablaze', called for the raising of storm troops or 'leopard' squads to butcher and bolt on foreign soil. By the end of the month, a handful of resolute volunteers had visited Boulogne and Le Touquet as part of Operation Collar, yet for the most part the few raids mounted during 1940 were inconsequential and no prisoners were brought back from France. Whether the offending passage was deleted from the British edition of *They'll Never Quit* for reasons of military secrecy, or because the estaminet story was patently ridiculous, remains unclear.

'Well-known American correspondents and broadcasters came over to this country in an unending stream from the autumn of 1940,' carped Thomson in *Blue Pencil Admiral*. 'Before they went back to America we would tell them what we were banning from publication in this country.' It was assumed, correctly, that few wished to print anything beneficial to the Nazi cause. 'Nonetheless, when they felt that what we were banning was somewhat far-fetched, they very naturally used their discretion when they got back to the USA – and made things rather awkward for me in my dealings with British editors.'

The censor was also apparently powerless to control public lectures by itinerant American reporters. On 7 April 1942, a jobbing journalist named Charles M. Barbe gave a talk advertised as 'None So Blind' to a small audience at the Royal Institute of International Affairs, the private think-tank better known as Chatham House. Like Lars Moen, Charles Barbe was a man of many parts, describing himself as a former musician who had volunteered as an ambulance driver early in 1940, followed by active service in France. The text of his talk included the following paragraphs:

Along with a few others who did not feel like the show was over I stayed on in Paris, and during the last part of August this curiosity I speak of got the better of me again, and along with another chap – a Frenchman, believe it or not, who felt an equal curiosity – we had been hearing stories of something which was going to happen round the 15th of September, during the first, second or third week in September. So we went up into the military zone, which was something I would not do again.

From about the 10th to the 16th September we were in a small house about 10 kilometres south of Dunkirk, a good healthy stone's throw from the Channel, during what is commonly termed the Battle of Britain. Maybe you remember it. Now I have broadcast several times for the BBC since I have been in London and I have written the story of what we saw happen there and what I was able to confirm later on in Paris and Berlin, but it has always been cut out of my scripts. I understand that I might be able to mention it here. Anyway I'll take a chance. The 161st and 197th Schleswig-Holstein SS divisions and the 67th Hessian Division, three of the prime, crack SS divisions, never bothered anyone after the 15th September. The better part of 33,000 men started out from the shores of France, and not one of them ever got back to the shores of France alive.

I do not know what happened. About the 17th or 18th September on our way back to Paris we saw something strange … At a point on the coast quite near to Dieppe, we saw bodies on the shore like driftwood, something which could in some cases be identified as once having been human, while others looked like blackened tree stumps, and I don't believe I shall ever get the stench out of my nose, not if I live to be 1,000 years old. They were just burned beyond recognition. I had previously spoken to a couple of German soldiers just north of Paris, who had told me that they had been badly burned during the latter part of August. One of the boys said he would be shot before he went back. He said he was out in a rowing boat, fishing, that is the official word, fishing, when, in his words, the sea exploded in flames. As I say, I do not know what happened. I only know what the results were.

Barbe went on to explain that 'None So Blind' was the title of an abandoned book project based on his experiences in France:

I had thoroughly determined when I came to England to be unique among journalists in that I was not going to write a book; but I had been in England less than two weeks when a book was talked over as a sequel to *Berlin Diary* by one of England's better publishers

Alas, having dashed off 50,000 words, Barbe found his text rejected on the basis that it was unlikely to help the war effort. The lecture at Chatham House failed in its presumed purpose to excite fresh interest from London editors.

Barbe was little more than a huckster: musician, ambulance driver, broadcaster and latterly failed author. Certainly few of the purported facts in his account suggest a reliable witness. For example, the three Waffen SS divisions confidently identified never existed, and the given names and numbers bear no resemblance to any units raised before or during the Second World War. And how, or why, did the Admiralty, the RAF or the Petroleum Warfare Department manage to target a lone Wehrmacht angler in a small rowing boat? Barbe's fanciful talk did not escape the attention of the censor. 'An American broadcaster,' Thomson wrote drily, 'one of our many visitors from the United States in those days, evidently believed that Chatham House was an excellent place to make a name for himself in London, and that his audience wouldn't examine too closely the accuracy of his statements. He certainly made a most moving speech.'

Fact and fiction became hopelessly entangled. As early as 1940, the celebrated author Graham Greene, then a serving MI6 officer, published a short story called

The Lieutenant Died Last. The plot revolved around 'an unrecorded victory in 1940' in the fictional village of Potter, where a detachment of German paratroopers are swiftly bagged by a lone poacher, thus providing 'a discouraging failure for the German High Command'. Greene developed this theme in a superior screenplay for the film *Went The Day Well?*, a notable success on release in November 1942, and went on to lend Jack Higgins inspiration for his runaway 1975 bestseller *The Eagle Has Landed.* A broadly similar novel, *When the Bells Rang*, was published anonymously in May 1943. The plot turned on a German landing in April 1941, during which the Kentish village of Russocks is occupied by jackbooted Nazi thugs. Neither Greene nor the unknown author of *When the Bells Rang* made any reference to floating corpses or flaming oil, although a popular Will Hay comedy film from 1942, *The Goose Steps Out*, contained a pointed reference to visiting Germans receiving the 'warmest welcome' of their lives, apparently a nod to the burning sea sib released two years earlier.

By then the fiery phantom menace was no longer required. Following the Japanese attack on Pearl Harbor in December 1941, America finally joined the war against Germany and the Axis powers, making an eventual Allied victory inevitable – as indeed it had been since June, when Hitler invaded the Soviet Union, in doing so opening up an unwinnable war on two fronts. Flame played no part in the calamitous Canadian landing at Dieppe in August 1942, and although German propaganda magazine *Signal* later printed pictures of a barrage (*flammensperre*) apparently installed to protect a harbour in Brittany, nothing similar was encountered in July 1943, when the first major seaborne landings of the war delivered Sicily to the Allies in just six weeks. Instead, a very different kind of deception played a central role in the capture of this key Mediterranean island, thanks to false plans planted on the body of a fake British officer, burdened with posthumous infamy as The Man Who Never Was.

A half-page photo spread in *Signal* aside, no record exists of any German scheme to bolster the vaunted Atlantic Wall with flame or petroleum weapons as the Allies prepared for the invasion of Europe. With limited reserves and supplies of fuel products, Germany faced an unending struggle to procure enough gasoline to keep its tanks on the move in Russia and the Luftwaffe in the skies above the Reich to defend cities and industrial centres. Simply put, even if any had been installed, there was no oil available for *flammensperre* to protect likely landing beaches in Normandy and the Pas de Calais in June 1944.

The question of whether Hitler's invasion armada had actually sailed in 1940 was raised in the House of Commons for the first time three years later. Besides sitting as the Conservative member for West Leeds, Major Vyvyan Adams was a barrister at law and a serving officer in the Duke of Cornwall's Light Infantry. Under the cryptic pen-name Watchman, he was also an occasional author of opinionated political biographies, including *Right Honourable Gentleman* and *Churchill: Architect of Victory*. On 29 July 1943, Major Adams enquired whether the government was by now prepared to 'describe the character and extent of any attempt at the invasion of these islands' made by the enemy during the summer and autumn of 1940. With the invasion of Sicily now under way, Adams reasoned, issues of military secrecy were surely no longer involved.

Watchman found his question brushed aside by the deputy prime minister, Clement Attlee. According to Attlee, it was already 'well known throughout the world' that Hitler's preparations for invasion had been frustrated by the RAF, an assertion greeted with a volley of cheers from the benches. However, Churchill's mild-mannered coalition deputy went on to assert that since the staffs of all three armed services were 'heavily engaged' on current duties, the prime minister was 'reluctant to impose on them the additional work of preparing a detailed answer'. Moreover, military secrecy remained very much an issue, since a detailed response would risk 'disclosing to the enemy the extent of our sources of information'.

These certainly included Enigma decrypts, a source classified as Ultra Top Secret until 1974, as well as intelligence gathered by MI6, double-agent networks and perhaps even the Abwehr itself via the Swiss corridor. There followed a brief exchange, during which Watchman derided Attlee's evasive reply, and was in turn accused of impudence. Major Adams plainly harboured suspicions of what might today be termed a cover-up, for soon after the Normandy landings in June 1944 he returned to the subject of Operation Sealion, demanding that Churchill himself now indicate 'in broad terms' the nature and scale of any German invasion attempt in 1940. Once again, he found himself effectively stonewalled:

CHURCHILL: I have nothing which I can usefully add at this stage to the reply which my right honourable friend [Clement Attlee] gave to my honourable and gallant friend on 29 July last.

MAJOR ADAMS: May I ask my right honourable friend if he cannot tell at this interval of time, as a matter of historical interest, whether the enemy ever set in motion the apparatus of a sea-borne invasion?

CHURCHILL: Well, Sir, it is a matter on which I should not like to take people off other current jobs in order to use their time today. I do not know what my honourable and gallant friend means by 'set in motion'. 'Set in motion', in the sense of crossing the Channel, no; 'set in motion', in the sense of making very heavy concentrations, both of troops and ships, to cross the Channel, yes.

EMANUEL SHINWELL: Can the right honourable gentleman say that, if such an attempt was made, at any rate, was it unsuccessful?

CHURCHILL: Yes, sir.

MAJOR ADAMS: Can my right honourable friend add this – did any of that shipping emerge from the ports across the Channel?

CHURCHILL: Not to my belief. A great deal of it was smashed in the ports and then they changed their minds.

Adams never did receive a straight answer. With cruel irony, six years after the end of the war the inquisitive major would himself be drowned while swimming in heavy seas off Gunwalloe in Cornwall.

Unlike Operation Sealion, planned in haste over no more than a dozen weeks, the Allied landings in Normandy on 6 June 1944 took fully two years to prepare, and gained the added benefit of operational dress rehearsals in North Africa, Sicily and Italy. By the time D-Day took place, the engineers, mechanics and mixtures specialists of the Petroleum Warfare Department had graduated from hastily improvised flame traps to far more sophisticated projects, including thickened and smokeless fuels for conventional flame-throwing systems, as well as FIDO installations for fog dispersal on airfields, and PLUTO, an acronym for Pipe Line Under The Ocean. Laid between Shanklin Chine on the Isle of Wight and Cherbourg, the first PLUTO pipeline came on stream during the middle of August. Ultimately, another seventeen would be laid across the Pas de Calais, capable of delivering a combined total of 4,000 tons of fuel each day.

The sea flame barrage programme had long since become a white elephant. Not only was the PWD Experimental School at Studland Bay unable to perfect a reliable ignition system until 1941, but sea temperatures and swell made the operation of barrages all but impossible during the winter months. Deep water also presented significant problems, as did huge volumes of choking black smoke. Despite the fact that Operation Sealion was dead in the water, in March 1941, the chiefs of staff approved the installation of 50 miles of barrage, the respective allotment to each regional command being 25 miles (South Eastern), 15 miles (Eastern) and 10 miles (Southern). With labour and steel scaffolding in short supply, however, next to no progress was made, and the original figure of 50 miles was successively reduced to 30, then 15, and finally a mere 3½ miles. By the end of the year, just three sea barrages were listed as operational, these being Deal (520 yards installed between Kingsdown and Sandwich), 400 yards on Rye marshes operated by a complex system of remote controls and the test-bed at Studland Bay itself.

The whole amounted to less than a mile. Beach flame barrages were more numerous, yet both types required regular and substantial maintenance. 'Our big problem was the beach moving,' recalled PWD engineer Bernard Kimpton. 'We had constant problems with the pipes either being buried or exposed.' At Porthcurno in Cornwall, where vital transatlantic telephone cables came ashore, a small gravity-fed section was installed to guard against German commando raids. Planned stretches in Scotland at Wick and Thurso, as well as in South Wales, were never completed, while smaller tanks at sites including Tenby and Freshwater Bay were installed but never filled.

Of the highly visible barrage at Dover, running between the Shakespeare Cliff and the Admiralty Pier, Bernard Kimpton recollected:

> This was the most spectacular of all, as we had the height, and troops behind that. There were fears that the tests would crack the concrete on the Admiralty Pier, but the heat went out to sea. There were other problems as the cliff kept crumbling and we had to keep sheering pieces off the pipes, or else divert them. Later on in the war Churchill and General Patton came down to watch a demonstration. Patton looked mightily impressed, and remarked, 'That'll burn the bastards!'

In Normandy the enemy were burned not by flame barrages, or latter-day Greek Fire, but by Wasp carriers and Crocodile flame-throwing tanks. Utilising cumbersome Churchill Mk IV infantry models, coupled to an armoured trailer charged with 400 gallons of gelled fuel, the Crocodile was developed as one of several types of specialist engineer vehicle tasked with breaching Hitler's vaunted Atlantic Wall. Other so-called 'Funnies' operated by the 79th Armoured Division on D-Day included tanks that could swim, clear mines, bridge ditches and lob hefty 'flying dustbin' demolition charges at bunkers and other strongpoints. In the latter role' flame-throwing Crocodiles proved devastatingly effective, neutralising enemy positions by starving the occupants of oxygen or simply by burning them alive. Before long, most ordinary German troops took to surrendering after an initial burst of flame intended as a ranging – or warning – shot.

Strictly speaking, the flame-throwing tank was not a British innovation, having been tested by the Germans in North Africa, where their short range made them of little use in the wide open spaces of the desert. In the closed *bocage* countryside of Normandy, however, the Crocodile was king. Three full regiments operated in France after D-Day, sometimes on the cusp of legality. Crews were obliged to sign the Official Secrets Act, and risked summary execution if captured. 'It was our job to take out the strongpoints with flame,' recalled Ernie Cox, a driver/operator with 141st Regiment, Royal Armoured Corps (The Buffs). 'Farmhouses would be turned into strongpoints by the Germans, and with the enemy well dug-in just shelling would not move them.' As well as hardened positions, Cox and most other Crocodile crews also flamed enemy troops concealed in hedgerows. 'When our infantry had been over the ground, one of the majors came over and asked if we wanted to inspect our handiwork. We declined.'

Andrew Wilson, a troop commander with 141 RAC, did so only once, and found himself sufficiently disgusted to adopt the third person when writing his powerful post-war memoir *Flame Thrower*.

Ever since his first action in Normandy he'd been drawn by a fierce curiosity to see what happened where they'd flamed. Yet he'd never done so, because always they'd be switched from one place to another, and there was never a chance to explore the objective.

He walked down the front of the trees, where here and there the brushwood still smouldered among the blackened trunks. The burning away of the undergrowth had completely uncovered some trenches. He looked in the first and for the moment saw only a mass of charred fluff. He wondered what it was, until he remembered that the Germans were always lining their sleeping-places with looted bedding.

Then, as he was turning to go, he saw the arm. At first he thought it was the charred and shrivelled crook of a tree root; but when he looked closer, he made out the hump of the body it was attached to. A little way away was the shrivelled remains of a boot.

He went on to the next trench, and in that there was no concealing fluff. There were bodies which seemed to have been blown back by the force of the flame and lay in naked, blackened heaps. Others were caught in twisted poses, as if the flame had frozen them. Their clothes had burned away. Only their helmets and boots remained, ridiculous and horrible.

He wanted to vomit.

From July 1944 onwards, Allied ground attack aircraft also made limited use of napalm and other prototype gelled fuel weapons. Unsurprisingly, appalling realities such as those described by Andrew Wilson were nowhere to be found in the jocund histories of the Petroleum Warfare Department offered by Geoffrey Lloyd and Sir Donald Banks. With the Second Front secure by the end of August, the existence of the PWD was revealed to the public for the first time on the 25 July at a dramatic press conference staged by Lloyd at Moody's Down Farm near Winchester. There, various flamethrowers in use in Normandy – Wasps, Crocodiles and Lifebuoy man-packs – were demonstrated to journalists, as well as anti-invasion weapons such as the Fougasse, and footage released for inclusion in newsreels. The *Daily Express* professed utter astonishment: 'A man in a bowler hat, it was disclosed, headed a committee which has produced Britain's newest secret weapon, the flamethrower, which is now helping the British and Canadian forces to burn their way through France. That man has been known to those who still run cars as the man responsible for their petrol allowances.'

The Petroleum Warfare Department itself was also unmasked as a hitherto secret body set up to produce stop-gap anti-invasion weapons using surplus fuel stocks. 'All this has developed from our first crude experiments to improvise burning oil defences on the beach at Ramsgate on a June afternoon in 1940,' the dapper minister explained. 'All of us who were there became keen believers in the effectiveness of flame warfare. That band grew, and included people with the most varied and, indeed, unorthodox qualifications.'

Another unnamed source talked up the importance of the Department to the *Evening Telegraph*:

> Often Mr Lloyd would take part in the experiments with a boiler suit over his ordinary clothes. There was one occasion when the Germans became interested in one of our earliest experiments. They decided to try and dive-bomb us on the beach and very nearly succeeded. They sheered off when, very fortunately for us, our flames shot up and almost scorched them.

Lloyd, too, seems to have been prone to exaggeration. By his reckoning, a total of 20 miles of sea flame barrage had been installed around the coast of Britain, along with 'several hundred miles' of pipe-work on land. With the press of a single button, 'millions of gallons of oil' would have risen to the surface of the sea, flaring into an 'all-consuming mass of fire' off vulnerable beaches in Kent, Dorset and the South-West. Ignition could be delayed 'until the landing craft were right among it', or else 'lit to force them into "safe" channels where they could be dealt with by guns shooting accurately under the daylight conditions created by the mighty glare'.

These tales sounded almost as tall as the sibs launched by British intelligence four years earlier. That side of the story, however, would never be told. In April 1945, with the war in Europe drawing to a close, Sefton Delmer, the head of the Political Warfare Executive, quietly shut down his *Soldatensender* black propaganda operation (broadcasting from Milton Keynes), as well as the *Nachrichten* newspaper (printed in Luton), before gathering together his disparate staff for a final briefing. Here, the assembled linguists, dissidents, forgers and psychological warriors were warned against bragging of their clandestine achievements, even after the final defeat of Germany. This, Delmer said, was to avoid repetition of previous errors made by Lord Northcliffe, whom he disparaged as 'hungry for public glory' after 1918. Triumphalist boasts about the potency of British propaganda during the Great War by its greatest exponent, it was reasoned, served only to fuel a dangerous myth that Germany had been 'stabbed in the back' by deceit and trickery, rather than beaten on the field of battle. It was a point laboured time and again by Hitler in *Mein Kampf.*

'It made them anxious to have a second go,' Delmer warned. 'It prepared the way for Hitler and this present war. If we start boasting of the clever things we did, who knows what the result of that will be? So mum's the word. Propaganda is something one keeps quiet about.'

Those privy to the momentous secrets of Enigma codebreaking at Bletchley Park were sworn to silence for much the same reason. At the end of May 1945, Churchill personally ordered Group Captain Frederick Winterbotham to contact each and every Allied commander and their staffs in the European theatre, giving strict instructions not to divulge the nature or detail of any ULTRA intelligence received over the previous five years. This embargo was intended to ensure that there might be 'neither damage to the future operations of the Secret Service, nor any cause for our enemies to blame it for their defeat'.

The need for absolute secrecy is also borne out by John Baker White. A year before *The Big Lie* was published in book form, an early draft was serialised in *Reynolds News.* 'I have since talked to former members of the German intelligence,' the major revealed. 'I have no doubt from what they told me that six deceptions launched from London in 1940, "planted" with great care and backed up with apparent confirmation from other quarters, were believed by the German High Command.' These six, in the opinion of Baker White, were sufficiently misleading to convince Hitler and his advisors to call off plans for the invasion of Britain.

Frustratingly, the precise nature of the other five deceptions remains unclear. For when the long-form version of *The Big Lie* was eventually published in 1955, this intriguing passage had mysteriously disappeared.

7

THE MEN WHO NEVER WERE

Following the Allied breakout from Normandy, and the liberation of Paris in August, victory in Western Europe seemed only a matter of time. Indeed the pace of the Allied advance across Belgium during September 1944 even outstripped that of the German blitzkrieg in May 1940, with much of the country freed in the space of a few days. In many places delirious crowds of civilians held up the advancing armies more effectively than enemy action, while at the same time reviving interest in the myth of the invasion that failed. W.A. Birkbeck, a British soldier who took part in the liberation of Antwerp in September 1944, recalled later:

> While we were enjoying the gaiety and celebrations a friend and I were invited to take tea with an old Londoner who had married a Belgian soldier after the First World War. Their daughter was a nurse in an Antwerp hospital. During our walk around the district, watching collaborators tried, the nurse remarked, 'the best thing you ever did was set the sea on fire.' I asked when it was that we set the sea on fire, to which she replied 1940, and that, 'I know because I was on duty in the hospital. The British set the sea on fire, and they were all so terribly burned.'

Parliamentary answers given by Winston Churchill and Clement Attlee had stopped short of an outright denial, while Geoffrey Lloyd's dramatic press call in August studiously avoided any mention of charred corpses or fatal practice drills. After speaking with a different Belgian nurse, this time in Brussels, an American reporter named John A. Parris (of United Press) laid claim to having uncovered 'final details' of Hitler's 'calamitous' attempt to invade Britain on 16 September 1940. The *News of the World* ran his dispatch on its front page:

Thousands of German soldiers – 50,000 so it is said – were burned to death or maimed for life on that September day. 'A nightmare in hell' was how German soldiers described it after the RAF, catching the Nazi fleet in mid-Channel, dumped oil on the water and set fire to it with incendiary bullets.

Belgians with whom I talked were surprised to learn that the British people had never been fully told of the attempt, which appeared to be common knowledge in Belgium. I heard one side of the story from Renée Meurisse, a Belgian Red Cross Nurse, in charge of a group of refugees at the time.

'During September 17th,' Renée told me, 'we heard rumours that thousands of bodies of German soldiers were being washed ashore along the Belgian beaches. At seven o'clock that night a German Red Cross train of 40 coaches pulled into Brussels Station. We had been expecting a refugee train, so we were surprised when we saw a train-load of Germans. The commandant, tired and in crumpled uniform, approached me and asked if we could help his wounded. He said that the train had been shunted on to the wrong line, and his men were dying for lack of treatment. We agreed to help, sent a call for more nurses and ambulances, and began taking the wounded from the train. The moans and screams were terrible.

'I personally helped to carry a young German soldier from the train. He was horribly burned about the head and shoulders. A doctor assisted me to put him in a corner, and we determined to find out, if we could, exactly what had happened to him. We began by inquiring about his mother and sweetheart, and after each answer I would ask, "Where were you going and what happened?" Finally we managed to piece the story together.

'He said they had been told they were going to invade Britain, that nothing was going to stop them, that it was just a matter of getting into boats and crossing the Channel. He told me: "It was horrible. The sea was ablaze. The British they bombed and machine-gunned us. Hell couldn't be worse." Then he died, there on the stretcher. We looked after more than 500 soldiers as best we could. Many of them died in Brussels railway station, others in our hospitals.'

Renee explained that other nurses told her more stories they had picked up from German soldiers. 'Thousands of us started out and we expected to be in England tonight,' they said. For days afterwards the bodies of German soldiers, their heads and shoulders burned, were washed ashore, and it was impossible for the Nazis to preserve the secret any longer. 'The German Red Cross trains passed through Brussels for three days,' Renee went on. 'We asked for a supply of medical equipment for the Germans, but they didn't have much.'

The arrival of hospital trains at the Gare du Nord in Brussels during September 1940 was also recalled by Agnes Mann, then a teenage schoolgirl. 'One day I saw up to four hospital trains in the sidings, all containing these burnt German soldiers,' she told this author more than fifty years later. 'They were all bandaged up like the invisible man. That morning in Brussels has always stayed clearly in my mind.'

All are apparently eyewitness reports, yet all present just as many problems for historians as the hospital trains reported from Berlin by William Shirer. The official history of the German Army medical service (*Sanitätsdienst*) does not record any large-scale casualties caused by burning in September 1940, while primary research by American military historian Walter Ansel during the late 1950s confirmed that the testing of flame countermeasures produced no 'noteworthy casualties'. In 1957, BBC researchers placed press adverts in French and Belgian newspapers appealing for eyewitnesses to the failed invasion, or its aftermath, yet none came forward with first-hand evidence. Nor is any such catastrophe mentioned in the published memoirs of senior German commanders charged with the organisation of Sealion, such as Manstein or Blumentritt.

If trains carrying up to 500 casualties each continued to arrive in Brussels for three days, it beggars belief that no German veterans subsequently came forward to tell – or sell – the story of a disaster on the scale of the Dieppe raid. Indeed, even the most unreconstructed conspiracy theorist must surely baulk at the notion that, in the years since 1945, all mention of a large-scale amphibious operation, which resulted in trainloads of German casualties, can have been expunged from every memoir, history and official file. A far more likely explanation is that the Parris report circulated by United Press was another deliberate plant by British intelligence, designed to undermine German military morale, and safe to revive now that all key ports on the Channel coast were in Allied hands.

Thus colourful reports continued to surface. At the end of October 1944, the *Sunday Post* ran yet another piece on 'the war's biggest mystery', describing a devastating bombing raid on Antwerp docks during which 'ammo and petrol boats blew up with such force that bodies of soldiers were blown clear of the port'. At Cherbourg, according to the paper's correspondent, the RAF had played a hidden trump card. 'From our planes poured thousands of gallons of a special petrol and oil mixture. Tracers and incendiaries were poured into it.'

As the war drew to a close the following year, another journalist wrote of an encounter with a man who claimed to have watched Hitler's invasion gambit unfold over the course of a lively weekend in 1940. A spot on the coast near Bognor Regis afforded a grandstand view. 'He gave me a graphic description of coastal guns in action against a fleet of German invasion barges, while RAF bombers roared overhead. He said he saw hundreds of uniformed bodies washed up on the shore.'

Others were keen to debunk such voodoo history. Following the great heroism of the Dambusters raid by 617 Squadron in May 1943, Wing Commander Guy Gibson was commissioned to write an account describing in realistic fashion the work of aircrew in both Fighter and Bomber Command. Unfortunately, Gibson was killed over Holland in September 1944 and publication of his ghost-written memoir, *Enemy Coast Ahead*, was delayed until 1946. Discussing the Battle of the Barges in September 1940, Gibson confirmed that he had taken part in a devastating raid on an oil depot at Antwerp, but was at pains to debunk talk of bodies on beaches:

> There were rumours that they actually had moved out and that we had sunk them. There were rumours that thousands of German soldiers were buried on the east coast of England, soldiers who had been hit by Bomber Command, who had drowned and washed ashore. These rumours were untrue, and no-one in this country will even know anyone who saw a dead German soldier, although many a man will claim to know someone who knows someone else who buried one.

Evidently Guy Gibson was not a reader of *The Times* in 1940 and had missed the arrival of Heinrich Poncke, the Wehrmacht anti-tank gunner, at Littlestone-on-Sea.

The war in Europe finally ended on 8 May 1945, a week after Hitler committed suicide in a fetid bunker beneath the ruins of Berlin. Geoffrey Lloyd found himself appointed Minister of Information in Churchill's short-lived caretaker administration, albeit briefly, and on 3 June devoted another press conference to revealing further details of the various petroleum weapons devised for the defence of Britain in 1940. Copies of the air-delivered leaflet *Short Invasion Phrasebook* were distributed, as well as stills of mobile flamethrowers in action at Newhaven harbour and dramatic footage from Studland Bay. National and provincial papers, particularly tabloids, afforded the story blanket coverage next day. According to the *Daily Express*, the 'biggest secret' of the war was at last revealed; elsewhere, headlines proclaimed in 36-point type that 'Wall of Fire Saved Us From Invasion' and 'Germans Burned Own Troops'. Most journalists painted a highly exaggerated picture of the flame defences available in 1940, describing an extensive double defence line of sea and beach barrages along the south coast, deadly in and of themselves, and positioned to draw German invasion barges into killing zones covered by pre-ranged artillery.

Nowhere was it mentioned that less than a mile of sea flame barrage had actually been installed. Nevertheless, these fresh disclosures and images served to fix the story of an invasion foiled by flame in the public mind, and also made waves in the States, not least because Lloyd for the first time hinted that British agencies had deliberately spread the burning sea rumour overseas:

> We on this side, by leaflets and other means, let the German troops on the French coast know about the inferno awaiting them if they tried to invade us. There is evidence that the whole thing had a great morale effect on them. But it was not true that they ever tried an invasion. I am told that they had ordered 100,000 asbestos suits, but apparently their experiments were abandoned.

Lloyd made no mention of covert American help, but took care to acknowledge the contribution made by Lord Hankey. For the rest, however, the new Minister of Information carefully avoided anything which smacked of victory by trickery, or stabs in the back, and fell instead to recycling old sibs:

> It always seemed to happen that when we were conducting full-scale experiments and making a tremendous blaze there was a German aeroplane about. On many occasions it came and bombed us. In this way the Germans must have known what we were doing, and in fact they showed us they expected us to use flames as a defence, for they carried out experiments with asbestos suits. But there was some defect in the helmets used and their own men got badly burned about the face.
>
> This gave rise to a rumour that an invasion had been attempted, and when we heard of it we used it to the full. Leaflets were dropped in France assuring the German soldiers that there was a warm reception awaiting them should they attempt invasion.

Given its close working relationship with British Security Co-ordination in 1940, the *New York Times* was better placed than most to separate the fact from the fiction: 'History does not turn on so simple a matter as an asbestos uniform that will not keep out fire.' Hyperbole aside, the writer also praised Britain's valiant leaders and the unconquerable spirit of her people. 'The petroleum defence worked out by Mr Lloyd, Lord Hankey and others may have saved the world years of bloodshed and suffering.'

Sir Donald Banks had his say in October at the opening of a dedicated Petroleum Warfare Exhibition, held within the precincts of the still-closed Imperial War Museum. Most of the displays were concerned with flame-throwing tanks such as the Churchill Crocodile, as well as Pipe Line Under the Ocean and fog-dispersing FIDO, said to have safely landed 2,500 aircraft with 15,000 aircrew aboard. In his opening address, Banks also described something of the improvised flame defences of 1940, in doing so confirming the intelligence aspect which Lloyd had merely hinted at and featured nowhere in *Flame Over Britain*, his unofficial history of the PWD published while the Imperial War Museum exhibition was still running:

> Intelligence of these developments reached the Germans and gave rise to the widespread legend that vast numbers of them had been burnt to death in crossing the Channel. In fact steps were taken by the British propaganda authorities to spread this story within the enemy ranks, and there is little doubt that it acted as one of the contributory factors in deterring the German authorities from pursuing their invasion plans.

Geoffrey Lloyd had lost his seat in the general election upheaval of July 1945, as had Major Vyvyan Adams, the inquisitive member for West Leeds also known as Watchman. With the House of Commons now under Labour management, the invasion question was again raised in May 1946, this time by two surviving Conservative backbenchers, Wing Commander Norman Hulbert and Sir Hugh Lucas-Tooth, representing Stockport and Hendon respectively. A leading member of the Anglo-German Fellowship pre-war, Hulbert would later damage his reputation still further by attacking the popular BBC satirical programme *That Was the Week That Was*. Lucas-Tooth had only recently returned to the Commons after serving in the Queen's Own Cameron Highlanders. Like Major Adams, both men seemed to think that the true facts of the Cromwell alarm on 7 September 1940 had not yet been fully disclosed.

By now there was a new prime minister. Having fielded inconvenient questions from Adams in 1943 and 1944, Clement Attlee was already well versed on the subject of the mid-September mystery, while the Joint Intelligence Committee now had ample time to draft a detailed response. Six whole months, in fact. The lengthy document was signed off by the chiefs of staff in November and given as a written answer. Following a brief resume of the Sealion operational plan, and of British defence strategy, Attlee informed the House:

> It has been widely believed in this country that a German invasion attempt was actually launched in 1940. This belief is based partly on the fact that a number of German bodies were washed up on the south coast of England in August and September 1940; and partly on the knowledge that the 'invasion imminent' signal was issued by General Headquarters, Home Forces on 7th September. The facts are as stated in the following paragraphs ...

In August 1940, the Germans were embarking their army in the barges in harbours along the French coast, but there is no evidence that they ever left harbour as a fleet to invade this country. Bombing raids on those harbours were carried out by Bomber Command and some barges which put to sea, probably to escape the raids, were sunk either by bombing or on encountering bad weather. During the next six weeks bodies of German soldiers were washed up at scattered points along the coast between Cornwall and Yarmouth (amounting to about thirty-six over a period of a month).

A figure of 'about thirty-six' dead Germans over the course of six weeks seemed far more plausible than 80,000, and many British papers printed the whole of the lengthy written answer verbatim. Yet even this lower figure of three dozen defies verification. The arrival of Heinrich Poncke alone was reported in the British press in 1940, and no official confirmation exists of the ten or so bodies Gunner William Robinson helped to recover from St Mary's Bay at about the same time. Did Attlee mean actual soldiers, or simply personnel from all three German armed services? The figure of 'about thirty-six' was endorsed by Air Marshal Sir William Dickson, who chaired the meeting of the Chiefs of Staff Committee at which the written answer was approved, though he referred only to bodies rather than soldiers.

Three years later, Churchill himself muddied the waters still further in *Their Finest Hour*, the second volume of his lengthy (and highly subjective) war history. Back in August 1940, Britain's war leader had been favourably impressed by the content of David Kelly's cipher telegram from Berne, and on the strength of it made several pointed references to flame in a speech broadcast on 11 September. In print, however, Churchill simply repeated the substance of Attlee's written answer to the Commons, rounding up the number of bodies washed ashore, while at the same time adding a little embroidery of his own:

During August the corpses of about forty German soldiers were washed up at scattered points along the coast between the Isle of Wight and Cornwall. The Germans had been practising embarkations in the barges along the French coast. Some of these barges put out to sea in order to escape British bombing and were sunk, either by bombing or bad weather. This was the source of a widespread rumour that the Germans had attempted an invasion and had suffered very heavy losses either by drowning or by being burnt in patches of sea covered with flaming oil. We took no steps to contradict such tales, which spread freely through the occupied countries in a wildly exaggerated form and gave much encouragement to the oppressed populations. In Brussels, for instance, a shop exhibited men's bathing suits marked 'For Channel Swimming'.

The bathing costumes were, of course, cut from whole cloth spun by the great man himself. Churchill (or perhaps his researchers) also muddled the timing, as well as confusing Great Yarmouth in Norfolk with the smaller port of Yarmouth on the Isle of Wight. Despite these schoolboy errors, Churchill's forcible imprimatur meant that this brief, guarded mention in *Their Finest Hour* came to be accepted as the last word on the failed invasion myth for almost a decade. Even though *Flame Over Britain* (Banks), *Blue Pencil Admiral* (Thomson) and *The Big Lie* (Baker White) appeared in 1946, 1947 and 1955 respectively, none of these books sold in large quantities and were all but ignored by mainstream historians.

As in 1940, a rush of hot air filled the information vacuum. A friend and disciple of Sigmund Freud, author and psychoanalyst Marie Bonaparte, published *Myths of War* in France in 1947, the basic premise of which was that in wartime all mankind is prone to revert to a state of barbarism. '350,000 men were burnt alive by fuel oil spread on the sea,' Bonaparte vouched, without citing any sources:

> The British collected the corpses, identified them by their identity discs, loaded them into planes and dropped each corpse in its own village to strike terror into their families and undermine German morale … From Calais to Honfleur, the German soldiers could be seen swimming ashore upright. It was an army of the drowned. Their heavy equipment had slipped to their feet and so they were kept upright.

The story also found its way into at least one serious novel. Published in 1952, *Men at Arms* by Evelyn Waugh formed the first part of his masterful trilogy *Sword of Honour*, and despite being a work of fiction closely mirrored the author's own war service in the Royal Marines. In September 1940, Waugh had taken part in an ill-fated expedition to Dakar in French West Africa, and in his later fictional version observed through his protagonist Guy Crouchback:

> Wireless news from England was full of air raids. Some of the men were consumed with anxiety; most were consoled by a rumour, quite baseless, which was travelling the whole world in an untraceable manner, that the invasion had sailed and been defeated, that the whole Channel was full of charred German corpses.

Rumours of a failed invasion bid were no less entrenched in Germany, and gained new currency in 1954 with the release of *Canaris*, a superior monochrome feature directed by Alfred Weidenmann. The film offered up a liberal account of the career of Admiral Wilhelm Canaris, the German chief of intelligence who acted, albeit sporadically, as an Allied informant, and whose mistress in Berne was supported by MI6. During scenes concerned with the planning of Operation Sealion, an Abwehr agent is seen to remove a canister of secret film from an unguarded Whitehall office. On closer examination in Berlin, this is found to contain graphic evidence of flamethrowers, Fougasses and sea flame barrages. While the film is genuine footage shot at Studland Bay and Moody's Down Farm, the scale model of a complicated flame barrage installation at Hastings surpasses anything actually constructed by the PWD. Canaris has only to exhibit these several 'beast-eating' weapons to the German High Command to secure the cancellation of Sealion as 'suicidal'.

In a letter to this author, Weidenmann claimed that the PWD footage was sourced from an archive in Paris. He could shed no light on why screenwriter Erich Ebermeyer (who died in 1970) attached such significance to the role of flame warfare in foiling Sealion. Herbert Reinecker, who also worked on the shooting script, offered the caustic observation that 'history is like a tart – it chases the man who pays most'. Given that rumours of Channel firing may have been deliberately planted on Hitler's chief of intelligence, at least according to Sefton Delmer, the scenario in *Canaris* is not easily dismissed. Rather less credibility attaches to subsequent accounts of an actual landing, such as that published by one Konrad Burg in a controversial German military magazine called *Der Landser*. This unattributed tale of a thwarted Waffen SS raid on the east coast of England may in turn have informed the opening chapter of *Death's Head*, a pulp novel by Leo Kessler published in 1972, wherein an SS raiding party are routed by clouds of flammable gas. Folkloric tales of bodies on beaches subsequently inspired other works of fiction, including *Sea Wrack*, written by Raymond Hitchcock in 1980, and *The House at Sea's End* by Elly Griffiths, published in 2012.

The first serious attempt to uncover the truth about bodies burned and washed ashore was made by Peter Fleming in his book *Invasion 1940*, published in America as *Operation Sea Lion*. A wartime intelligence officer, Fleming was among those charged with co-ordinating stay-behind auxiliary units during the hectic invasion summer of 1940, and later oversaw a number of deception operations in the Far East. In 1941, his short satirical story *The Flying Visit* had anticipated the surprise arrival of Rudolf Hess on British soil by parachute, although in Fleming's fictional version the hapless visitor was Hitler himself. Fleming's younger brother Ian, who later achieved global celebrity as the creator of suave superspy James Bond, served in the Naval Intelligence Division throughout the war years and was a frequent visitor to BSC in New York, as well as a close friend of Dennis Wheatley. Peter Fleming knew Evelyn Waugh, and may have been reminded of the failed invasion myth by the publication of *Men at Arms* in 1952. In his detailed study of Operation Sealion, published in 1957, Fleming devoted considerable space to debunking the mid-September mystery. His account is its own best historian:

> In one strange case credulity found itself allied not with fear but with hope. At the beginning of September a rumour spread swiftly through the country that large numbers of dead German soldiers had been washed up on the south coast. In many accounts the corpses were said to be burnt or charred, and it was widely believed that the RAF had somehow 'set the sea on fire' at the very moment when an invasion was being launched. 'The Channel is white with dead' was a phrase in common use to describe a grim but satisfactory spectacle.

An adventurer and travel writer in civilian life, Fleming had joined a 1932 expedition to Brazil in an attempt to ascertain the fate of explorer Colonel Percy Fawcett, whose own party vanished without trace while searching for the lost city of El Dorado. Digging deeper into yet another tantalising mystery, this time from the invasion summer of 1940, Fleming found that:

> Here again, as so often in this period, we find the flinty soil of fact bearing a crop of legend. Not only was it believed in Britain that the countless German corpses washed up in the south coast had suffered burning in the sea, but on the other side of the Channel rumours of deaths or injuries to German troops from this cause were current. An American correspondent in Germany [William Shirer] saw a hospital train all of whose occupants were said to be suffering from burns, and a story circulated in various forms that the Germans had been testing flame-proof asbestos suits with disastrous results. It is inconceivable that tests of untried equipment of this type would have been carried out on a large scale or caused a noticeable number of casualties, and the origins of this particular legend remain inscrutable.

All of which was broadly accurate. Unfortunately, Fleming then allowed scepticism to cloud his judgement, stating incorrectly that a 'characteristic feature' of the rumour was that the legendary corpses seemed always to arrive on municipal seafronts and harbours, rather than deserted beaches, thereby causing a 'public nuisance'. If Fleming was aware of the arrival of Heinrich Poncke's body at Littlestone-on-Sea on 20 October 1940, he chose to ignore this inconvenient detail. Indeed, the former intelligence officer also overlooked published texts such as *Blue Pencil Admiral* or *The Big Lie*, and even Attlee's statement to the Commons in 1946. The result was a catalogue of errors spread over several pages.

Bizarrely, Fleming seized on the muddled account given by Churchill in *Their Finest Hour*, inferring 'with respect' that Britain's venerable wartime leader had fallen to believing his own propaganda:

> In fact the whole business was much odder than would appear from Churchill's narrative, for his first sentence – which gives the rumour some foundation in fact – has no such foundation itself. The recovery from the sea of forty dead German soldiers would have had at least four consequences which would still be traceable today. It would have been reported in the war diaries of the Army formations in whose sectors they were washed up; the casualties would have been notified to the German Government through the International Red Cross in the same way as casualties to aircrews or prisoners of war in British territory; the pay books and other personal documents of the dead men would have been studied and commented on by MI14; and particulars of the West Country churchyards or cemeteries where the bodies were buried would have been recorded by the Imperial War Graves Commission. None of these consequences ensued.

Just how far these avenues were explored is open to question. In 1957, both regional war diaries and MI14 files remained firmly closed, even to men of trust such as Fleming. Moreover, Red Cross records remain strictly confidential in all territories, while the registers maintained by the Imperial War Graves Commission and *Deutsche Dienstelle* do not specify the armed service to which German casualties belonged. The confusion between Great Yarmouth in Norfolk and Yarmouth on the Isle of Wight, begun in *Their Finest Hour*, also served to muddle Fleming's geography:

> To reach the coast 'between the Isle of Wight and Cornwall' the forty corpses, assuming that they started from the nearest German embarkation area (Le Havre), would have to drift a minimum distance of over 100 miles in a north-westerly direction; and they must, with respect, be written off as not less imaginary than their countless fellow-victims who were said to be whitening the whole Channel.

Again, the lonely corpse of Heinrich Poncke at Littlestone-on-Sea proved Fleming quite wrong. In Britain, *Invasion 1940* arrived in a striking dustcover featuring a colourised image of a flame barrage trial at Studland Bay, which in turn served to spur fresh debate on the mid-September mystery – and flush out startling new evidence. In November 1957, the BBC devoted an entire edition of a factual television programme called *First Hand* to the heady invasion summer of 1940. After advertisements were placed in coastal newspapers on both sides of the Channel, hundreds of people came forward to offer reminiscences and information. Just one of the respondents shed new light on the mystery: former Royal Artillery gunner William Robinson. By then a jobbing gardener living in Brighton, Robinson recalled that:

> I helped to collect the bodies of Germans from the beach between Hythe and Hastings. I was among a party of soldiers sent to search for bodies. The first day we found two soldiers. They had no badges. Later we found five more.

The programme itself, titled *The Finest Hour*, was spiced with familiar footage of PWD demonstrations staged at Moody's Down Farm and Studland Bay, as well as interviews with Gunner Robinson and Peter Fleming. After running through the birth and death of Operation Sealion, and recounting the legend of thousands of charred bodies clogging the Channel, presenter Peter West continued:

> But 1553826 Gunner Robinson, 333 Battery, coastal artillery, was actually detailed to the collect the bodies from the beaches in late September.

> ROBINSON: I was stationed at Herne Bay at the time, and one day I was called into the office and sent to Folkestone. I reported to Folkestone and the following day I was sent out with a party – another six or seven men – to St Mary's, also in Kent, and told to walk along the beach and collect bodies. My part of the beach was back towards Hythe. During the course of that day we found two bodies. We took them back in the lorry to a field at the back of New Romney. We left them there at a canvas screen arrangement, and there went on ... and during the course of the next few days we had seven or eight more.
>
> WEST: Were the bodies badly burned?
> ROBINSON: No, slightly. On the lower part of their bodies.
> WEST: How were you sure that they were German bodies?
> ROBINSON: By the field-grey uniform.
> WEST: Did you think that they'd been in the water very long?

ROBINSON: Yes, a considerable time.

WEST: What about identity discs, paybooks and that kind of thing?

ROBINSON: They were collected by the NCO and handed in to one of the officers at the camouflaged screen.

WEST: Do you think they might not have been pilots or aircrew of the Luftwaffe?

ROBINSON: Well, I'd seen a considerable amount of pilots both dead and alive of the Luftwaffe at the time.

WEST: What do you think yourself had happened to these Germans?

ROBINSON: Well I was told – and I believe – that they were caught by the RAF on a pre-invasion manoeuvre.

WEST: Purely on manoeuvres?

ROBINSON: Yes.

WEST: Now, I believe you were given a special sort of inducement for a rather grisly assignment.

ROBINSON: Yes – twenty Woodbines, which we collected each day, and two shillings a day, which we collected some considerable time later.

WEST: Peter Fleming is especially interested in Mr Robinson's evidence because when he was doing the research for his book *Invasion 1940* he could get no official confirmation of it whatsoever.

FLEMING: Well, I am very interested. Gunner Robinson is the first man I have ever come across with first-hand experience of this particular fatigue – collecting dead Germans – and I gather that you've had evidence in the last couple of days from three or four other people all pointing to the same date at the end of September or early October.

Well, there are two interesting points. One is that Sir Winston in his great book refers to this legend which we've been talking about, and specifically says that at the end of August about forty German bodies were washed up. And it's fairly clear that the rumour which swept the country started in late August/early September before any bodies arrived at all.

Fleming then repeated his position on unit wardiaries, Red Cross notifications, the Imperial War Graves Commission and intelligence reports:

WEST: So the whole thing remains a very fishy business?

FLEMING: No, I wouldn't say that, but it's still surrounded by the mystery in which it started.

WEST: Well anyway, the legend helped to keep up morale here at home.

Robinson's appearance on national television provoked no little debate in the vicinity of Romney Marsh, which now held the promise of irregular – even clandestine – wartime burials. According to a diarist in the *Folkstone and Hythe Gazette*:

> I hope you didn't miss Friday night's excellent BBC television programme *The Finest Hour* … One of those taking part, Mr W.L. Robinson, said he was serving in the Royal Artillery in 1940 when he was sent to Folkestone and then on to St Mary's Bay to keep a watch for German bodies. One day, Mr Robinson said, two bodies were found and then later seven or eight more. As far as he knew they were buried in a mass grave at New Romney.

However, the mystery of the bodies was destined to remain unsolved. Chief Inspector L.A. Hadlow of Kent County Constabulary, in charge of the Hythe Sub-Division throughout the war, told the paper that he only recalled the discovery of one body, at Littlestone, in October 1940. This was of course Heinrich Poncke, the anti-tank gunner, who may have drowned when a flak trawler positioned off Calais was pinched out by the Royal Navy. Intrigued, the *Gazette* traced an ex-soldier named Cyril Goodburn, formerly of the 7th Battalion, Somerset Light Infantry. The same unit had taken part in the apprehension of Charles van den Kieboom and Sjoerd Pons, two of the four ill-starred invasion spies who landed by boat near Dymchurch:

> Wondering whether ex-Private Goodburn could throw any light on the mystery of the bodies I traced him to his home at 16 Hawkins Road, Cheriton, during the weekend. He served with his battalion first at Dymchurch and then at Littlestone, from the last week in June to the following November, but he knew nothing of any German bodies being washed up, although they maintained constant patrols from Littlestone to almost Dungeness.

Goodburn, then, knew nothing even of Heinrich Poncke, and the origin of the corpses in field-grey uniforms collected by Gunner Robinson remained obscure. Were these 'Men Who Never Were' ten of 'about thirty-six' washed ashore over a six-week period in September and October? Was Poncke really the only dead German soldier to arrive, with the rest merely imagined or mistakenly identified? Or could it be that the corpse deception mooted by John Baker White was actually carried out? Despite his flawed methodology in *Invasion 1940*, Peter Fleming's overall assessment survived intact: the whole business was still shrouded by the mystery in which it had started.

So mysterious, indeed, that half a century later the very same legend of foiled landings and charred German bodies would emerge like an unquiet ghost from the mists of time, now to rattle chains – and cages – on the Suffolk coast at Shingle Street.

8

SHINGLE STREET

The isolated fishing hamlet of Shingle Street sits astride a wild and desolate stretch of the Suffolk coast, 12 miles east of Ipswich. Many maps omit to mention the village by name, perhaps justifiably so, for visitors will find there few amenities besides stout Martello towers of Napoleonic vintage. Its public house, the Lifeboat Inn, was blasted by scientists from the Chemical Defence Research Establishment in 1943, while many of the surviving properties are now fair-weather holiday homes.

Yet this apparently tranquil beauty spot is surrounded by sinister mystery. To the north lies the longshore shingle spit of Orford Ness. A secret site since the First World War, the straggling peninsula has played host to a bewildering variety of hush-hush military installations, including an RAF experimental flying field and, in 1935, the very first Air Ministry radar station. Post-war residents came to include the Atomic Weapons Research Establishment, as well as a vast Anglo-American over-the-horizon radar known as Cobra Mist. In 1993, Orford Ness, by then half wilderness, half military junkyard, was sold by the Ministry of Defence to the National Trust for £292,500, and since then has been a protected conservation area.

It was at Orford, too, that Lord Maurice Hankey first tried his hand at setting the sea on fire. A senior Whitehall naval secretary in 1914, 'fired' and inspired by Edward Gibbon's account in *Decline and Fall of the Roman Empire*, Hankey corralled several of the best petroleum experts of the day in an effort to reformulate Greek Fire. The endgame was to flood and fire suitable rivers running into enemy territory, such as the Rhine. Ten barrels of fuel – some 300 gallons – were mixed by specialists at Chatham naval dockyard before being driven to Orford for a trial on 5 December, a day on which newspapers reported fierce fighting around Antwerp and Lodz, as well as 'lively intermittent cannonades' at Ypres. Unfortunately, due to a strong wind and choppy waters on the River Ore, the results were disappointing. 'Part of the raft became detached and drifted away before getting thoroughly alight. In the result three centres of flame, each of great intensity, were formed, instead of a single mass of flame as had been intended.'

The project was quietly abandoned. 'They worked for a month doing nothing else on a pond lent by the Admiralty near Sheerness,' Hankey rued later of this disappointing failure. 'Gibbon's prescription was quite useless.'

A few miles to the south of Shingle Street, on the mouth of River Deben, stands Bawdsey Manor. This flamboyant neo-Jacobean mansion succeeded Orford Ness as the principal Air Ministry radar research establishment in 1936, and after the outbreak of war served as a regular Chain Home radar station. During the 1960s, three of the four 360ft steel transmitting masts were demolished to make way for a large underground ROTOR air defence bunker, as well as a Bloodhound missile site. After decommissioning, RAF Bawdsey was sold for use as a language school, the last transmitting mast finally being demolished in 2000 amidst some controversy.

Situated halfway between Bawdsey and Orford Ness, at the centre of Hollesley Bay, Shingle Street boasts a secret history of its own. In the bowels of The National Archives in London lies a slim, yellowing Ministry of Home Security dossier detailing the 'Evacuation of civil population from the village of Shingle Street in East Suffolk'. Indexed as HO 207/1175, the file was first noted by alert researchers at Kew in 1974, this at a time when it was due to remain sealed until 2021. The existence of a top-secret government file boggled minds across the Eastern region. It was all to do with a type of experimental bomb, some hinted, while others found room for the ULTRA secret. In his book *East Anglia at War*, first published in 1978, a local historian named Derek Johnson even suggested that it was 'on the cards' that primitive atomic missiles had been tested in the area.

Then, in 1992, allegations that a German raiding force had been incinerated by a flame barrage at Shingle Street in 1940 exploded across the national press. At the height of the furore, normally sober television news anchors broadcast tales of charred German bodies washed ashore, this the apparent aftermath of an 'attempt to invade the Suffolk coast in regimental or brigade strength'. These sensational reports soon multiplied to include fatal chemical warfare trials and a suppressed friendly fire disaster in 1944. The result was the kind of undignified media scramble triggered by the notorious *Hitler Diaries*, involving public outcry, the tabling of fresh questions in the House of Commons, robust denials of a conspiracy by the Ministry of Defence and the early declassification of file HO 207/1175.

To those with longer memories, stories of foiled landings and charred German corpses all sounded strangely familiar.

In truth, the facts about Shingle Street's secret wartime past are rather more prosaic. Prior to the outbreak of the Second World War, the village had subsisted as a moderately prosperous fishing hamlet for close on 200 years. The area also boasted a colourful smuggling history, much of which revolved around Dumb-Boy Cottage on the Hollesley road. In 1860, the Reverend Richard Cobbold chose Shingle Street as the setting for climactic scenes in his historical melodrama *The History of Margaret Catchpole*, during which arch-smuggler Will Laud is shot down by Revenue agents while attempting to escape out to sea. A decade later, the village found itself vigorously promoted as Shingle Street-on-Sea, a 'delightful resort' with the 'grandest sea views possessed by any place on the Suffolk coast'. Shortly before the outbreak of the First World War, in May of 1914, five of seven coastguards stationed there were drowned when their whaler overturned on a routine payroll run to Aldeburgh. Two decades later, in 1934, the village featured prominently in *Black August*, a pacy adventure thriller by Dennis Wheatley, set against the background of a violent communist coup, after which Shingle Street is turned into an improvised fortress.

By 1939 the village still consisted of only twenty-three dwellings, the largest of which was the stoutly built coastguard station. The Mission Hall, where gatherings were held once a month, was tended by a visiting parson from Alderton. Save for visiting charabancs, very few cars passed through to disturb the peace, and even the humble bicycle was an uncommon sight. The only pub, the Lifeboat Inn, had been built by Francis Langmaid on the proceeds of salvage money gained from the operation of a private lifeboat prior to the foundation of the RNLI.

Initially, the outbreak of the Second World War affected only coastguard personnel. Although part of the barracks had been sold off previously, the observation building was retained for use by the four local men who continued to act as auxiliaries: Eric Andrews, Ronald Harris, Bert Simpson and Will Lucock. Their duties included patrolling the beach as far as Bawdsey East Lane each evening, a return distance of approximately 4 miles; their counterparts from Bawdsey were responsible for the morning patrol. This wearying routine proved short-lived, for in November 1939 a battalion of the Essex Regiment arrived to defend a lengthy stretch of the East Suffolk coastline. A Territorial unit, battalion headquarters was located at Saxmundham, with forward companies deployed to Leiston and Aldeburgh. The regimental history recalls:

That curious period of lull and unreality which occurred after the outbreak of war, with little to enliven the long hours of guard duty and training. There was the occasional mine on the shore, flares and gunfire well out to sea as some

East Coast convoy was attacked, and the sound of aircraft engines by night as enemy aeroplanes flew in to drop magnetic mines in harbours or on the coastal sea routes. There was also an occasional spy scare to break monotony and keep sentries on their toes.

In *East Anglia at War*, tirelessly inventive local historian Derek Johnson wrote that on a bleak winter night an entire patrol from the 2/4th Essex vanished without trace from Hollesley Bay. According to his source, never precisely revealed, wireless-equipped patrols numbering half a dozen men were dispatched to watch over isolated beaches during the long hours of darkness. The patrol covering Shingle Street ceased to report, and were put on a charge in their absence. The following morning, a search party discovered scattered equipment on the beach but no trace of the lost patrol.

No official records confirm this incident. Tom Abram, an infantry soldier stationed on the coast at Bawdsey during the summer of 1940, puts this apocryphal tale in its proper perspective. 'I never heard of any patrols equipped with wireless sets, although rumours of shore patrols missing from their positions were commonplace. We heard the same thing when we were stationed at Norman's Bay, near Bexhill-on-Sea.'

In April 1940, the 2/4th Essex moved on to Northumberland, and were replaced until November by troops from the Liverpool Scottish. Meanwhile, June 1940 saw the fall of France and the hurried creation of a coastal defence area roughly 20 miles deep between Southend-on-Sea and King's Lynn. The following month, this evacuation zone was extended south as far as Portland in Dorset. In East Anglia alone no less than 127,000 people would be obliged to leave coastal towns to make way for an extensive network of fixed defences, including deadly minefields. In line with this policy, the Regional Commissioner for the Eastern Region, Will Spens, ordered the complete evacuation of Shingle Street on 22 June 1940. Issued under Regulation 16(a) of the Defence Regulations 1939, the order was to take effect before midnight on 25 June, leaving villagers just three days to arrange alternative accommodation. Only the coastguard personnel were exempted.

While draconian, these measures were entirely necessary. Work had already begun on an extensive minefield running east from Oxley Farm towards the shingle beach, then south along the shore ridge to Bawdsey East Lane. The danger posed by these primitive devices was underlined by the death of one of the Royal Engineers tasked with laying them. Worse still, the only road leading out of the village towards Hollesley crossed a narrow humpback bridge at Dumb-Boy Sluice. This, too, was now mined, and at Action Stations would be blown sky high. Since several natural watercourses had also been widened to create an anti-tank ditch, the hamlet and its inhabitants would have been rapidly – and hopelessly – cut off in the event of a genuine emergency.

Nevertheless, the sudden evacuation caused no little hardship. A majority of the villagers opted to move inland to Hollesley, 2 miles away, while others found billets in Bawdsey and Alderton. With just one lorry to assist in the hasty exodus, most were able to remove only the barest essentials, leaving behind larger items such as beds and furniture. In a plaintive letter addressed to the regional commissioner in August, one elderly widow complained:

Dear Sir. I am writing to ask if you can help me in the evacuation of Shingle Street. Mr Hocking and Mr Collett came round and told us to take 48 hours' notice to get out. The military helped me move some of my furniture. I am a widow getting ten shillings a week and lived in my own home. Now I am turned out and having to pay six shillings a week rent.

Since our evacuation my house has been broken into by the soldiers, windows smashed and doors broken from hinges, and also goods taken from the house. Can you give me the paper with the orders to quit my home which I should have had at the time, or can you help me and give me advice on what steps to take?

Regrettably, over the next few months extensive looting continued, though thankfully troops who behaved in this way formed a small (but callous) minority. Tom Abram, a private with the Liverpool Scottish stationed at Bawdsey East Lane, recalls the humdrum routine of Home Defence units stationed on the Suffolk coast during the tense 'invasion summer' of 1940:

Our platoon was ordered to man certain points near and on the beach. We were billeted in tents which had been erected alongside a field near the beach road. Other platoons were stationed near Shingle Street. We were close to the Martello tower, which was manned by the coastguard. There was also a cottage in which lived two sisters who provided much-needed tea and cakes.

We hadn't been there long when the Royal Engineers turned up with very unsophisticated anti-tank mines, which were laid in the field alongside our tents, with our help and a little instruction. They then mined the beach, although with the movement of the shingle it became a very dangerous place. I often wonder if all the mines were ever lifted.

There was a profound lack of action. Whenever enemy fighter planes passed over on their way to Martlesham Heath we had a go with our Bren gun, but with only one tracer bullet to every ten rounds it was futile. In June, and later on, we had Stand To from sunset to dawn with orders to hold on at all costs. It must be remembered that in those days we had no wireless, never saw a newspaper, never received information from our superiors and never saw any road signs or maps. We simply lived from day to day and did as we were told.

Although there were constant warnings about imminent invasion the only German we saw was a dead airman, who we fished out of the sea and carried back to camp on a hurdle.

The German flyer, washed ashore at Bawdsey on 30 October 1940, almost certainly belonged to the same crew as a second man found near Hollesley on the same day, as well as a third at Shingle Street on 29 October. A fourth body had arrived two days previously at Aldeburgh. All had been in the water for almost a month, their Heinkel 111 bomber having come down off the Suffolk coast on 4 October. This sad quartet, the only Germans officially acknowledged as having landed near Shingle Street during the Second World War, posed no great military threat.

Ronald Harris, an Auxiliary Coastguard stationed at Shingle Street throughout the war, recalled that on one occasion written instructions were received from the area coastguard headquarters at Walton-on-the-Naze to watch the shoreline for bodies. Interviewed by this author in 1992, Mr Harris could not recall the precise date, and in any case saw none. Indeed, the only enemy landing in Hollesley Bay took the form of a theoretical II Corps exercise staged on 29 July, when the imagined action unfolded as follows:

14.50 Enemy troops landing in Dovercourt Bay … 15.10 Confused fighting in Woodbridge … 15.22 Frinton and Mersea captured … 15.23 Ipswich heavily damaged and many casualties. Strong enemy force arrived on outskirts of town from Harwich … 15.47 Sniped en-route at Ashbocking and Otley … 16.00 Enemy landing one mile south of Shingle Street.

Regrettably, the outcome of this close-run paper battle is not recorded. On 25 September, however, an equally interesting entry appeared in the war diary of the 165th Infantry Brigade, whose sector included Hollesley Bay:

Received a letter from [55] Division stating that a scheme was afoot to produce an impenetrable barrage of flame on the sea to prevent or destroy enemy ships attempting a landing.

The same message was sent to all units in Southern and Eastern Commands at the behest of the Petroleum Warfare Department, at the time still dreaming of mile upon mile of beach and sea barrage. The unit replied the following day, suggesting that flame might prove useful at four locations:

a) Bawdsey 8057
b) Mouth of River Deben 7855
c) Mouth of River Orwell 7249
d) Felixstowe, from Ferry 7755 to Landguard Fort 7350

There is no evidence that any of these barrages were installed. Indeed, in October 1941, with the threat of invasion now remote, the War Office wrote to inform the Ministry of Home Security that Shingle Street could be de-requisitioned. Unfortunately, none of the long-suffering villagers were allowed to return to their homes due to the continued danger posed by mines, which had by then accounted for another two soldiers and a trespassing civilian.

These rusted mines also found their way into 'Dawn on the East Coast', a poem by Welsh-born writer Alun Lewis, then serving in the Royal Engineers. Like much of his work, these Suffolk lines explore the effect of new postings and places on the poet, evoking perfectly the 'grey disturbance' and 'frozen fields' running between Orford Ness and Shingle Street during the third year of war. Lewis later took his own life while on active service in Burma, and in September 1942 events at Shingle Street would also take a more sinister turn. At this time the Chemical Defence Research Establishment (CDRE) at Porton Down was casting around for an area of land on which to conduct trials with a new chemical weapon. On their behalf, the Ministry of Home Security approached each of the twelve Regional Commissioners, seeking locations replete with:

> Suitable evacuated dwelling houses in reasonably good repair, which [the CDRE] could use for the purpose of dropping trials of 250lb HE/Chem. bombs. The height of release of the bombs would be between 500 ft and 1,000 ft. The bomb wall thickness would be ¼ inch, and its content would be 75lbs TNT, together with a charging of either mustard or a substitute.

Quite why Porton Down wished to test a new form of chemical weapon at this time is unclear. Two years earlier, faced with the prospect of invasion, Churchill had authorised Plan Y, by which landing beaches in Britain would have been sprayed with blister gas. This 'lively terror' would have slowed down the enemy, if not quite stopping them dead, but risked appalling forms of retaliation. By 1942, scientists at the CDRE were also engaged in research into biological warfare, and in July of that year detonated several small 30lb bombs charged with live anthrax spores on a remote Scottish island called Gruinard, uninhabited save for a few dozen black-faced hill sheep. The chair of the committee supervising these highly secret experiments was veteran secret statesman Lord Maurice Hankey.

For the 'HE/Chem.' bomb trial brokered by the Ministry of Home Security, Porton Down were said to prefer existing battle training areas, from which civilians had already been evacuated, and considerable damage inflicted on buildings. Following assurances that inmates of the nearby borstal at Hollesley would not be affected by blast or poison gas, at the close of 1942 the CDRE was granted leave to test the new hybrid device on the hapless hamlet of Shingle Street.

Trials were expected to last between seven and ten days, and involved pinpoint low-level bombing. Conscientious to a fault, Porton Down was informed of the approximate value of all twenty properties, so that the vexed question of compensation could be taken up with the Ministry of Home Security at a later date. Weather conditions meant that the trial was then delayed for several months. Nevertheless, a measure of the importance of the new device was supplied in 1974 by the late Nora Pierce Butler, a native of Woodbridge. In 1943, Miss Pierce Butler was introduced to Air Commodore Patrick Huskinson, the director of the Air Armament Board, who had been blinded by a bomb splinter during the Blitz. Their encounter took place in Canterbury, in a social context, yet on learning that Butler knew the village of Shingle Street well, Huskinson told her in confidence that a new type of bomb would shortly be dropped on it. 'There won't be any Shingle Street next week,' he warned ominously.

The actual trial took place on 28 March 1943. Following evacuation of the coastguard personnel, large yellow target markers were painted on the ground around the Lifeboat Inn. Percy Darvell, then a member of the Auxiliary Fire Service, recalls that his unit was called out from Woodbridge for several dry runs before a twin-engined aircraft flew in low from the south and released a bomb, scoring a direct hit on the abandoned pub. The blast damage to the building and the surrounding cottages was extensive, yet apparently precise, causing the scientist overseeing the trial to rub his hands with glee. In 1992, Darvell identified the boffin concerned as none other than Sir Barnes Wallis, the legendary aircraft and bomb designer, whose creations included the so-called 'bouncing bomb' deployed by 617 Squadron against the Ruhr dams in May 1943 – the Dambusters. Unfortunately, no evidence confirms that Wallis worked with Porton Down, while his diaries and personal papers record no visits to Suffolk during 1943. The white-haired civilian in the photograph kept by Darvell appears to resemble the inventor, yet surviving members of the Wallis family deny any connection. Be that as it may, Wallis certainly knew Air Commodore Huskinson well, and the brilliant scientist may have travelled up to Suffolk the following year during ballistic tests of his giant 12,000lb 'Tallboy' bomb, conducted on Orford Ness.

Fifty years later, Porton Down confirmed to this author that the bomb dropped at Shingle Street was an experimental 250lb device, intended to enhance the tactical use of mustard gas by combining a vesicant charge with ordinary high explosive. This disagreeable combination, it was hoped, would result in both physical contamination and blast damage, thus dispensing with the need to co-ordinate a mixed stick of separate chemical and explosive munitions. The CDRE charged the bomb with 4 gallons of dyed methyl salicylate, otherwise known as oil of wintergreen, an innocuous mustard substitute which could be readily traced by sight and smell to show the extent of the chemical splash. Ultimately, however, the test drop at Shingle Street in March 1943 was judged to be a failure, since the instantaneous fusing necessary to prevent the chemical charge being buried in the ground reduced the effectiveness of the high explosive.

Damage of another kind was inflicted on the village after the arrival of the US Eighth Air Force in East Anglia. In the scramble to build new airfields across the region, many thousands of tons of shingle were removed from the beach to provide hardcore for runways and perimeter tracks. This was achieved at some cost to the environment, since the sea began to creep steadily closer to the houses after extraction ceased in 1944. 'At this rate,' one villager was moved to complain some years later, 'Shingle Street will have no shingle, and no street.'

In addition to an uncharged chemical bomb, spring 1943 saw other secret weapons arrive in the area. Situated to the north of Shingle Street and Hollesley, the Orford Battle Training Area played host to the 79th Armoured Division, an armoured engineering unit equipped with 'Funnies' – specially adapted tanks designed to breach the Atlantic Wall during the D-Day landings in France. The division remained in the Orford area until early 1944 and carried out intensive training, pitting their vehicles against replicas of obstacles likely to be encountered on the beaches of Normandy. On at least one occasion, waterproofing trials with amphibious DD tanks were conducted at Shingle Street, as well as mine-clearing flails, but no evidence exists of flame-throwing Crocodile tanks in the village, nor any fatal accidents.

The approach of the end of the war in Europe brought no relief for the long-suffering population. By October 1944, Shingle Street had been prioritised for mine clearance before the end of the year, yet in April 1945 the military informed the Ministry of Home Security that the village remained off-limits, being an 'extremely dangerous and awkward minefield'. Moreover, most of the houses were by now uninhabitable. Those not damaged by the 1943 bombing trial had suffered equally from five long years of weather and neglect. Many would be written off as total losses. A 1945 report by the Regional Commissioner on the state of each property in the village made for gloomy reading:

> A small bungalow of brick and slate construction owned by Mrs S. Curtis. Damaged by bombing beyond repair. Walls fractured, doors and window frames blown in and slates off. Evidence of some chattels which had obviously been looted. Still contains three chairs, one bed, an old settee and useless personal effects.
>
> Bungalow of wooden construction with pan-tiled roof, owned by Mr R. Harris. All windows smashed and end demolished by bombing. Total loss.
>
> The Lifeboat Inn, of wood and lathe and plaster construction with pan-tiled roof. Completely demolished.

The partial devastation wrought on the Lifeboat Inn by Porton Down and the RAF was largely completed two years later, when a high-spirited raiding party from Bawdsey Manor dynamited the shell of the pub and took the timber to build an extravagant bonfire on VE Day.

The removal of the beach mines lasted well into 1945, and residents who wished to return to the blasted village would be obliged to wait years, rather than months. The compensation packages offered were meagre, and much delayed due to Whitehall wrangling between the War Office and the Ministry of Home Security. Ronald Harris, whose bungalow Ronina beside the Lifeboat Inn was one of the properties damaged beyond repair, had to wait until 1949 for a new, more sturdy house to be completed. Even as late as 1948, travel writer Archie White described the once 'busy and prosperous' hamlet as 'blown to pieces', with nothing left but 'large deep ponds between the houses and the sea to show where the river once ran'.

Plans to build a new Lifeboat Inn were thwarted when a Mrs Pritchard-Carr won the only available victualler's licence and opened a tea shop. Shingle Street never did regain its status as a working fishing village, or well-to-do seaside resort, becoming instead the domain of the weekend angler, the watercolour artist, the naturalist and the hardy rambler. 'A sea-bathing and fishing hamlet along the ridge of the beach since 1810,' noted Norman Scarfe in his popular *Shell Guide to Suffolk*, 'where the ancient shore-line dips into the marsh.'

Shingle Street's curious wartime past first made headlines in August 1974, when the existence of file HO 207/1175 was noticed at the Public Record Office. In a prominent article titled 'War File on Hamlet Closed for 40 Years', the *East Anglian Daily Times* made much of the discovery that a Ministry of Home Security dossier, indexed as 'Evacuation of civil population from the village of Shingle Street, East Suffolk', remained subject to a seventy-five-year embargo. This seemed puzzling given that large numbers of previously classified military and War Cabinet files were now being released to the PRO under the thirty-year rule, while several other closely guarded wartime secrets had recently entered the public domain thanks to books such as *The Double-Cross System* and *The Ultra Secret*.

'Officials responsible for the government archives say that embargoes of this duration are generally imposed on papers believed to contain matters of "personal sensitivity" likely to cause embarrassment or even distress to members of the public,' wrote reporter Margaret Warren. 'Records remained closed on two other general grounds – because they contained matters affecting state security, or information given to government departments under a pledge of confidentiality. They did not know which category the Shingle Street file came under. The maximum embargo is 100 years.'

Digging deeper into the mystery, Warren caught the Ministry of Defence in an unusually playful mood. From Whitehall an enigmatic spokesman hinted darkly that 'this has been classified as Top Secret, and as we are not going to release it for another forty-five years you might say that it is Top Top Secret'. An embargo of seventy-five years, added the Man from the Ministry, 'usually only applies when it comes to something of national importance'.

Historian Norman Scarfe, a resident of the village himself since 1963, admitted to being mystified:

> What happened was that everyone had to move out when the army took the place over as a battle training area. There was only a very small population and most of them went to Hollesley, only a mile or two away. When the war was over they came back here. I have never heard anyone grousing about what happened. Some of the houses were badly knocked about because in some mysterious way they were used as a target for bombing, I believe.

Another villager, Robin Usher, a retired Royal Navy commander, was renowned for raising a Union Jack outside his cottage each day at dawn. 'I cannot understand why there should be secrecy for so long,' he told a reporter. 'It just makes people think that the military authorities may have made a terrible blunder.'

'The military authorities kept me out of the village if there was anything special going on,' added Eric Andrews, one of the auxiliary coastguards who had remained in situ throughout the war.

Phrases as loaded as 'Top Top Secret' and 'national importance' tickled fancies across East Anglia, with talk of 'sinister secrets' soon picked up by *The Sun* and *The Guardian*. Yet nowhere was it mentioned that the seventy-five-year embargo placed on HO207/1175 was far from unique. Indeed, all files relating to the wartime requisition of land and property by the military remained sealed. That innocuous dossiers on the 'Immobilisation of boats' and 'Agricultural damage: Thetford battle training area' also remained closed should have provided clues that the yellowing flimsies within contained little which might affect national security.

Some thought the puzzle solved when Nora Pierce Butler contacted Norman Scarfe to report her wartime encounter with Air Commodore Patrick Huskinson, the sightless RAF armaments specialist. Thirty years earlier, during a walk by a lake in Canterbury, Huskinson had confided details of a new sort of 'fragmentation' bomb and the imminent destruction of the village. 'Until now I have kept this secret,' Miss Butler told the *East Anglian Daily Times*. 'But I firmly believe this is why the files are to remain closed for another forty-five years. After all, what else can it be?'

Readers had to wait another decade for an answer, proposed this time by journalist David Henshall. The trigger was renewed public interest in Exercise Tiger, a disastrous D-Day rehearsal staged off Dorset in April 1944, when German motor torpedo boats struck at three crowded troop transports, resulting in the deaths of 749 American servicemen. In truth, the Slapton Sands tragedy was less secret than simply obscure. Nevertheless, beneath the headline 'D-Day: Suffolk's Own Sinister Secret', the paper now speculated on:

Another D-Day exercise in which British barges were blown out of the water by British gunners who had not been told what was going on ... Defenders set fire to the sea in the belief that the enemy was about to land on British soil. The soldiers were said to number about 100, dying when trapped by a new invention code-named PLUTO.

Henshall was vague about his sources, hinting that rumours around the violent demise of a considerable number of British troops at Shingle Street had circulated in the area 'for many years'. Gladys Andrews, widow of coastguard Eric Andrews, could offer only guarded comment: 'There have been rumours and stories about soldiers being killed, but the only things I know about for sure were the land mines killing men on the beaches when they were working on them.'

PLUTO had indeed been a secret D-Day device, the development of which was supervised by the Petroleum Warfare Department. In all, some 500 miles of piping was laid between Dungeness and Boulogne, a remarkable feat of engineering which allowed Geoffrey Lloyd to boast of its tremendous utility on revealing its existence at the end of the war. However, PLUTO was simply a fuel supply system and shared nothing in common with the PWD flame barrage programme of 1940. Moreover, not a single one of the twenty-odd pipelines laid ran from the east coast across the North Sea. Thus the 'major security blunder' proposed by Henshall seemed no less fanciful than the tall tales of atomic missile tests retailed by Derek Johnson in *East Anglia at War*.

Thereafter the story lay dormant for another decade, only to be revived during a quiet news week in 1992. On 7 March, the tranquil slumber of Hollesley Bay was again disturbed by another sensational exclusive in the *East Anglian Daily Times* (*EADT*). Beneath the arresting headline 'Dozens of Soldiers Killed in Nazi Invasion Blunder', journalist Henry Creagh informed readers that:

Dozens of British soldiers were burnt to death by one of their own men in a wartime exercise on the Suffolk coast which went tragically wrong, it was claimed yesterday. New information has come to the EADT about the secret of Shingle Street, an isolated coastal hamlet which was evacuated in 1940 for use by the armed forces. The incident allegedly occurred during a training exercise near the radar installation at Bawdsey, just south of Shingle Street.

Part of the base's defences consisted of drums of petrol chained to concrete blocks under the sea and wired to detonators. In case of an enemy assault from the sea, the drums would be blown and the petrol would rise to the surface, where it could be set alight using tracer rounds.

The army had decided to carry out a mock assault on Bawdsey, and contacted the base to say it would be doing so, but somehow the message was not passed on. Later that night, a sentry saw rubber dinghies approaching the base, and, assuming it was the enemy, detonated the charges. The petrol was set alight by tracer bullets from a machine gun post. Many soldiers died in the inferno and their bodies were carried out on the tide, only to be washed up at Shingle Street.

Mr Ron Harris, one of the few residents to remain in Shingle Street after the evacuation, was a coastguard at the site throughout the war. He can remember being given an order to look for charred bodies, but cannot recall the date or any incident where the sea was set on fire.

A file on the mystery has lain in the Public Record Office since the Second World War under a seventy-five-year embargo lasting until 2014. Such an embargo can only be granted for reasons of national security, to protect confidential information supplied by the public, or where publication of records would distress or embarrass any living person. The Ministry of Defence could not comment on the claims.

The *EADT*'s source was said to be an anonymous telephone caller 'close to the Ministry of Defence', who had gained sight of the classified papers by chance. Although the MoD mole allegedly rang through on a second occasion, the *EADT* news desk was given no name or contact number and the informant fell silent after the blunder/inferno story broke nationally in wildly exaggerated form.

Crucially, Henry Creagh's report obscured one important detail: that the mysterious incident was said to have occurred during a D-Day training exercise in 1944. Phrases such as 'Nazi invasion blunder' painted a very different picture, and served to revive long-dormant memories of the mid-September mystery in 1940. In truth, the mystery 'Deep Throat' call bore all the hallmarks of a hoax. No record exists of any beach or sea flame barrage at Bawdsey, while the PWD never developed a system based on tethered submarine drums, fired by tracer rounds. It does, however, chime with the fictive account by Boris Nikolaevsky printed by the *New York Times* in December 1940, headlined 'Nazi Invaders Held "Consumed By Fire" – Dead Are Put At 80,000', which portrayed the English Channel as 'sowed … with oil tanks sufficiently beneath the surface to be hidden from view'. Nikolaevsky's article also talked of the doomed German force striking 'the oil and gasoline line about midway between the French and British coasts' – a phrase which might cause confusion with PLUTO.

Had the potential of the rumour as a news story ended there, coverage of this apparently cyclical tale might well have died away for another ten years. But like all good sibs, it simply grew in the telling. On the strength of the *EADT* report by Henry Creagh, the owner of a small art gallery in Long Melford named John Rux-Burton came forward with information passed on by his late grandfather, John Edgar Burton. His story was broadcast on *Anglia News*, the facts of which (as stated to this author) ran as follows. When war broke out in 1939, Burton suddenly abandoned his London accountancy practice to scour the countryside for timber. This innocuous task served as cover for oblique undercover duties on behalf of the Naval Intelligence Division. According to his grandson, one day during the autumn of 1940, Burton received word that:

A German force had attempted to invade Suffolk and [he] was dispatched to Shingle Street to find out what had happened. When he arrived the beach was covered with dozens upon dozens of bodies, most of them charred beyond recognition. The defenders believed the men to be Germans dressed as British soldiers. A senior officer then arrived on the scene and said that the bodies were really those of British troops, and that there had been a friendly-fire incident. My grandfather was not convinced, since the markings on a burned-out dinghy nearby appeared to be German. The dinghy was then heaved onto the back of a truck and driven away, along with the bodies. He thought that the government were very keen on not allowing it out that these men had died by burning in oil in the sea.

Although he carried on working as an intelligence officer, John Edgar Burton heard nothing more of the incident. According to his grandson, he came to discuss Shingle Street with his family only later in life, by which time memories of the horrific scene had begun triggering nightmares.

Like the bodies described by Gunner William Robinson on BBC television in 1957, the Burton story is impossible to verify. Nevertheless, the re-emergence of the myth of a failed invasion attempt four decades later set the media hares running. The first national on the scene was *The Sunday Telegraph*, whose defence correspondent, Christy Campbell, pulled together an impressive double-page spread, touching on the hospital trains spied in Berlin by William L. Shirer, the close proximity of Bawdsey Manor and the mystery bombing trial supposedly overseen by Barnes Wallis. 'Wartime rumours of a failed Nazi invasion have resurfaced,' Campbell mused. 'Was there a cover-up, or is the story just too good to be left alone?'

Ironically, the most astute commentary came from Jack Higgins, author of *The Eagle Has Landed*, a runaway bestseller in 1975 and a major motion picture the following year. Taking its lead from *Went the Day Well*, Higgins' plot revolved around the occupation of a remote Norfolk village by German paratroops in a desperate bid to kill, or kidnap, Winston Churchill. 'The really astonishing thing is how fiction and reality can blur,' the millionaire writer told *The Telegraph*. 'A retired postman who claimed to have been at the Battle of Studley Constable was interviewed on television, and I still receive the occasional letter from Germans and Americans claiming that fathers or uncles had been at the "battle".'

A comprehensive overview of media coverage of the Shingle Street stir between March and July 1992 reveals a bewildering array of wild theories and voodoo history. Besides endless variations of the failed invasion sib concocted by British propagandists in 1940, it was variously claimed that: civilians spent two whole days clearing bodies from the beach at Felixstowe; a skeleton found by a canoe party from the Hollesley borstal in 1985 was that of a Nazi; Germans had landed in Suffolk on motorcycles and lobbed grenades at coastal gun batteries; the dead men at Shingle Street dressed in British uniforms were German *Brandenburg* commandos engaged in a false flag operation; British troops were used as guinea pigs in a chemical warfare trial; the RAF bombed civilians by accident; and tragedy overtook sea trials with amphibious DD tanks by the 79th Armoured Division. Juxtaposition of the 1940 failed invasion myth, the bombing of the Lifeboat Inn in 1943 and a supposed training disaster in 1944 served to cloud already muddied waters, resulting in the publication of a catalogue of errors and half-truths.

Anglia Television, *The Sunday Telegraph* and the *East Anglian Daily Times* together received more than a hundred letters from members of the public, all supporting one version of events or another. Undoubtedly these correspondents were well intentioned, yet none had witnessed anything significant at first hand. Meanwhile, unreliable local historian Derek Johnson appeared to operate as a one-man underground propaganda committee. During the 1950s, dubious German pulp magazine *Der Landser* had printed a story attributed to one Konrad Burg, who made brief mention of a doomed east coast foray by troops of the dreaded Waffen SS. The detail, such as it was, seemed to have been lifted from wartime newspaper copy and the *Canaris* biopic from 1954. Johnson passed off this pamphlet to the press as a genuine historical document, and was rewarded with headlines such as 'Invasion Met Fire Wall' and 'Nazi Landing Attempt Disaster Report Found'. Having rushed out a revised edition of his earlier book *East Anglia at War*, Johnson revealed next that staff at Ipswich Crematorium had been instructed to rush all available coffins to Shingle Street. Subsequently, the industrious historian also claimed to have uncovered evidence that bodies had been interred in a mass grave in nearby Rendlesham Forest. Thankfully, the *Sunday Sport* lent its weight to the investigation, with their intrepid reporter able to locate without effort 'near Ipswich ... the unmarked grave where 100 kraut stormtroopers lie secretly buried – on the orders of Churchill himself'. This story became the basis of a ribald lampoon in *Viz* magazine. Unfortunately, the suspicion remains that publicity-hungry Derek Johnson simply fabricated conspiratorial stories of burial pits, atomic tests and sinister telephone calls as a means of selling books.

Others, too, stumbled across secret Nazi graves. *Anglia News* broadcast pictures of the headstones of several unknown German servicemen dotted around the region. In truth, the generic inscription *Eine Deutsche Soldat* was applied to casualties from all three services, not merely soldiers, and their presence in local graveyards was due to nothing more mysterious than practical difficulties around the removal of all German remains to Cannock Chase after 1959. Nevertheless, fuelled by fading memories of the original wartime Big Lie, the dominant narrative came to be that German troops had, in the words of *Anglia News*, 'attempted to invade the Suffolk coast in regimental or brigade strength to establish a toehold and/or act as a decoy for a main invasion on the south coast'.

The key to the enigma, it was widely held, lay hidden between the buff manila covers of HO 207/1175 at the PRO, although with few prepared to wait until 2021 to examine the contents of the sealed file, pressure began to mount for its early declassification. The burden initially fell on two local MPs, Shingle Street itself falling within the Suffolk Coastal constituency of John Gummer, then the minister for agriculture. In May 1992, after several media prompts, Gummer promised to raise the matter privately with the home secretary, Kenneth Clarke. A more robust campaign was launched by Jamie Cann, the newly elected Labour MP for Ipswich and something of a latter-day Watchman. After writing to Clarke to request that the sealed file be opened, Cann told reporters that he believed 'the people of Suffolk have a right to know what went on in their own back yard over fifty years ago'. Clarke told Cann that the matter would be given due consideration, thanks in part to the Waldegrave Initiative, a new governmental proposal aimed at promoting greater openness around official secrecy. Unfortunately, classified files on the Rudolf Hess affair released in June proved innocuous, leaving sceptics and conspiracists convinced that files would be diligently weeded of any sensitive material long before entering the public domain.

Anticipation reached fever pitch on the evening of 6 July, when the Home Secretary announced that HO 207/1175 would be opened the following morning. 'The wartime mystery behind the unexplained evacuation of a Suffolk fishing hamlet will soon be solved,' trumpeted *The Daily Telegraph*. 'It was thought the dead men were German commandos sent to attack an RAF radar station at nearby Bawdsey Manor.' Having invested heavily in the Shingle Street story, the *East Anglian Daily Times* puffed its own 'relentless campaign' to uncover the sinister wartime secret:

> The file will explain exactly what happened during WW2 at Shingle Street, when dozens of charred bodies in British uniforms were washed up on the beach … Whitehall has until now refused to say who the men in British uniforms were, how they died or where they came from … EADT reporters were travelling to the PRO in London this morning to view the files for the first time.

While the sudden release of the file caught many unawares, a red-eye wire from Associated Press drew a crowd of reporters to the Public Record Office. Sadly, those eager for an historic scoop would be sorely disappointed. Instead of a thwarted German commando raid, the coveted file merely detailed mundane wrangles over compensation for damaged property and the minor revelation that a mustard gas bomb – uncharged – had been dropped on the Lifeboat Inn in 1943.

Six other HO 207 series files relating to the Eastern Region were released on the same day. They were, if anything, even less revelatory than the Shingle Street papers. HO 207/1183, concerned with the requisition of Iken Hall near Woodbridge, disclosed a bizarre wartime complaint:

> The lady has always been very reasonable in her questions with regard to military activities around her house, and in view of the use of it as a residential war nursery, I think it will be appreciated how important it is not to involve the children in risk of damage or unnecessary alarm.

Had such high-value secret material fallen into unscrupulous foreign hands, the consequences might scarcely be imagined. Indeed, so damp was the squib that few national newspapers even bothered to follow up the story next day. Left with egg on their faces, Anglia Television News cried foul, voicing concerns that the content of the file had been 'raided in an official cover-up', with all reference to a German landing attempt removed by the Ministry of Defence.

Having held the front page, the following day the *East Anglian Daily Times* made do with a desultory résumé of 'sinister theories' beneath the misleading headline 'Secret File Deepens War Tragedy – Hamlet Used for Mustard Gas Tests'. An apparently genuine photograph of 'a lone angler on the beach at Shingle Street yesterday' did little to assuage local disappointment. Ipswich MP Jamie Cann declared himself equally unhappy: 'I think there has been an error made, because the Ministry of Defence have told me they are not aware of any other files relating to Shingle Street. There are so many reports about bodies being found on the beach that it must have happened, and if it happened there will be reports. And if there are reports there must be files.'

Like so many others, Cann seemed blind to the inconvenient truth that not a single first-hand, eyewitness report confirmed charred or multiple bodies at Hollesley Bay during the Second World War. In any event, this defiant mood proved short-lived. A week later, the Army Historical Branch provided Cann with a detailed summary of wartime events at Shingle Street, signed off by Viscount Cranborne, a junior defence minister. In essence, the document drew on: (a) Eastern Command unit war diaries for 1940; (b) a resume of wartime activity by the Petroleum Warfare Department; (c) Porton Down and the 1943 bombing trial; (d) the 79th Armoured

Division war diary; (e) Clement Attlee's lengthy written reply to the Commons in November 1946; and (f) Winston Churchill's skewed paragraph on beached bodies in *Their Finest Hour*.

Since the report prepared by the Army Historical Branch was specific to Suffolk, no reference was made to the arrival of Heinrich Poncke at Littlestone-on-Sea, nor to the several bodies collected by Gunner William Robinson from St Mary's Bay. Cautious to a fault, the overall summary concluded:

> There is no evidence in either the most highly classified contemporary British records, or apparently in the contemporary German records, of an actual attempt by the Germans to land in Britain … The contemporary authoritative records provide no evidence to support the claims that a number of burnt, British uniformed bodies were washed up on the Shingle Street beach in the summer or autumn of 1940, or that the 1943 events also considered provide any evidence to support the general allegations made.

The full text of the AHB report is reproduced here as Appendix 3. Viewed with the benefit of hindsight, this slight document carries little weight. With the exception of the 1943 bombing trial, details of which had only recently surfaced through HO 207/1175, none of the material on which the Ministry relied had been classified since 1974. Indeed, writing in haste, its single author even managed to overlook significant published sources, notably *Blue Pencil Admiral* and *The Big Lie*. Nevertheless, Jamie Cann chose to accept these findings and at a press conference in Ipswich confirmed that there had been no invasion attempt at Shingle Street. 'The truth is that not very much happened,' he added later. 'I am convinced we now have all the information available. The only remaining mystery is why anyone wanted to cover it up for seventy-five years.'

John Gummer too dismissed as 'nonsense' the suggestion that Nazi commandos had attempted to wrest his constituency fifty years earlier: 'There is no reason at all to believe other than the Home Office statement. Clearly that's what did happen. I can't understand why anybody objects or disagrees.'

Recognising that the puzzle was now solved, or simply unsolvable, the Fourth Estate beat a tactical retreat. 'War Riddle of Bodies on Beach is Solved' wrote *The Daily Telegraph* on 20 July, a conclusion echoed by *The Times* in a piece on the Public Record Office and the thirty-year rule. The back-peddling executed by the *East Anglian Daily Times* was even more vigorous. At the end of July, hidden away on page 22, the headline 'Shingle Street Riddle Was Unravelled 45 Years Ago' prefaced an article in which all recent claims were dismissed as conspiracy theories.

'It's like UFOs or corn circles,' their correspondent stated with authority. 'People want to believe it.'

That it is easier to believe than to know is a well-worn truism. Since the first edition of this book in 1994, the advent of the internet has ensured that countless exaggerated versions of the Shingle Street myth remain in circulation. The author's own primary research was plagiarised by Peter Haining in a slipshod work, *Where the Eagle Landed*, published in 2004. Even as late as 2010, Anglia Television news felt able to devote five minutes of airtime to a familiar round of baseless stories, broadcasting – unchallenged – claims that the Lifeboat Inn was destroyed during a 'firefight' with German troops. Fortunately, the true story of the remarkable propaganda victory instigated by John Baker White has now been absorbed into the accepted historical narrative of 1940. 'Like all good lies it was simple,' the unsung major concluded. 'Imagination is a very powerful thing, as we were to discover many times before the war was over ... The burning-sea story was our first large-scale attempt at a Big Lie, and it proved amazingly successful.'

Ultimately, the Shingle Street fiction is a story of smoke without fire, and of two near-identical myths separated only by time. The first, from the dark days of 1940, stands as testament to the potent effect of Big Lies and black propaganda. The second, more recent, bears witness to the boundless credulity of the modern age, while dealing a mortal blow to Sophocles' ancient dictum that a lie never lives to be old.

SHORT INVASION PHRASEBOOK (1940)

DER KLEINE INVASIONS- DOLMETSCHER	PETIT MANUEL DE CONVERSATION POUR L'INVASION	TAALCURSUS ZONDER LEERMEESTER VOOR DUITSCHE SOLD [...]

I. Vor der Invasion

1. Die See ist gross — kalt — stürmisch.
2. Wie oft müssen wir noch Landungsmanöver üben?
3. Ob wir wohl in England ankommen werden?
4. Ob wir heil zurückkommen werden?
5. Wann ist der nächste englische Luftangriff? Heute morgens; mittags; nachmittags; abends; nachts.
6. Warum fährt der Führer nicht mit?
7. Unser Benzinlager brennt noch immer!
8. Euer Benzinlager brennt schon wieder!
9. War hat schon wieder das Telefonkabel durchgeschnitten?
10. Haben Sie meinen Kameraden in den Kanal geworfen?
11. Können Sie mir eine Schwimmweste — einen Rettungsring — leihen?
12. Was kosten bei Ihnen Schwimmstunden?
13. Wie viele Invasionsfahrten brauch' ich für das E.K.I?
14. Sieben — acht — neun.
15. Wir werden gegen Engelland fahren!

I. Avant l'invasion

1. La mer est vaste — froide — houleuse.
2. Combien de fois encore devrons-nous faire des exercises de débarquement?
3. Pensez-vous que nous arriverons jamais en Angleterre?
4. Pensez-vous que nous reviendrons jamais d'Angleterre?
5. Quand le prochain raid anglais aura-t-il lieu? — Aujourd'hui, dans la matinée, à midi, dans l'après-midi, dans la soirée, dans la nuit.
6. Pourquoi est-ce que le Fuehrer ne vient pas avec nous?
7. Notre dépôt d'essence continue de brûler!
8. Votre dépôt d'essence a recommencé à brûler!
9. Qui a encore coupé notre ligne téléphonique?
10. Avez-vous jeté mon camarade dans le canal?
11. Pouvez-vous me prêter une ceinture, — une bouée de sauvetage?
12. Quel prix prenez-vous pour les leçons de natation?
13. Combien d'invasions dois-je faire pour recevoir la Croix de Fer de Ière classe?
14. Sept — huit — neuf.
15. Nous partirons pour l'Angleterre! (Qu'ils disent.)

I. Vóór de invasie

1. De zee is groot — koud — stormachtig.
2. Hoe vaak nog moeten w'exerceeren om 't landen op een kust te leeren?
3. Zullen we ooit in Engeland komen?
4. Zullen we heelhuids wéerom komen?
5. Wanneer komt de volgende Britsche luchtaanval? Heden — morgen, middag, namiddag, avond, nacht.
6. Waarom reist de Führer niet met ons mee?
7. Ons benzinedepot staat nog steeds in lichter laaie!
8. Uw benzinedepot staat alweer in lichter laaie!
9. Wie heeft ons telefoonleiding nou weer doo, geknipt?
10. Heeft [ ] mijn [...] ecaal in de gracht gesmot n?
11. Kunt U mij een zwemvest — een reddinggordel leenen?
12. Hoeveel kost het om bij U zwemmen te leeren?
13. Hoe dikwijls moet ik aan een invasietocht meedoen om het Ijzeren Kruis te winnen?
14. Zeven — acht — negen keer.
15. Wij zullen gauw naar Engeland varen! (Plons! Plons! Plons!)

II. Wahrend der Invasion

1. Der Seegang. — Der Sturm. — Der Nebel. Die Windstärke.
2. Wir sind seekrank. Wo ist der Kübel?
3. Ist das eine Bombe — ein Torpedo — eine Granate — eine Mine?

II. Pendant l'invasion

1. Le gros temps — la tempête — le brouillard — la violence de l'ouragan.
2. Nous avons le mal de mer. Où est la cuvette?
3. Est-ce une bombe — une torpille — un obus — une mine?

II. Tijdens de invasie

1. De deining — de storm — de mist — de orkaan.
2. Wij zijn zeeziek. Waar is de kwispedoor?
3. Is dat een bom — een torpedo - granaat — een mijn?

4. Achtung! Englische E-Boote—Zerstörer—Kreuzer — Schlachtschiffe —Bom ber !

5. Unser Schiff kentert — versinkt — brennt — explodiert !

6. Unsere Gruppe — unser Zug — unsere Kompanie — unse. Bataillon — unser Regiment geht unter !

7. Die Anderen — die ganze Division — das ganze Armeekorps auch !

8. Schon wieder geht eins unter !

9. Wo ist denn unsere Flotte — unsere Luftwaffe ?

10. Hier riecht die See so nach Petroleum !

11. Hier brennt sogar das Wasser !

12. Schauen Sie, wie schön der Herr Hauptmann brennt !

13. Der Karl — der Willi — der Fritz — der Johann — der Abraham ist verkohlt — ertrunken — von den Schiffsschrauben zerfleischt.

14. Wir müssen umdrehen !

15. Wir fahren gegen Engelland !

III. Nach der Invasion

1. Wir haben genug !

2. Sie sind noch immer im Lazaret t.

3. Wo haben Sie sich den schönen Schnupfen — den Hexenschuss — die Lungenentzündung — den Nervenschock geholt ?

4. Mehr ist von uns nicht übrig geblieben.

5. Bitte, wo kann man hier die Totenlisten mal einsehen ?

6. Wie sieht England eigentlich aus ?

7. Es gab einmal eine deutsche Flotte.

8. Es gibt sehr viele englische Luftangriffe.

9. Wann findet die nächste Invasion statt ?

10. Am 1., 15., 30. Januar, Februar, März, April, Mai, Juni, Juli, August, September, Oktober, November, Dezember — 1941, 1942, 1943, 1944, 1945 . . . usw.

11. nicht ! Du nicht ! Er nicht ! Wir nicht ! Sie auch nicht ! Aber Ihr vielleicht !

12. Wir fuhren gegen Engelland !

13. Wir wollen heim !

Zur Beachtung : Ein englischer Taschendolmetscher wird jedem deutschen Englandfahrer bei seiner Ankunft in einem englischen Kriegsgefangenenlager unentgeltlich ausgehändigt werden.

---

4. Attention ! ce sont des vedettes lance-torpilles — des contre-torpilleurs, des croiseurs — des cuirassés — des bombardiers anglais !

5. Notre bateau chavire — coule — brûle — fait explosion !

6. Notre escouade — notre section — notre compagnie — notre bataillon — notre régiment est englouti (ou engloutie) !

7. Les autres — toute la division — tout le corps d'armée — !est (ou le sont) aussi !

8. Un autre bateau est en train de couler.

9. Où est notre flotte — notre aviation ?

10. La mer empeste le mazout, ici !

11. Même l'eau brûle ici !

12. Regarde comme notre capitaine brûle bien !

13. Charles — Guillaume — Frédérique — Jean — Abraham est carbonisé — est noyé — est déchiqueté par les hélices.

14. Il faut faire demi-tour !

15. Nous partons pour l'Angleterre. (Tant pis pour vous !)

III. Après l'invasion

1. Nous en avons assez !

2. Ils sont encore à l'hôpital.

3. Où avez vous attrapé ce beau rhume — ce lumbago — cette pleurésie — cette commotion cérébrale ?

4. Nous sommes les seuls qui nous nous en soyons tirés.

5. Où peut-on consulter la liste des tués et disparus, ici, s'il-vous-plaît ?

6. Pouvez-vous me décrire l'Angleterre ?

7. Il y avait une fois une flotte allemande.

8. Il y a un très grand nombre de raids anglais.

9. Quand la prochaine invasion doit-elle avoir lieu ?

10. Elle doit avoir lieu le 1er, 15, 30 janvier, février, mars, avril, mai, juin, juillet, août, septembre, octobre, novembre, décembre — 1941, 1942, 1943, 1944, 1945, etc.

11. Pas moi ! Pas toi ! Pas lui ! Pas nous ! Pas eux ! Mais peut-être vous !

12. Nous sommes partis pour l'Angleterre !

13. Nous voulons rentrer chez nous !

N.B. Un manuel de conversation en langue anglaise sera distribué gratuitement à chaque envahisseur lors de son arrivée au camp de prisonniers en Grande-Bretagne.

---

4. Pas op ! Britsche E-booten — torpedojagers — kruisers — slagschepen. — bommenwerpers !

5. Ons schip kapseist — zinkt — brandt — vliegt in de lucht !

6. Onze groep — afdeeling — compagnie-bataillon — regiment verdrinkt !

7. De anderen— de heele divisie — het geheele legercorps verdrinkt ook !

8. Daar zinkt weer een schip !

9. Waar is onze vloot — onze luchtmacht !

10. Wat stinkt de zee hier naar olie !

11. Hier staat waarachtig het water in brand !

12. Kijk eens hoe mooi de kapitein in brand staat !

13. Karel Willem Frits Johan Abraham is verkoold — verdronken — tot pap gemalen door de schroeven van het schip.

14. We moeten omdraaien !

15. Wij varen gauw naar Engeland. (Arme bliksems !)

III. Na de invasie

1. Wij hebben er tabak van !

2. Zij liggen nog steeds in het hospitaal.

3. Waar heb je die mooie verkoudheid opgeloopen — spit — longontsteking — zenuwstoring ?

4. Dat's alles wat er van ons over is.

5. Kunt U mij ook zeggen waar ik de verlieslijsten kan nakijken ?

6. Hoe ziet Engeland er eigenlijk uit ?

7. Er was ereis een Duitsche vloot.

8. Er zijn veel Britsche luchtaanvallen.

9. Wanneer is de volgende invasie ?

10. Op den 1 sten, 15 den, 30 sten Januari, Februari, Maart, April, Mei, Juni, Juli, Augustus, September, October, November, December — 1941, 1942, 1943, 1944, 1945, enzoovoorts.

11. Ik niet ! Jij niet ! Hij niet ! Wij niet ! Niemand van ons ! Misschien jij wel ?

12. We wilden gauw naar Engeland !

13. Wij willen naar huis !

N.B. Iedere Duitsche reiziger naar Engeland krijgt een Engelsch zakwoordenboekje cadeau, zoodra hij in het krijgsgevangenkamp is aangekomen.

APPENDIX 2

LOOKED, DUCKED, VANISHED

If this book seeks to prove anything at all, it is that there was no actual attempt at an invasion of the British Isles in 1940, and no fiery destruction of Hitler's Sealion armada in the middle of the English Channel. Rumours of smaller German landing parties, and of missing British patrols, were also commonplace at the time, and at first glance seem just as fantastical. However, original research by this author in 1992 did unearth several stories no less remarkable than others related in this book.

Edward Sharpin, who served as a private in the Royal Army Service Corps, had the misfortune to be captured in Greece in 1941, spending the remainder of the war in captivity in several prisoner-of-war camps in Austria, notably 18A and 18B. It was there that Sharpin had an unexpected encounter:

> I spoke German and was often used as an interpreter. In late 1943 or early 1944, I was sent down to the railway junction at Selzthal to do something or other. While there I noticed an old-looking man. He looked a dead-ringer for the actor John Le Mesurier so far as I remember, with grey hair, and didn't seem very well. I went over and asked him who he was. He didn't have a pay book and said he was in the Home Guard. He told me that he had been on guard duty on the Kent coast and that a squad of Germans had landed and taken him away.
>
> I think he was being paraded around different PoW camps to try to reduce the prisoners' morale. I don't think he was a plant – you could usually sense it if people were. I think he was a Londoner originally, as he mentioned something about Fulham football club.

Eddie Sharpin's subsequent escape from captivity is related in *Greece 1941: To Fight Another Day*, a book by William Frick. A similar man with a similar story was encountered by Jack Driscoll of the 12th Royal Lancers, this time at Stalag IIIVB in Upper Silesia:

> I myself met this poor old man in Lamsdorf camp in about 1943, while I was also in captivity. I was walking in the compound when I saw this chap with Home Guard on his shoulder. I stood back in amazement and asked if it was a joke. He told me that a party from a U-boat had landed and snatched him, while he was on duty on the Kent coast. I gather later he was repatriated via Sweden by the Red Cross.

Could this be the same man whose story was related by George Hearse to his son, also named George Hearse:

> From 1943 to 1945 my father worked in London in a government department. Being a 1914–18 war veteran he took part in Home Guard duties. Sometime late in 1943 there was an appeal for Home Guard personnel to volunteer for weekend guard duty in a sensitive location on the coast. One man said goodbye to his wife on the station platform in London, expecting to be home in a few days' time. His wife heard nothing more about him until several weeks later, when she was informed he was a prisoner of war in Germany. My father told me this story some time before his death in 1945, and I have no reason to doubt its authenticity.

If he ever existed, and was not a clever German plant, this unfortunate Home Guard seems not to have been an isolated case. In 1945, Mr E.C. Leslie was an administrative subaltern at a transit camp at Barry in South Wales, where returned prisoners of war were processed. When asked when and where he had been captured, one soldier in his twenties told Lieutenant Leslie that he had been snatched by Germans at St Margaret's Bay in Kent in 1940. 'He seemed a bit embarrassed about it,' Mr Leslie recalled in 1992.

But can these reports really have any foundation in fact? Despite the frequency with which Allied commandos and other raiders probed the enemy-occupied coastline between 1940 and 1944, there are no recorded incidents of German soldiers landing in Britain while still alive. This, of itself, seems curious, given that Germany threatened a full-scale seaborne invasion in 1940. It would not even have been very difficult, a fact proved by the 'four men in a boat' spies who landed at Dungeness and Dymchurch in early September, and by the remarkable private raid on France in April 1942 staged by two foolhardy enthusiasts from the Army Dental Corps, both of whom managed to return to England. Yet had German reconnaissance teams landed in Britain at any time during the Second World War, let alone returned home with prisoners, surely surviving participants would have come forward to tell – or sell – their story? And why would it still remain secret?

There is no easy answer. Nonetheless, if one chooses to believe that one or two isolated sentries were snatched by German raiding parties, their absence could have been put down to simple desertion. Obscurity, rather than secrecy, could explain why such fleeting incidents are lost to history. As for the abductees, perhaps they were simply not believed on returning to Britain, just as Private Albert Pooley of the Royal Norfolk Regiment was disbelieved in 1943, when he was repatriated on medical grounds, having survived the now-infamous massacre of almost 100 unarmed prisoners by Waffen SS troops at Le Paradis in May 1940. Somewhat shamefully, Private Pooley had to struggle for three years before his story was finally accepted and investigated, even then only after corroborative evidence from France and another survivor came to light.

In the case of the snatched Home Guards, however, the final verdict must remain Not Proven.

APPENDIX 3

ARMY HISTORICAL BRANCH REPORT (1992)

Report prepared by the Army Historical Branch in July 1992 and released to Mr Jamie Cann, Member of Parliament for Ipswich.

SHINGLE STREET SUFFOLK IN WW2: HISTORICAL NOTES

1. **INTRODUCTION**

   Shingle Street is a village on the Suffolk coast south of Orford. In recent months there has been local interest and considerable press speculation about 'incidents' reported to have occurred at Shingle Street. However the main allegation which we have to address is that in the summer or autumn of 1940 a number of bodies in British uniforms were washed up on the beach at Shingle Street; they had been badly burnt.

2. **1940: BACKGROUND**

   a. It was only after the German offensive in the West of May 1940, the subsequent withdrawal of the BEF through Dunkirk and the surrender of France in June 1940, that Britain's South and East Coast areas came to be considered as being 'in the Front Line' of the war. As a result of the need to take defensive measures against any possible German invasion of the UK, in the summer of 1940 an extensive coastal area of East Anglia was largely evacuated of its inhabitants to enable the creation of extensive minefields and defensive works. This measure could be adopted in this area because it was not heavily populated or industrialised, whereas the South Coast, which included many large centres of population, could not be so treated. In addition plans were drawn up for the evacuation of the inhabitants of certain East Coast towns if the need arose.

b. **SHINGLE STREET**

Shingle Street was among those villages which were evacuated in the initial scheme mentioned above, following a declaration by the 'Regional Commissioner' on 22 June 1940. With the exception of the coastguard station, all properties in this area were requisitioned by the military authorities, apparently to permit the payment of compensation to the inhabitants which would otherwise not have been possible – evacuation carried with it no entitlement to compensation.

c. **BAWDSEY**

Within the area around Shingle Street, the main military site of significance was the 'Radar' station at Bawdsey to the south-west. This site had in fact been one of the UK's experimental radar establishments for some years but, following the Fall of France and the possibility of invasion, its research staff had been moved to locations in Scotland and it remained in use as a routine radar establishment under RAF control with the Army providing troops for the general defence of the site. Bawdsey's records make no mention of any attempted German raids, or of any special defence measures being prepared at the site.

d. **DEFENCE OF SHINGLE STREET/BAWDSEY AREA & OCCURRENCES POST-MAY 1940**

Our research has covered the relevant War Office and Service files. These include the contemporary, and initially highly classified, War Diaries of the Corps, Division, Brigade and Battalions that were responsible for the defence of the area, as well as the files of 'Eastern Command' which had overall control of this part of the UK. These War Diaries are all available in the Public Record Office under the normal conditions governing use of War Diaries.

From April 1940 until November the same year, the defence of the area including Shingle Street was the responsibility first of the 1st Battalion the Liverpool Scottish and subsequently of the 2nd Battalion the Liverpool

Scottish. In addition the 7th York & Lancs Battalion was deployed in the area in a general, rather than direct, coastal defensive role. In due course Home Guard units also provided additional troops.

The examination of the War Diaries reveals plentiful evidence of: (a) defensive activities by the British units, primarily mine-laying along all coastal areas and the erection of coastal defences; (b) aerial activity overhead by both British and enemy aircraft, including the crashing of such aircraft both on land and in the sea; (c) the washing up of the **occasional** body on the local beaches.

In connection with the latter point, between May and December 1940 there are mentions in the records of **five** bodies, all of German airman in their proper uniform, being found at the following points: Shingle Street (one body) on 29th October 1940; Hollesley (one body) 30 October; Bawdsey (one body) 30 October; south of Walton Pier (one body) 30 October/1 November; Landguard Point, Felixstowe (one body) 15 December.

There are however no reports to support the claim of a number of badly burned bodies in British uniform being washed up at Shingle Street, whether from aircraft, from the Dunkirk battles of late May–early June, or any other source. Indeed there is no record of any large number of bodies being recovered from the beaches in the area in the summer, autumn or winter of 1940.

e. **HISTORICAL BASIS FOR STORIES OF 'LARGE NUMBERS OF BODIES' – BURNT OR OTHERWISE – CIRCA 1940**

The question of the contemporary documentary evidence for bodies washed up on the coast-line in the Shingle Street area has been discussed above. Bodies were also found at a number of other locations on the South and East Coasts of Britain during the summer and autumn of 1940. Some, as at Shingle Street, were those of aircrew lost over the Channel. Others were apparently from German units based in France whose invasion training exercises may have been disrupted by British bombing of the Channel ports. Whatever the source, the total number of bodies for the entire coastline of South and South-East England was fairly small. Winston Churchill in his *History of the Second World War* similarly records the discovery of small numbers of dead bodies around the coastline.

The contemporary **rumours** that bodies had been found on the coasts of German troops who had been killed during a failed invasion attempt, are typified by the extract from the 11 Corps War Diary for September 1940. This example is particularly important as it demonstrates the existence of such rumours not that far from the Shingle Street area. One of the reasons given in these rumours for the Germans' alleged failure to succeed in their attempt included the use by the British of 'Flame Defences' along the shoreline – such rumours were also current on the German-held continent. This aspect is considered more fully below, but it should be noted that these rumours and how Britain did nothing to quash them, for understandable propaganda reasons, are also mentioned by Churchill in his account.

f. **ALLEGED 'INVASION' ATTEMPTS**

There is no evidence of any German invasion attempt in the Shingle Street area, or even German 'commando' style raids by sea or air. Indeed there is no evidence in either the most highly classified contemporary British records, or apparently in the contemporary German records, of an actual attempt by the Germans to land in Britain, apart from the Channel Islands which were occupied by the Germans after the Fall of France. The British official study of the German preparations for the invasion, produced shortly after the war with the benefit of contemporary German records and the interrogation of relevant German commanders, and a more recent German study on the German preparations for invasion, confirm this.

g. **GERMAN RAFTS FOUND ON BEACHES**

There have also been suggestions that a German 'raft' was found on Shingle Street's beach in 1940, perhaps associated with 'burnt bodies'. The implication is that this was used in an abortive invasion attempt or 'raid' by German troops. The contemporary records for the Shingle Street area make no mention of any such item being found. However, the intelligence reports for Eastern Command for November 1940 do record two rafts found elsewhere on the South Coast of Britain. The contemporary assessment was that these rafts had been sited in the English Channel by the Germans in a 'life-saving' role for the use of any of their airmen forced to crash-land in the Channel.

h. **FLAME DEFENCES**

Claims about 'burnt bodies' are naturally associated with the British experimentation with 'flame defences' in 1940. While it is true that experiments were made in 1940 with ignited oil on the sea and flaming oil on the fore-shore, throughout 1940 these were experiments only.

Trials took place on the South Coast in the Solent on 24 August. In the winter of 1940 less successful trials took place at Studland Bay, Dorset. As a result the emphasis was placed on 'shore-line flame barrage' apparatus. However, none were provided for the East Coast area in 1940, although initially there were plans to erect some of this apparatus on the East Coast and local commanders were keen to have such additional defensive obstacles if available, as the September 1940 War Diary for the Brigade HQ covering the Shingle Street area illustrates. The 'rumours' about such defences have already been mentioned in 'e' above.

In addition in 1940 there were experiments at a local level with a number of other 'ad hoc' flame defences including a 'submerged anti-flying boat' system which was tried on the Norfolk Broads but not deployed elsewhere. This system is mentioned because one recent article on the Shingle Street allegations spoke of a system allegedly deployed at Shingle Street to defend Bawdsey radar station. The report called this system 'PLUTO'. In fact 'PLUTO' (Pipe Line Under the Ocean) was only produced in 1943/44 for the precise purpose its name suggests, that is to transmit fuel through a pipeline between the South Coast of Britain and our forces in France after the successful invasion of Normandy in June 1944. Thus 'PLUTO' was not based anywhere near Bawdsey or Shingle Street. However, the design of a system mentioned in the claim about 'PLUTO' in fact resembles that trialled in the Norfolk Broads and detailed in a book on Britain's flame warfare experiments and operations which was published in 1946. The relevance of the term 'PLUTO' in a Shingle Street context is further considered in paragraph 4 below.

What is clear is that there were no formal British 'flame defences' in the sea or on the shore-line in the Shingle Street area during this period, nor is there evidence of any casualties, British or German, in the area in 1940 resulting from such weapons or from the ignition of oil from fractured pipelines.

i. **BRITISH TRAINING/ANTI-INVASION EXERCISES**

It is interesting to note that the contemporary records show there was a 'paper' exercise concerning only the headquarters of British Army units in the area in July 1940 that had as its theme a German invasion attempt and that the **exercise** story included mentions of German troops landing at Shingle Street. However, there is no contemporary evidence to support any claims of such exercises using British troops as 'enemy' actually took place against the Shingle Street area, let alone that troops were killed during such training in 1940.

j. **SUMMARY**

The relevant contemporary records covering the defence of the area, all of which are in the public domain, contain nothing to support the claims of an alleged incident at Shingle Street in 1940 which was outlined in paragraph 1. Nor do the records of subsequent analysis of Britain's defence operations and German invasion preparations support the claims.

However, given the above-mentioned wartime rumours of failed invasions, flame defences, the occasional German body washed up on the shore, and 'anti-invasion' exercises by British forces in the Shingle Street area, the basis for such stories leading to the current allegations become more clear.

3. **BRITISH CW ACTIVITY IN THE SHINGLE STREET AREA**

There have also been suggestions that the 'bodies in the Shingle Street area' are in fact related to British chemical warfare experiments. The Home Office file relating to Shingle Street which spans 1940–43 mentions a proposal for a chemical warfare experiment at Shingle Street in 1943. Therefore although the incident dates from 1943, not 1940, it is covered in outline here.

In late 1942 it was decided to use the empty dwelling houses of Shingle Street as targets for a trial of a bomb designed to combine High Explosive (HE) and a chemical (Chem) filling. The trial took place in the spring of 1943 using trial bombs containing HE, **but no chemical warfare filling**; the space in the trial bomb for such a filling in fact contained **a harmless substitute** ('oil of wintergreen'). The trial resulted in some HE damage to buildings in Shingle Street, but as there was no chemical warfare agent in the bombs dropped there, there was no chemical warfare agent contamination or residual hazard. Further, the target area was completely cleared of human beings and there were **no casualties** to personnel either during the trial or subsequently.

4. **79TH ARMOURED DIVISION IN ORFORD/SHINGLE STREET AREA 1943–44**

Although the main allegations concerning the Shingle Street area claim that the incident occurred in 1940, there have been some suggestions that subsequent activity by 79th Armoured Division in the area later in the war might have resulted in some similar incident. Accordingly this aspect is considered here briefly.

In 1942 the Army's need for extensive 'battle training' areas led to the requisitioning of fairly large areas of the UK countryside. Among these was the 'Orford' Training area to the north of Shingle Street.

In early 1943, 79th Armoured Division had been reorganised as a 'special' armoured division to be equipped with special engineering tanks designed to assist in the breaching of the German 'Atlantic Wall' defences on the French coast. The Division was based in the Orford area in 1943 and early 1944 and carried out training there. The Division's contemporary War Dairies are all available in the public domain. A check of these for 1943 and 1944, up to the landing in France in June, reveal nothing to support the claims of any 'accidents' during training in the area which resulted in the loss of large numbers of servicemen's lives. Indeed the Division's training in the area appears to have included very little use of live ammunition; the 'live firing' of the major weapons appears to have taken place on the Castlemartin ranges in Wales.

It is however interesting to note that the Division's records include the Divisional 'anti-raid' orders for both 1943 and 1944. The 1943 orders note that 'raids on this country from the sea or air [that is parachute/glider attacks] have not occurred but remain, nevertheless, a possibility'. In addition these orders detail both the defensive measures and defences available in the area and there is no trace of any flame barrage equipment deployed in the area.

Further, in relation to the Divisional records, these note the use by 79th Armoured Division of the code-word 'PLUTO' as the 'trigger' for unit level anti-invasion exercises. It is possible that this may have some bearing on the association in local memories of the word 'PLUTO' with a German invasion.

5. **OVERALL SUMMARY**

As explained above, the contemporary authoritative records provide no evidence to support the claims that a number of burnt, British uniformed bodies were washed up on the Shingle Street beach in the summer or autumn of 1940, or that the 1943 events also considered provide any evidence to support the general allegations made.

Notes added by Author

2g – for 'rafts' read dinghy, and the story told by John Rux Burton. This seems to be a misreading by the AHB. One of the rescue rafts washed ashore in 1940 was at St Margaret's Bay.

2h – 'throughout 1940 these were experiments only' – incorrect; a few beach flame barrages were operational by August 1940.

BIBLIOGRAPHY

All titles published in London unless otherwise stated.

Addison, Paul & Crang, Jeremy A., *Listening to Britain – Home Intelligence Reports on Britain's Finest Hour, May to September 1940* (Bodley Head, 2010)

Agar, Captain Augustus, *Footprints In the Sea* (Evans, 1959)

Alanbrooke, Field Marshal Lord, *War Diaries 1939–45* (Weidenfeld & Nicolson, 2001)

Ansel, Walter, *Hitler Confronts England* (Durham, NC, USA: Duke University Press, 1960)

Baird, Jay W., *The Mythical World of Nazi War Propaganda 1939–45* (Minneapolis, USA: University of Minnesota Press, 1974)

Balfour, Michael, *Propaganda in War 1939–1945* (Routledge & Kegan Paul, 1979)

Banks, Sir Donald, *Flame Over Britain* (Sampson Low Marston & Co., 1946)

Blumentritt, Günther, *Von Rundstedt* (Odhams, 1952)

Bomber Command September 1939 to July 1941 (HMSO pamphlet, 1941)

Bove, Charles, *A Surgeon in Paris* (Museum Press, 1956)

Bowyer, Michael, *2 Group RAF – A Complete History* (Faber, 1974)

Bradley, General Omar, *A Soldier's Story* (New York: Rand McNally, 1951)

Brooks, Andrew, *Photo Reconnaissance – The Operational History* (Ian Allan, 1975)

Brown, R. Douglas, *East Anglia 1939* (Lavenham: Terence Dalton, 1981)

Brown, R. Douglas, *East Anglia 1940* (Lavenham: Terence Dalton, 1981)

Brown, Richard, *Mr Brown's Diary* (Stroud: Sutton, 1998)

Bryant, Arthur, *The Turn of the Tide* (Collins, 1957)

Cairncross, John, *The Enigma Spy* (Century, 1997)

Churchill, Winston S., *The Second World War Vol. II – Their Finest Hour* (Cassell, 1949)

Collier, Basil, *The Defence of the United Kingdom* (HMSO, 1957)

Collier, Richard, *1940 – The World in Flames* (Hamish Hamilton, 1979)

Colville, John, *The Fringes of Power* (Hodder & Stoughton, 1985)

Cruickshank, Charles, *The Fourth Arm – Psychological Warfare 1939–45* (Davis-Poynter, 1977)

Cruickshank, Charles, *Deception in World War II* (Oxford: OUP, 1980)

De Vries, Kelly & Smith, Robert, *Medieval Military Technology* (Toronto: University of Toronto Press, 2012)

Deacon, Richard, *British Secret Service* [Revised Edition] (Grafton, 1991)

Delmer, Sefton, *Black Boomerang* (Secker & Warburg, 1962)

Doherty, Richard, *Hobart's 79th Armoured Division at War* (Pen & Sword, 2011)

Draper, Alfred, *Operation Fish* (Cassell, 1979)

Feuchter, Georg, *Geschichte des Luftkriegs* (Germany: Athenaum Verlag, 1954)

Fleming, Peter, *Invasion 1940* (Rupert Hart-Davis, 1957)

Fletcher, David, *Churchill Crocodile Flamethrower* (Osprey Publishing, 2007)

Ford, Corey, *Donovan of OSS* (Robert Hale, 1971)

Foster, Rodney, *The Real Dad's Army – The War Diaries of Colonel Rodney Foster* (Viking, 2011)

Foynes, Julian, *The Battle of the East Coast 1939–45* (private printing, 1994)

Fulter, Geoffrey, *The Funnies* (Bellona, 1974)

Garlinski, Jozef, *The Swiss Corridor* (J.M. Dent, 1981)

Garnett, David, *The Secret History of PWE* (St Ermin's Press, 2002)

Gash, Norman, *Geoffrey Lloyd – A Short Biographical Appreciation* (Leeds Castle Foundation, 1986)

Gibson, Guy, *Enemy Coast Ahead* (Michael Joseph, 1946)

Gillies, Midge, *Waiting for Hitler* (Hodder & Stoughton, 2006)

Glover, Michael, *Invasion Scare 1940* (Leo Cooper, 1990)

Graves, Charles, *The Home Guard of Britain* (Hutchinson, 1943)

Grinnell-Milne, Duncan, *The Silent Victory* (Bodley Head, 1958)

Hanson, Neil, *First Blitz* (Doubleday, 2008)

Harris, Robert & Paxman, Jeremy, *A Higher Form of Killing* (Chatto & Windus, 1982)

Hastings, Max, *Bomber Command* (Michael Joseph, 1979)

Hayward, James, *Myths & Legends of the First World War* (Stroud: Sutton, 2002)

Hayward, James, *Myths & Legends of the Second World War* (Stroud: Sutton, 2003)

Hayward, James, *Double Agent Snow* (Simon & Schuster, 2013)

Heazell, Paddy, *Most Secret – The Hidden History of Orford Ness* (Stroud: The History Press, 2010)

Hinsey, F.H., *British Intelligence in the Second World War* (HMSO, 1979)

Hodgson, Vera, *Few Eggs & No Oranges* (Dobson, 1976)

Hogben, Arthur & MacBean, John, *Bombs Gone* (PSL, 1990)

Hohne, Heinz, *Canaris* (Weidenfeld & Nicholson, 1979)

Horne, Alistair, *To Lose a Battle – France 1940* (Macmillan, 1969)

Howe, Ellic, *The Black Game* (Michael Joseph, 1982)

Hoyt, Edwyn, *The Invasion Before Normandy* (Robert Hale, 1987)

Hyde, H., *Montgomery: The Quiet Canadian* (Hamish Hamilton, 1962)

Hyde, H., *Montgomery: Secret Intelligence Agent* (Constable, 1982)

Ironside, Sir Edmund, *The Ironside Diaries 1937–1940* (Constable, 1962)

Jackson, Robert, *Before the Storm – The Story of Bomber Command 1939–1942* (Arthur Barker, 1972)

Jeffrey, Keith, *MI6 – The History of the Secret Intelligence Service 1909–1949* (Bloomsbury, 2010)

Johnson, Derek, *East Anglia at War 1939–1945* [First Edition] (Norwich: Jarrold, 1978)

Johnson, Derek, *East Anglia at War 1939–1945* [Second Edition] (Norwich: Jarrold, 1992)

Kelly, David, *The Ruling Few* (Hollis & Carter, 1952)

Kent, Peter, *Fortifications of East Anglia* (Lavenham: Terence Dalton, 1988)

Kinsey, Gordon, *Orfordness – Secret Site* (Lavenham: Terence Dalton, 1981)

Kinsey, Gordon, *Bawdsey – Birth of the Beam* (Lavenham: Terence Dalton, 1983)

Knight, Dennis, *Harvest of Messerschmitts* (Wingham Press, 1990)

Knightley, Phillip, *The First Casualty* [Revised Edition] (Quartet, 1982)

Lampe, David, *The Last Ditch* (Cassell, 1968)

Last, Nella, *Nella Last's Diary* (Bristol: Falling Wall Press, 1981)

Leckie, Robert, *Delivered From Evil* (New York: Harper and Row, 1987)

Levine, Joshua, *Forgotten Voices of the Blitz and the Battle of Britain* (Ebury, 2007)

Longmate, Norman, *How We Lived Then* (Hutchinson, 1971)

Longmate, Norman, *If Britain Had Fallen* (BBC/Hutchinson, 1972)

Longmate, Norman, *Island Fortress – The Defence of Great Britain 1603–1945* (Hutchinson, 1991)

Lumsden, Malvern, *Incendiary Weapons* (Sweden: SIPRI, 1975)

Macintyre, Ben, *Operation Mincemeat* (Bloomsbury, 2010)

Macksey, Kenneth, *Invasion – The German Invasion of England, July 1940* (Greenhill, 1980)

Mahl, Thomas, *Desperate Deception – British Covert Operations in the United States 1939–44* (Brassey's, 1998)

Manstein, Field Marshal Erich von, *Lost Victories* (Methuen, 1955)

Martienssen, A., *Hitler & His Admirals* (Secker & Warburg, 1948)

Martin, Colonel T.A., *The Essex Regiment 1929–1950* (Essex Regiment Association, 1952)

Masterman, J.C., *The Double-Cross System* (New Haven, USA: Yale University Press, 1972)

McKee, Alexander, *Strike from the Sky – The Battle of Britain Story* (Souvenir Press, 1960)

Middlebrook, Martin & Everitt, Chris, *The Bomber Command War Diaries 1939–1945* (Viking, 1985)

Moen, Lars, *Under the Iron Heel* (Robert Hale, 1941)

Morgan, Sir Frederick, *Overture to Overlord* (Hodder & Stoughton, 1950)

Morpurgo, J.E., *Barnes Wallis* (Longman, 1972)

Moyes, Philip, *Bomber Squadrons of the RAF* (McDonald, 1964)

Neillands, Robin, *The Battle of Normandy 1944* (Cassell, 2002)

North, Richard, *The Many Not the Few* (Continuum, 2012)

Partington, J.R., *A History of Greek Fire and Gunpowder* (Cambridge: Heffer, 1960)

Pawle, Gerald, *The Secret War 1939–45* (Harrap, 1956)

Ramsay, Winston (ed.), *The Blitz Then and Now (Vol. 1)* (After the Battle, 1987)

Ramsay, Winston (ed.), *The Blitz Then and Now (Vol. 2)* (After the Battle, 1988)

Rankin, Nicholas, *Churchill's Wizards – The British Genius for Deception 1914–1945* (Faber, 2008)

Richards, Denis, *Royal Air Force 1939–1945 Vol. One – The Fight at Odds* (HMSO, 1953)

Roberts, A. & Guelff, R. (eds), *Documents on the Laws of War* (Oxford: Clarendon Press, 1989)

Robertson, G.W., *The Rose & the Arrow – A Life Story of the 136th Field Regiment Royal Artillery 1939–1946* (Private Printing, 1988)

Rolf, David, *Prisoners of the Reich* (Leo Cooper, 1988)

Roskill, Stephen, *The War at Sea Vol. I* (HMSO, 1954)

Roskill, Stephen, *Hankey – Man of Secrets Vol. 1* (Collins, 1970)

Roskill, Stephen, *Hankey – Man of Secrets Vol. 3* (Collins, 1974)

Ruge, Friedrich, *Sea Warfare 1939–1945 – A German Viewpoint* (Cassell, 1957)

Scarfe, Norman, *Suffolk – A Shell Guide* (Faber & Faber, 1960)

Schenk, Peter, *The Invasion of England 1940* (Conway Maritime Press, 1990)

Shirer, William, *Berlin Diary* (New York: Alfred Knopf, 1941)

Shirer, William, *The Rise & Fall of the Third Reich* (Secker & Warburg, 1960)

SIPRI, *Incendiary Weapons* (MIT Press, 1975)

Skidmore, Ian, *Marines Don't Hold Their Horses* (W.H. Allen/Virgin Books, 1981)

Small, Ken, *The Forgotten Dead* (Bloomsbury, 1988)

Smith, Michael, *Station X* (Pan Macmillan, 2004)

Smith, Richard Harris, *OSS – The Secret History of America's First CIA* (Oakland, USA: University of California Press, 1972)

Spaight, J.M., *The Battle of Britain 1940* (Geoffrey Bles, 1941)

Speer, Albert, *Inside the Third Reich* (Weidenfeld & Nicholson, 1970)

Stafford, David, *Churchill and Secret Service* (John Murray, 1997)

Stevenson, William, *A Man Called Intrepid* (Macmillan, 1976)

Sutcliffe, Sheila, *Martello Towers* (David & Charles, 1972)

Tarrant, V.E., *The Red Orchestra* (Cassel, 1995)

Taylor, Frederick, *Dresden* (Bloomsbury, 2004)

Thomas, Andy, *Effects of Chemical Warfare – A Selective Review and Bibliography of British State Papers* (SIPRI, 1985)

Thompson, Laurence, *1940 – Year of Legend, Year of History* (Collins, 1966)

Thomson, Rear Admiral George, *Blue Pencil Admiral* (Sampson Low, Marston & Co., 1947)

Tooze, Adam, *The Wages of Destruction – The Making and Breaking of the Nazi Economy* (Allen Lane, 2006)

Waller, Douglas, *Wild Bill Donovan* (New York: Free Press, 2011)

Waugh, Evelyn, *Men at Arms* (Chapman & Hall, 1952)

Weeks, John, *Men Against Tanks – A History of Anti-Tank Warfare* (David & Charles, 1975)

West, Nigel, *MI5 – British Security Service Operations 1939–45* (The Bodley Head, 1981)

West, Nigel, *MI6 – British Secret Intelligence Service Operations 1939–45* (Weidenfeld & Nicolson, 1983)

West, Nigel, *Unreliable Witness* (Weidenfeld & Nicolson, 1984)

West, Nigel, *Secret War – The Story of SOE* (Hodder & Stoughton, 1992)

West, Nigel (ed.), *British Security Co-ordination* (St Ermins Press, 1998)

Wheatley, Dennis, *Black August* (Hutchinson, 1934)

Wheatley, Dennis, *Stranger Than Fiction* (Hutchinson, 1959)

Wheatley, Dennis, *The Time Has Come 1919–1977* (Hutchinson, 1979)

Wheatley, Ronald, *Operation Sealion* (Oxford: OUP, 1958)

White, Archie, *Tideways and Byways in Essex and Suffolk* (E. Arnold, 1948)

White, John Baker, *The Big Lie* (Evans, 1955)

White, John Baker, *True Blue* (Frederick Muller, 1970)

Wick, Steve, *The Long Night – William L. Shirer and the Rise and Fall of the Third Reich* (Palgrave Macmillan, 2011)

Wilson, Andrew, *Flame Thrower* (William Kimber, 1956)

Winterbotham, F.W., *The Ultra Secret* (Weidenfeld & Nicolson, 1974)

SOURCES

IWM = Imperial War Museum; TNA = The National Archives

Introduction
THE SMOKE AND THE FIRE

'I picked up …' Shirer (1941), pp.505–6
'In the whole …' Thomson (1947), p.73
'The burning sea …' White (1955), p. 22

Chapter 1
SUBTERRANEAN ACTIVITIES

siphon – De Vries & Smith (2012), pp.130–1
'The principal ingredient …' Gibbon (1776–1789)
Quincy Gillmore – https://markerhunter.wordpress.com/tag/greek-fire/
'On the first … ' TNA, WO 279/203 (1952 document on 'Special Weapons and
    types of Warfare' Vol. II)
Hankey/1914 – TNA, CAB 63/170. This file includes Hankey's lengthy report,
    catalogued as CID Paper 199-B, dated 11 December 1914
French fears – Roskill (1970), p.149
'submarines should …' quoted in Roskill (1970), p.224
Geneva Protocol – see SIPRI (1975), pp.23–4
'Depending on the …' TNA, ADM 116/4571

'Any such action …' TNA, ADM 116/4571, document dated 13 March 1940

'The American navy …' TNA, ADM 116/4571, document dated 16 December 1939

Geneva/legalities – SIPRI (1975), pp.23–4; Roberts & Guelff (1989)

brandbomben – see Hanson (2008)

WW1 myths – see Hayward (2002)

Elmwood – *The Times*, 27 February 1917; *Derby Daily Telegraph*, 28 February 1917. Although the targeting of Northcliffe was not reported at the time.

'sharpest and most urgent …' quoted in Howe (1982), p.26

Ministry of Information – Knightley (1982), p.202

Woburn Abbey – Howe (1982), p.39

Noël Coward – Garnett (2002), p.14

'If the policy …' quoted in Dick Richards (ed.), *The Wit of Noël Coward* (Sphere, 1970), p.105

'good Germans' – Garnett (2002), p.3

'bomphs' Rankin (2008), p.313

20 million – Howe (1982), p.44; Liddell (2005), p.21

Göring/Himmler – Taylor (2004), pp.106–7 (October 1939 leaflet)

Siegfried Line – Hayward (2003), p.33

Luftwaffe aviation spirit – Garnett (2002), p.211

U-boats – *Western Morning News*, 5 December 1939

German pilots – Hayward (2003), pp.11–12 & 64

magic lantern – Howe (1982), p.46

wood/canvas tanks – White (1955), p.39

Hankey/SOE summit – West (1983), p.90

Hankey MI5/MI6 review – Jeffrey (2010), pp.337–43

Hankey/Churchill – Colville (1985), p.119 & 556; Stafford (1997), p.155

'Lord Hankey had been …' Cairncross (1997), pp.85–8

'volcanic' TNA, CAB 63/170, letter Hankey to Hastings Ismay dated 1 July 1940

Lloyd clothes/carpets – *Dundee Evening Telegraph*, 28 August 1944

'I learned from …' TNA, SUPP 15/2, quoted in 9-page PWD history dated 1 October 1940

Hankey/Anderson – TNA, SUPP 15/2, dated 30 May 1940

'rough storage' – TNA, CAB 63/170, dated 27 June 1940

town gas – TNA, CAB 63/175

'subterranean activities' – Jeffrey (2010), pp.342–3

friction – see Garnett (2002), pp.8–9

£11,000 – Jeffrey (2010), p.340

Sweden/arrest – Stafford (1997), p.173

'To pit such …' Jeffrey (2010), p.352

UPC – Cruikshank (1977), p.109; TNA, FO 898/69–71

'sibs' – TNA, FO 898/70, Letter to the Minister of Economic Warfare from
 Reginald Leeper, 30 September 1940; Cruikshank (1977), p.108

'The object of …' TNA, FO 898/69 (document on 'Rumours' dated
 7 February 1942). This paper also states: 'Rumours vary immensely in their
 degree of credibility, the wideness of their diffusion and the type of audience
 for which they are designed. But they have these factors in common: that
 they are intended for verbal repetition through all sorts of channels, and that
 they are expected to induce a certain frame of mind in the general public,
 not necessarily to deceive the well-informed.' TNA FO 898/69 purports
 to contain minutes of UPC meetings between 1940 and 1945, but there is
 hardly any material from 1940 and little more from 1941

'important rules' – quoted in West (1998), p.111

White/circus – *Who Was Who, 1981–1990*, p.807

'A somewhat varied …' White (1955), pp.10–11. The Section D to which White
 belonged should not be confused with Section D (aka Section IX) of MI6 –
 see Jeffrey (2010), p.320. White made clear in *True Blue* (1970) that although
 he was recruited into 'Military Intelligence' (i.e. the DMI) during WW2, he
 was 'never a member of the British secret service' (p.164). For details of his
 private, pre-war Section D see pp.142–3. Unfortunately the narrative in *True
 Blue* ends with the outbreak of war in 1939

'Our task was …' White (1955), pp.12–13. That John Baker White was the
 originator of the burning sea rumour is confirmed by Garnett (2002), p.214

Chapter 2
ROASTING THE NAZIS

'God knows what …' Baker White (1955), p.12. This story is often told and
 probably true, though many different versions of the wording have been given

'There is no …' TNA, WO 193/734

Wheatley – Wheatley (1959), p.26; Wheatley (1979), pp.188–90

Desmond Morton – Stafford (1997), pp.184–5

'Mr Geoffrey Lloyd …' TNA, PREM 3/264

'petroleum warfare executive' TNA, CAB 63/170 (letter Morton to Hankey,
 5 July 1940)

poison gas – Colville (1985), p.213 (diary entry 1 July 1940)

'It is sheer ...'TNA, WO 32/5184 (minute dated 12 May 1919)

Geneva Protocol – Hayward (1994), p.50

'Enemy forces ...'TNA, WO 193/732 (memo on The Use of Gas in Home Defence)

'It was death ...' correspondence with author, December 1992. Spong was an army liaison officer attached to 225 Squadron, then flying Lysanders equipped with Smoke Curtain Installation apparatus (i.e. gas spray)

'I obtained the ...' Medlicott, unpublished paper dated 1 August 1946 held by the BP Society. Medlicott also seems to have had some mining expertise. That only one division stood between the coast and London is an exaggeration, though probably only one division was fully equipped

Sinclair and Henry Hodges – West (1992), pp.21–2; Ian Skidmore (1981), pp.8–33 (*Marines Don't Hold Their Horses*); Banks (1946), p.29

'It is not a ...'TNA, CAB 63/170 (letter Hankey to Churchill, 1 July 1940)

Colonel Livens – Harris and Paxman (1982), pp.22–3

'While Livens was ...' Banks (1946), pp.33–4

Wroxham Roaster – Banks (1946), p.39

PO Malders – TNA, AVIA 15/588 (documents from June and July 1940)

Nuttall – www.wolverhamptonhistory.org.uk/people/at_war/ww2/fighting3

July 2/ULTRA – Colville (1985), p.214

'Secret Service ...' Colville (1985), p.214 (diary entry 2 July 1940)

25,000 – *Aberdeen Journal*, 2 July 1940, quoted the *World Telegram*, a New York newspaper

'Troop-carrying aeroplanes ...' *Aberdeen Journal*, 1 July 1940

'great invasion scare' Colville (1985), p.225 (diary entry 12 July 1940)

'a good deal ...' Banks (1946), p.32

'An attempt to ...'TNA, WO 195/724

'A street is ...'TNA, CAB 63/170 (letter Hankey to General Pownall 8 July 1940)

JIC memorandum – Cruikshank (1979), p.15

'very large' – TNA, WO 193/734

'In conclusion ...'TNA, WO 193/734

Plan Y – Harris and Paxman (1982), pp.110–12; Thomas (1985), pp.53–5

'pretty shrewd ...'TNA, CAB 63/170, letter from General Robert Haining to Hankey dated 30 July 1940

'dropping light ...'TNA, CAB 63/170, undated document circulated in late July 1940; liquid oxygen – Pawle (1956), p.43

45lb petrol bomb – Hogben & MacBean (1990) p.66

'wholesale destruction' – Harris (1947), p.43

PWD formation – Banks (1946), p.29

Moody's Down Farm – later in the war this establishment would go on to become the principal proving ground for land-based flame weapons

Kroll Opera House – Stafford (1997), p.196

Das Engellandlied – Baird (1974), p.121

'The whole German …' Liddell (2005), p.86 (diary entry 13 July 1940)

German Embassy – Colville (1985), p.232 (diary entry 22 July 1940)

'A landing in …' Jodl, Nuremberg Documents IMT 1776-PS (1946)

'Rundstedt did not take …' Blumentritt (1952), pp.86–7

'Hitler did not want …' Manstein (1955), pp.153 & 169

sewerage system – IWM, 77/101

'Apart from a …' Banks (1946), p.33; TNA, CAB 63/171. Flame Over Britain seems to be an extract from a longer memoir planned by Banks called Across the Channel, itself preserved in rough manuscript at the IWM, 77/101/1

eight or nine Static Flame Traps – TNA, CAB 63/170

Hastings barrage – Dundee Courier, 5 June 1945; Western Morning News, 4 June 1945

St Margaret's barrage – author correspondence with Bernard Kimpton, 1992

'The burning beach …' White (1955), pp.16–17

Flame Fougasse – Banks (1946), pp.34–8. The Flame Fougasse spawned a litter of variants. Essentially the same as the Fougasse proper, the Demi-Gasse was instead sited in the open, and on ignition spread flame over 36 square yards. The Hedge-Hopper took the form of an upended drum with a charge set off-centre beneath it. Hidden and fired behind a convenient hedge or wall, the device could spring 10ft into the air, there to descend upon a passing column in a cascade of flame. There was even a Cliff-Hopper for use in certain elevated locations, notably St Margaret's Bay

'We are struggling …' TNA, CAB 63/171 (letter dated 9 August 1940)

'not at all …' TNA, CAB 63/171 (letter dated 15 August 1940)

'Admiralty flares …' Banks (1946), p.41

Thirty-five minutes/300 yards – TNA, CAB 63/172

'The psychological effect …' author correspondence with Bernard Kimpton, August 1992

'It was a glorious …' Banks (1946), p.41

'vast fires' – Aberdeen Journal, 26 August 1940

'I do not …' Baker White (1956), p.17

'the most widely …' Garnett (2002), p.214

'That the British ...' Garnett (2002), p.214

'Before the rumour ...' Baker White (1955), pp.18–19

Kelly/Red Cross – Kelly (1952), pp.271–4; North (2012), pp.18–20

'A story which ...' TNA, CAB 63/172 p.6 (telegram dated 27 August 1940)

'show' – Banks (1946), p.41

Charing flyer – Baker White (1956), p.19

'One early solution ...' Schenk (1990), p.140

'The *Kriegsmarine* reached ...' Ansel (1960), pp.244–5

'oil fires' Ansel (1960), p.278

'... extra investigation' Ansel (1960), p.245

'I am convinced ...' Baker White (1956), p.15

wooden rivets – TNA, FO 898/69 (sib dated 3 November 1940)

200 sharks – Garnett (2002), pp.214–15

'The vast majority ...' Garnett (2002), p.214. By comparison with lurid Allied
    propaganda of the Great War, much of the British effort in 1940 was anodyne.
    One rumour held that the German Army cooked food with fat rendered from
    condemned animal carcasses, triggering an epidemic of sore throats. Another
    told that foreign female workers entering Germany were obliged to have their
    heads shaved, this on the pretext that they might be carrying lice, but in fact
    because the thousand-year Reich now found itself desperately short of string.
    Scandinavian seamen leaving their ships at Lisbon, it was whispered, had been
    quietly murdered by Nazi agents. Somewhat fancifully, an Irish trawler fishing
    off Inishbofin was alleged to have dredged up an anchor from a Spanish
    Armada galleon wrecked in 1588, a timely discovery given contemporary
    spin as a 'relic of a former invasion that failed'. See: sore throats – TNA, FO
    898/69, sib dated 3 November 1940; female workers – TNA, FO 898/69, sib
    dated 8 May 1941; Scandinavian seamen – TNA, FO 898/69, sib/letter dated
    23 September 1940; Spanish anchor – *Aberdeen Journal* on 4 October 1940

Arthur Owens – Hayward (2013), p.141. Owens transmitted about Tommy
    guns on 26 July and 14 August 1940, and about 'super landmine adapted for
    marine use' on 22 July 1940

SUMMER/TATE – see generally Hayward (2013)

Tommy/1,500 rounds – *Aberdeen Journal*, 10 July 1940

'Home defence ...' Hayward (2013), p.150. Signal dated 14 August 1940.
    Unfortunately Snow signal traffic after 31 August 1940 seems not to have
    been preserved

'typically from selected ...' Howe (1982), p.47

George Thomson – Thomson (1947), p.73

Chapter 3
OPERATION LUCID

'most pleasing results' TNA, PREM 3/264

'The difficulty of ...' TNA, WO 193/734

Suffolk/petroleum barge – Banks (1946), p.48

'consuming itself ...' TNA, CAB 63/171 (report by H.W.Wildish)

'mystery VC' *Derby Daily Telegraph*, 10 March 1932

'Every effort was ...' TNA, PREM 3/264

'asked to volunteer' email letter to author from Richard T.G. Greenland dated
   7 April 2003.'I found myself in sole "charge" of a very dispirited and oil-
   drenched crew, and failed on three occasions to direct *Mytilus* into Boulogne.'

'We did so ...' Agar (1959), p.262

'Those four weeks ...' Apps quoted by Levine (2007)

'Make enquiries whether ...' TNA, PREM 3/264

'I explained the ...' Agar (1959), p.264

'By this time ...' Fell quoted in Agar (1959), p.267

Lucid II – TNA, PREM 3/264 (correspondence dated 17 February 1941)

'Looking back on ...' Agar (1959), pp.269–70

'Much of their ...' TNA, ADM 199/687 (document dated 8 January 1941)

Brooke/barrages – TNA, ADM 199/687 (document dated 26 December 1940)

Brooke/gas – Alanbrooke (2001), diary entry 22 July 1940

'various fiery forms ...' Banks (1946), p.53

coconut matting – TNA, CAB 63/171

'The sea erupted ...' McKee (1960), pp.203–4

Chapter 4
'BEACHES BLACK WITH BODIES'

'For two days ...' letter from Pat Barnes to Anglia TV dated 23 June 1992

'A convoy of ...' White (1955), pp.21–2

'There are plenty ...' White (1955), p.22

20th Flotilla – Roskill (1954), p.334

'not to lack ...' author interview in July 2002 with Lieutenant Thomas
   Waterhouse, then navigating officer on board HMS *Intrepid*, one of the five
   destroyers from the 20th Flotilla at sea that night

'after dinner the ...' Colville (1985), p.277

Texel casualty lists – *The Times*, 13 September 1940

'I was asked …' letter from Don Tate to Anglia TV dated 24 June 1992

'at an East Coast …' *Dundee Courier*, 6 September 1940

'part of a task …' Brown (1998), p.60 (diary entry 8 September 1940)

HMS Sturgeon – *Daily Mail*, 21 September 1940 (the supposed sinking was on 2 September 1940)

Cromwell – Hinsley (1979), p.185

'state of readiness' Alanbrooke (2001), p.105 (diary entry 7 September 1940)

MI6/Cromwell – Liddell (2005), p.93 (diary entry 7 September 1940)

'Rather falsely alarming …' Stephens (2000), p.134

Dungeness – Hayward (2013), pp.155–6

'The general German …' TNA, KV2/13 (Sjoerd Pons file), interrogation report dated 6 September 1940; see also Liddell (2005), p.93 (diary entry 6 September 1940)

'This made it …' Liddell (2005), p.94 (diary entry 8 September 1940)

'two main invasion …' Alanbrooke (2001), p.105 (diary entry for 8 September 1940)

Newport/Dover – Hayward (2003), p.144

92 aircraft – Middlebrook & Everitt (1985)

Daily Mirror – the issue for 3 September 1940 quoted a report from the *Svenska Morgenblatt* paper in Sweden, which quoted two Swedish businessmen lately returned from a trade fair in Leipzig: 'There is a recurrent rumour among the people that crack German troops have already landed in Britain.' A description that hardly matches the four invasion spies landed near Dungeness

Isle of Wight – on 30 September 1940 the tabloid *Daily Herald* (later re-branded as the *Sun*) reported wild rumours that the Isle of Wight had been overrun: 'The story of the mythical invasion has been growing and growing. It is being said now that there were nearly 5,000 island casualties when the invaders came.'

'The landing of …' *Yorkshire Post and Leeds Intelligencer*, 29 August 1940

'battle of the barges' Gibson (1946), Chapter 8

10 September – Winterbotham (1974), p.79

11 September etc. – Hinsley (1979), p.185

Great Moon Hoax – *New York Sun*, 25 August 1835 etc.

Poe/balloon hoax – *New York Sun*, 13 April 1844

'Revelation of an …' *New York Sun*, 11 September 1940

'I wonder if …' Last (1981), p.73 (diary entry for 12 September 1940)

'Tales begin to …' Brown (1981), p.120 (diary entry for 12 September 1940)

'I think by ...' TNA, CAB 63/172 (letter Morton to Hankey, 4 September 1940).
In a letter to Geoffrey Lloyd dated 2 September 1940, Hankey described the
contents of the Kelly telegram as 'rather amusing' before continuing: 'It so
chances that on most of the few occasions which we have demonstrated the
burning of oil on the sea or the sands, the Germans have come over. We also
did it once in sight of the French coast.'

Churchill flame speech – 11 September 1940 broadcast, available on YouTube

'All your work ...' Kelly (1952), p.277 (telegram dated 7 January 1941). In his memoir
Kelly admits to undertaking 'intelligence and propaganda activities' in Berne, but
makes no mention of the flame story, or Canaris, or the admiral's mistress.

'The Germans have ...' *Daily Mirror*, 14 September 1940

Bove/memoir – Bove (1956)

alarm and despondency – a point made by Thomson (1947), p.73

'Invasion is expected ...' Hodgson (1976), diary entry 14 September 1940

'What is the secret ...' Brown (1998), p.61 (diary entry 13 September 1940)

'I hear from ...' Perry (1972), p.134

Mass Observation – see Addison & Crang (2010), pp.425–33, reports dated 16 to
18 September 1940. On Scotland see also Brown (1998), pp.61–2 (diary entry
15 September 1940)

'we heard reports ...' Graves (1943), p.197

'There is no ...' *Daily Telegraph*, 16 September 1940

'The news coming ...' Shirer (1941), p.504 (diary entry 16 September 1940)

'British informants ...' *New York Times*, 17 September 1940

'Great things are ...' quoted in *Daily Mirror*, 18 September 1940

'Still no invasion ...' Brooke quoted in Bryant (1957), p.219

'until further notice' Wheatley (1958), p.89

Das Engellandlied – Baird (1974), p.133

'I was struck ...' Winterbotham (1974), p.81

'PM becoming ...' Colville (1985), p.288 (diary entry 20 September 1940)

'Thousands of German ...' *Daily Mirror*, 18 September 1940

'mild hurricane' Alanbrooke (2001), diary entry for 17 September 1940: 'Still no
invasion. And today a mild hurricane should be stirring up the Channel well.'

'There was a rumour ...' *Western Morning News*, 18 September 1940.

Cardozo – *Daily Mail*, 24 September 1940

official sources in London – *New York Sun*, 24 September 1940

Sicherheitsdienst/60,000 – Balfour (1979), p.192, citing *Meldungen aus dem Reich*,
a collection of SD weekly summary reports edited by Heinz Boberach in 1965
(at 7-x)

'But the British ...' *Daily Express*, 27 September 1940 (the report by Kenneth Downs, former Paris correspondent of the International News Service, was 'learned from a foreign observer why received eye-witness corroboration of the event')

'more American ...' *Eastern Daily Press*, 21 September 1940

Midlands stunt – Hayward (2003), p.65; Hayward (2013), p.149

'Each time I ...' Thomson (1946), p.74

'It was the ...' Thomson (1946), p.73. According to Thomson, the ban on reporting the invasion story at home was due to 'ticklish circumstances' (p.73), and the need to avoid spreading 'alarm and despondency' among the civilian population, a criminal offence under Emergency Powers Order number 938. In seeking to explain himself, however, Thomson found himself dancing on the head of a pin. 'We were not discouraging the circulation of this rumour in Germany. It was even contained in a pamphlet dropped over Germany by the RAF.' (p.71)

Russians in England – Hayward (2002), Chapter 2; Thomson (1946), p.73; White (1955), p.21

'Many things were ...' Firmin (1950), foreword by Thomson

'It began with ...' Royde Smith (1941), pp.78–9

Sandwich Bay – Thompson (1966), pp.233–4; White (1955), p.22; Hayward (2003), pp.144–5

'I suppose you've ...' Hodson (1941), p.330

Southampton – Klemmer (1941), p.188

'The fact is ...' quoted by Thomson (1947), p.70

'report the currency ...' TNA, WO 166/448

'an impenetrable ...' TNA, WO 166/1038

'It has been ...' TNA, WO 166/957 (document dated September 1940). Curiously, some within the British propaganda community were equally mystified. As late as 26 September, the Planning and Broadcasting Committee within Department EH declared itself unable 'to obtain the truth about the story of the sinking of 60,000 picked German invasion troops'. This surprising lack of knowledge tends to suggest that some within MI6 and the Foreign Office attached little importance to work being conducted at Woburn. See TNA, FO 989/8

William Robinson – BBC television programme *First Hand: The Finest Hour*, broadcast 22 November 1957; *Daily Mail*, 22 November 1957

'The body of ...' *The Times*, 22 October 1940. Six years later it was reported that a 'box of German ammunition' had been uncovered by holidaymakers on the beach at Littlestone – see *Taunton Courier and Western Advertiser*, 29 June 1946

Somerset Light Infantry – TNA, WO 166

BBC – Knight (1990), quoting diary entry by Mary Smith on 22 October 1940

'An examination of …' *Folkestone, Hythe and District Herald,* 26 October 1940

Heinrich Poncke – unfortunately identification is not entirely straightforward.

The death certificate issued by the registrar for the district of Romney Marsh on 24 October 1940 gives his name as Heinrich Poucke, aged about 27, as does the official registry of deaths for the period September to December 1940. Presumably this information came from the *Wehrpass* or *Soldbuch* found on the body (if this paper document survived several days or weeks in the water) and/or a metal identity disc (which generally gave details of unit, soldier number and blood type, but no name). The death certificate gives Poucke's unit as 'German Infantry Tank Defence Reserve Co. No. 19' and the cause of death as 'due to war operations'. In a letter to the author dated 5 February 2015, the Deutsche Dienstelle for the Notification of Relatives of the Fallen of the Former German Wehrmacht (aka WASt) stated that the death was formally notified by Britain to Germany only on 14 January 1942, by which time the spelling of the surname had somehow changed from Poucke to Poncke. His remains were moved from New Romney to Cannock Chase in December 1962, where the grave registration and headstone (Block 1, Row 5, Grave 151) also read Poncke. This confusion might be explicable as a simple spelling or administrative error, save that the *Deutsche Dienstelle* can find no record of any Heinrich Poucke or Poncke serving in the German Army at this time, nor can they make any sense of the unit identification stated on the British death certificate. In any event, the unit specified on an ID disc would normally be the first unit the holder was posted to, which was not necessarily the same unit they were serving in when killed

cutting-out operation – Foynes (1994), p.275

'Shortly before dawn …' Baker White (1955), pp.19–20

defeatist broadcasts – Garnett (2002), pp.164–5

'When we were …' White (1955), p.124

Glyndwr Michael – Hayward (2003), Chapter 9

John Charteris – Hayward (2003), p.127

Lewis Namier – Hayward (2003), p.94

Chapter 5
'THE STORY THAT IS SWEEPING AMERICA' (AND SWITZERLAND)

British Security Co-ordination – see generally West (1998); Jeffrey (2010), p.440–41; Mahl (1998); *New York Times*, 3 February 1989

International Building – BSC was situated on the 35th and 36th floors

'A man of …' quoted by Hyde (1962)

'The procurement of …' quoted in Hyde (1962), p.35

William Donovan – Waller (2011); Jeffrey (2010), pp.441–3; Hyde (1962), pp.34–7

'What's there to …' this is how some British papers (*Western Daily Press*, 14 November 1940) reported 'off the record' comments made by Kennedy to *The Boston Globe*

Tyler Kent – Stafford (1997), pp.177–80

A Man Called Intrepid – the reliability (or otherwise) of this biography is discussed by Nigel West in his expose *Counterfeit Spies* (1998)

procurement agents/aircraft – Tooze (2006), pp.405–6

'Because he was …' Ford (1971), p.91

'Much of what …' West (1983), pp.204–5

'a German invasion …' *Derby Daily Telegraph*, 10 August 1940

'If the picture …' TNA, CAB 65/10, War Cabinet minutes for 2 December 1940

'It was like …' *The Times*, 23 September 1940; *Sunderland Daily Echo*, 21 September 1940

'I give Britain …' *Dundee Courier*, 18 September 1940 via Press Association

American press agency – TNA, FO 898/69, document on 'Rumours' dated 7 February 1942

'This highly mechanised …' forward by Fleming in Hyde (1962)

'rendered service of …' West (1998), p.20

'Mr Solberg said …' *New York Sun*, 20 September 1940. Repeated in the *New York Times* and many British papers the following day

Robert Solborg - Smith (1972), pp.37–8

'I was surrounded …' Bove (1956), p.222

propaganda punch – see Knightley (1982), p.212

'important rules' West (1998), p.111

'Nazi dead said to …' *New York Times*, 29 September 1940

'Nazi losses seen in …' *New York Times*, 21 September 1940

'Letter to the editor …' *New York Times*, 20 October 1940

'Thousands of Nazi ...' *Daily Express*, 17 October 1940

'At dawn ...' *New York Sun*, 7 October 1940

'Channel losses denied ...' *New York Times*, 26 September 1940; *Chicago Tribune*, 26 September 1940. The original AP wire was dated 25 September 1940

'most reliable source' Colville (1985), pp.290–92 (diary entry 22 September 1940)

'queer stories' TNA, CAB 63/172 (letter Hankey to Morton, 12 September 1940)

'current everywhere ...' TNA, CAB 63/172 (telegram from Kelly dated 6 September 1940, in which Kelly noted a reluctance on the part of German troops 'to face the Channel crossing partly owing to stories such as that regarding oil, reported in my telegram No. 790, which is current everywhere')

'favourable' TNA, CAB 63/172 (letter Morton to Hankey, 4 September 1940)

'steady and consuming ...' WSC speech broadcast on 9 September 1940

'The stories there ...' Shirer (1941), pp.505–6. (diary entry 18 September 1940)

submarine scheme – via the 'latrinogram' the same rumour reached British prisoners of war held captive in Germany. 'There was a fine crop about the supposed invasion of England,' noted the camp diary kept by a Major E. Booth of the Royal Engineers. 'That 80,000 Germans had attempted to land and had been drowned in the Wash; that a strong naval attacking force had been completely routed by the skill of our own submarines which had spread oil on the sea around it and had then set fire to the oil.' Quoted in Rolf (1988), p.68

'partly owing ...' TNA, CAB 63/172 (telegram from Kelly dated 6 September 1940)

'Evidently your ...' TNA, CAB 63/172, memo DM to MH dated 13 September 1940

'short invasion phrasebook' reproduced in Banks (1946). A letter from Desmond Morton to Geoffrey Lloyd dated 24 February 1941 (IWM 85/49/6) suggests that the phrasebook had been dropped only 'recently', although other sources indicate 1940

'Crude stuff ...' Delmer (1962), p.20

Lucy spy ring – see generally Tarrant (1995)

Hans Bernd Gisevius – Jeffrey (2010), p.381; West (1983), pp.116–17

MI6/Szymanska – West (1983), pp.116–17; Jeffrey (2010), pp.380–1; Garlinski (1981), pp.90–1

'This tale first …' TNA, CAB 63/172 (telegram dated 27 August 1940). Bovet
    Grisel is probably Richard Bovet-Grisel, a Swiss writer and commentator

Bletchley Park – Smith (2004), pp.48–9

Paul Thümmell – Jeffrey (2010), pp.398–99

McCarthy/Ritter – Hayward (2013), pp.142–46

'extremely exaggerated …' TNA, KV 2/444–453

'His whole visit …' Liddell (2005), p.89 (diary entry 20 August 1940)

'subterranean' Jeffrey (2010), p.342–43

Wendell Willkie – Mahl (1998), chapter 8

Tyler Kent – Stafford (1997), p.178

Air Ministry news bulletin – *Hull Daily Mail*, 18 October 1940; Air Ministry
    Bulletin No. 2028 dated 18 October 1940

'There was evidently …' Foster (2011), p.70 (diary entry for 18 October 1940)

'Authorised German sources …' *New York Times* and also *New York Sun*,
    18 October 1940, citing an AP wire of same date

'terrific' *New York Sun*, 7 October 1940

'burned' *Daily Telegraph*, 19 October 1940

Telegraph/deliberate leaks – see TNA, FO 898/69, letter dated
    23 September 1940

'4,000 German patients …' *The Cornishman*, 23 October 1940

War Illustrated – 1 November 1940

glut of propaganda – Cruickshank (1977), p.109

William Whitney – Waller (2011), p.73; Garnett (2002), pp.119–22

'main purpose' Liddell (2005), p.196 (diary entry 20 November 1940)

'press and propaganda' Liddell (2005), p.196 (diary entry 20 November 1940)

'All this stuff …' *Dover Express*, 8 November 1940

Knox/gas – *Yorkshire Post and Leeds Intelligencer*, 1 February 1941

Shoeburyness barrage – TNA, CAB 63/170

'We drove ahead …' Banks (1946), pp.41–2

Zass/condoms – author correspondence with Bernard Kimpton, ex PWD, 1992

Chapter 6
FLAMING TO VICTORY

'mystery' *Sunderland Daily Echo*, 20 December 1940; *Aberdeen Journal*,
    21 December 1940; *Evening Telegraph*, 7 December 1940 and
    21 December 1940

Churchill/Donovan lunch – Stafford (1997), p.204

'After my last …' *Sunderland Daily Echo*, 20 December 1940

Compiegne – Knightley (1982), p.213

'uncensored account' Shirer (1941), dustjacket blurb

600,000 copies – Wick (2011), p.225

'the Germans have …' Shirer (1941), p.504 (diary entry 16 September 1940)

'the stories were …' Shirer (1941), pp.505–6 (diary entry 18 September 1940)

'wounded soldiers' Shirer (1960), p.773

'no fighting anywhere …' Shirer (1960), p.773

original typescript – contained in Shirer Papers, George T. Henry College Archives, Coe College, Cedar Rapids, Iowa. These issues are discussed in detail by Michael Strobl of the University of Berne in *Writings of History: Authenticity and Self-Censorship in William L. Shirer's Berlin Diary*, an article printed in German Life & Letters 66, 3 July 2013

'flyers' etc. original journal entries held at Coe College

'rendered service of …' West (1998), p.20

'The Nazis sprayed …' undated *Daily Telegraph* cutting from 1941 preserved in TNA, CAB 63/174

'In his desperation …' *Daily Mail*, 19 February 1941

Greece/April – *The Times*, 25 April 1941 (Axis claims that 30,000 Allied troops died at sea during the evacuation of Greece)

'In mid-September …' Spaight (1941), p.95

'One particular series …' Spaight (1941), pp.214–15

'stopped' Thomson (1947), p.73

book censorship – Knightley (1982), p.222 (fn)

'On or about …' Moen (1941), p.163. Little biographical information about Lars Moen is known. He may be the same Lars Moen as listed on www.imdb.com who was born (1901) and died (1951) in the United States, and is credited as a film editor on two British productions: *The Bells* (1931) and *Two White Arms* (1932)

faked landing film – Moen (1941), p.161

Reg Thompson – Chelmsford Chronicle, 19 September 1941

Ralph Ingersoll – Thomson (1947), p.87; West (1998), p.20

Klemmer/Kennedy – *The Independent*, 31 July 1992

Klemmer/Liddell – Liddell (2005), p.86 (diary entry 16 July 1940)

Klemmer/Sussex – *Dundee Courier*, 22 August 1940

'One thing which …' Klemmer (1941), p.189

'It seems that …' Klemmer (1941), p.270 (US edition)

'well-known American …' Thomson (1947), p.87

Charles M. Barbe – text of talk preserved in Chatham House archive, now transferred to TNA, RIIA/8/812 Apr 9 1942

'An American broadcaster …' Thomson (1947), p.71

The Man Who Never Was – see generally Macintyre (2010)

Signal/Brittany *flammensperre* – a copy of the Signal article was received by Geoffrey Lloyd and the PWD at the end of July 1943 – see IWM 85/46/11. That Germany had no fuel for flame barrages was noted in passing by a few papers at the end of the war, including the *Daily Dispatch* for 5 June 1945

'describe the character …' etc. Hansard, 29 July 1943 (pp.1770–01) (oral answers)

'Surely every member …' *Lancashire Evening Post*, 29 July 1943. *The Lion Roared Its Defiance*, a privately printed Home Guard memoir issued in 1944, recalled of 15 September 1940 that 'charred bodies of German soldiers were washed to the southern and eastern shores', adding in the light of Adams' Commons question that 'the events of that night may never be fully disclosed.

'in broad terms' etc. Hansard, 20 June 1944 (pp.22–2) (oral answers)

Adams/Gunwalloe – *Dundee Courier*, 14 August 1951

FIDO – Banks (1946), Chapter 7

PLUTO - Banks (1946), Chapter 8

Studland Bay – Banks (1946), pp.42–3

March 1941/50 miles – TNA, CAB 63/173 (document dated 11 March 1941)

barrage locations – a report by General Alan Brook dated 31 July 1941 (TNA, WO/193/374) lists only Studland Bay (200 yards), Deal (520 yards) and Rye (400 yards). Banks (1946) at p.46 also suggests sea flame barrages at Dover and St Margaret's Bay, but these seem to have been large beach barrages rather than true sea flame barrages. Meanwhile, mystery surrounds the large installation at Hastings, demolished in 1945. See also IWM documents 77/101/1

'Our biggest problem …' author correspondence with Bernard Kimpton, 1992

Crocodiles – Fletcher (2007)

Official Secrets Act – Wilson (1956), p.36

execution – Wilson (1956), p.60

'It was our …' quoted in Neillands (2002), p.166

'Ever since his …' Wilson (1956), pp.122–3

'A man in a …' *Daily Express*, 26 August 1944

'Often Mr Lloyd …' *Evening Telegraph*, 28 August 1944

'several hundred miles' *Daily Telegraph*, 5 June 1945

'millions of gallons …' *Daily Express*, 4 June 1945

'It made them ...' Delmer (1962), pp.218–19

'neither damage to ...' Winterbotham (1974), p.17

'I have since ...' *Reynolds News*, 16 May 1954. Apparently replaced on p.21 of *The Big Lie* by innocuous wording about conversations with 'ex-Wehrmacht officers' who had believed rumours of a failed invasion attempt

five deceptions – one other may have been the statement that 185 German aircraft were destroyed on 15 September 1940

Chapter 7
THE MEN WHO NEVER WERE

'While we were ...' letter W.A. Birkbeck to Anglia TV, 20 June 1992

'Thousands of German ...' *News of the World*, 1 October 1944

'One day I saw ...' *East Anglian Daily Times*, 13 June 1992; author correspondence with AM between June and September 1992

German Army medical service – Bundesarchiv, letter to author 9 September 1992

'noteworthy casualties' Ansel (1960), p.245. Rear Admiral Walter C. Ansel was a recently retired US Navy officer who undertook a study of Operation Sealion funded by the US Naval Academy's Forrestal Fellowship, and canvassed senior German naval personnel directly involved with the operational planning for Sealion

BBC – *Daily Mail*, 22 November 1957

Parris/safe to revive – e.g. the Signal photospread from 1943

'ammo and petrol ...' *Sunday Post*, 29 October 1944

'He gave me ...' quoted by Thomson (1940), p.73. Thomson does not identify the paper precisely but the Bognor Regis witness was mentioned by the *Daily Express* on 4 June 1945

'There were rumours ...' Gibson (1946), pp.105–6. The Antwerp raid to which Gibson referred was probably the large-scale operation on the night of 14–15 September

Geoffrey Lloyd press call – see generally papers in IWM 77/101/2

'biggest secret' *Daily Express*, 4 June 1945

'Wall of Fire ...' *Aberdeen Journal*, 2 June 1945

'Germans Burned Own ...' *Western Morning News*, 4 June 1945

'We on this ...' *Daily Telegraph*, 4 June 1945

'It always seemed ...' *The Times*, 4 June 1945. Sir Donald Banks also told the *Sunday Graphic* on 3 June 1945: 'Nazi planes snooped over at the crucial moment. They took a very frightened tale back to Germany.'

'History does not ...' *New York Times*, 5 June 1945

'Intelligence of these ...' IWM document 182.95; address by Banks on 4 October 1945

Joint Intelligence Committee – TNA, CAB 81, JIC (46) 89 (Final)

'It has been widely ...' Hansard 1946–47, Vol. 430, written answers, 18 November 1946. The same figure – 'about 36' – is referred to on p.53 of the Cabinet Office Historical Section volume on Defence Plans for the United Kingdom 1939–45 (TNA, CAB 44/47), which was itself part of the preparation for the Official History: The Defence of the United Kingdom 1939–1945

Sir William Dickson – TNA, CAB 79/52/14, minutes of CoS meeting on 10 October 1946. Dickson was then vice chief of the air staff and had no background in military intelligence

'During August ...' Churchill (1949), p.275

'350,000 ...' Bonaparte (1947), pp.109–17. Although the corpse collection story chimes with Gunner William Robinson, and a scheme to use Luftwaffe corpses is mentioned by White (1955) at p.124

'Wireless news ...' Waugh (1952), p.232

Weidenmann – letter to author dated 30 September 1992

Reinecker – letter to author dated 29 October 1992

Der Landser magazine – see Chapter 8

Peter Fleming – see Fleming (1957), chapters 7 and 13

'I helped to collect ...' *Daily Mail*, 22 November 1957

'But 1553826 ...' BBC *First Hand*, broadcast 22 November 1957

'Wondering whether ...' *Folkstone and Hythe Gazette*, 27 November 1957

Chapter 8
SHINGLE STREET

Orford Ness – see Kinsey (1981)

'fired up' TNA, CAB 63/170, letter Hankey to General Haining dated 31 July 1940

'lively intermittent ...' *Daily Telegraph*, 5 December 1914

'Part of the …'TNA, CAB 63/170, which contains a copy of the original report
    by the Oil Burning Committee dated 11 December 1914. Roskill (1974)
    states wrongly that the trial took place on the River Orwell

'They worked for …'TNA, CAB 63/170, letter Hankey to General Haining
    dated 31 July 1940

'on the cards' Johnson (1978), p.142

'attempt to invade …' Anglia TV news bulletin, 17 June 1992

'delightful retreat' *Ipswich Journal*, 30 June 1877; 18 May 1880

5 of 7 coastguards – *Daily Herald*, 4 May 1914

'That curious period …' Martin (1952), p.349

lost patrol story – Johnson (1992), pp.125–6. Absent from the original version of
    the book published in 1978

'I never heard …' author correspondence with Tom Abram, October 1992

127,000 – Collier (1957), p.144

'Dear Sir …'TNA, letter preserved in file HO 207/1175

'Our platoon …' letter Tom Abram to *Daily Telegraph*, 7 April 1992 (not printed)

Heinkel 111 – *After the Battle*, issue #84 (1994); TNA, WO 166/1038, WO
    166/329

Ronald Harris – author interview, 1992

'14.50 Enemy troops …'TNA, presumably WO 166/1038 (copy document
    circulated in 1992 as part of MoD Army Historical Branch report)

Alun Lewis – in 2015 poet Blake Morrison also published an east coast
    collection, simply titled *Shingle Street*

'Received a letter …'TNA, WO 166/1038. Brief details of the CDRE trial
    at Shingle Street are located in the following TNA files: WO 189/2385
    (Chemical Defence Experimental station: half-yearly report for October–
    December 1942) and WO 189/2446 (Chemical Defence Experimental
    station: half-yearly report for January–June 1943), both released to TNA
    in 2006

'Suitable evacuated …'TNA, HO 207/1175

Plan Y – Harris & Paxman (1982), pp.109–15; Thomas (1985), pp.52–5

Hankey/biological warfare – Hankey was involved as early as 1940, see Liddell
    (2005), p.76

Gruinard/1942 – Harris & Paxman (1982), pp.68–73

borstal – originally a labour colony, then an open borstal. Pre-war inmates included
    Brendan Behan, who described his time at Hollesley in *Borstal Boy* (1958)

Nora Pierce Butler – *Guardian*, 6 August 1974; *East Anglian Daily Times* (EADT),
    7 August 1974

Percy Darvell – *Evening Star*, 12 March 1992; *EADT*, 13 March 1992; author interview with Darvell in 1992

Barnes Wallis – in a letter to the author dated 31 July 1995, the CBDE stated that they were unaware of any work undertaken for Porton Down by Barnes Wallis. His personal papers are held by the Science Museum and are available for public inspection. The Dambusters raid took place after the CDRE trial at Shingle Street, not before, and Wallis was not a famous public figure at this time. Quite why the photo kept by Darvell was taken is unclear, and even if Wallis is indeed the man pictured then Darvell is unlikely to have appreciated his importance at the time

Tallboy – Heazell (2010)

Gruinard/1942 – Harris & Paxman (1982), p.71; TNA, DEFE 55/119. The tests on Gruinard in September 1942 also included tests with 'disintegrating' 20mm Hispano AP rounds charged with anthrax spores, intended to kill enemy AFV crews. The bomb casing used on Gruinard had been designed for liquid mustard, with the concentrated anthrax spores suspended in a thick brown sludge. Unfortunately, the bomb buried itself in a peat bog, and so the trial was repeated on estuary mudflats in South Wales in October and November. Of the Welsh test (which took place in the Burry estuary between Llanelli and the Gower Peninsula), a spokesman for the MoD told the BBC in 2009: 'The Gower coast was often used for munitions testing during WWII. However, a bacterial weapon was only tested once, in 1942, when a 30-lb bomb charged with anthrax spores was dropped from a Blenheim aircraft at 5,000ft. There was no residual contamination of the site as it was washed by the incoming tide. No other biological weapons trial was done at Penclawdd and no other species of bacteria were used.' Source: http://news.bbc.co.uk/1/hi/wales/south_west/8334592.stm and TNA, DEFE 55/120. Following these tests, and more dead sheep, the contaminated island of Gruinard remained off limits until 1990. In a letter to the author dated 4 February 2015, DSTL Porton Down stated that there was no connection between these anthrax trials and the bomb testing at Shingle Street

'At this rate …' *Daily Mail*, 10 April 1964. Erosion problems caused by shingle extraction had been noted as early as 1880 – see *Ipswich Journal* 18 May 1880

79th Armoured Div – see Fulter (1974); Doherty (2011); *Guardian*, 5 August 1974

'A small bungalow …' TNA, HO207/1175, undated 1945 report by coastguard to regional HQ

'busy and prosperous …' Archie White, *Tideways and Byways in Essex and Suffolk* (1948)

'A sea-bathing ...' Scarfe (1960), pp.59–61

'Officials responsible ...' *EADT*, 3 August 1974

'I cannot understand ...' *Sun*, 6 August 1974

'The military ...' *Sun*, 6 August 1974

Guardian – *Guardian*, 5 August 1974

'fragmentation' *Guardian*, 6 August 1974

'Until now I ...' *EADT*, 7 August 1974

'Another D-Day ...' *EADT*, 26 April 1984; *Evening Star*, 26 April 1984

PLUTO – *Western Morning News*, 24 May 1945

'major security ...' *Evening Star*, 26 April 1984

Derek Johnson – Johnson (1978), p.142. Subsequently, in 1989, Johnson claimed to have received a mysterious telephone call from an official called 'Mr Smith', politely warning him off further investigation of wartime events at Shingle Street. To their eternal regret, no other investigator has received such a call. For many years Johnson owned a militaria shop called Penny-farthing in Clacton-on-Sea, and was interviewed by this author in March 1992. By then, Johnson appeared fond of conspiracy theories and made anti-Semitic remarks. His contributions to the Shingle Street saga must be considered highly unreliable

'sowed with oil ...' *New York Times*, 15 December 1940

'A German force ...' author interview with John Rux-Burton, 4 April 1992; see also *EADT*, 10 March 1992. An email sent to JRB in 2014 elicited no reply. References to the Naval Intelligence Division raise the spectre of Ian Fleming and his superspy James Bond

'Wartime rumours ...' *Sunday Telegraph*, 5 April 1992. The author declares an interest here, having helped to research the article

'The really ...' *Sunday Telegraph*, 5 April 1992

Felixstowe – *EADT*, 6 June 1992

skeleton/borstal – human remains discovered on 8 June 1985

motorcycle raiders – letter to *Sunday Telegraph* from George ffoulkes, 3 May 1992

Brandenburg – *EADT*, 9 June 1992

guinea-pigs – *Sunday Sport*, 12 April 1992

RAF – *Evening Star*, 16 March 1992; 20 March 1992

79th/tragedy – *EADT*, 3 June 1992

Konrad Burg – *Der Landser*, issues 723 and 745 (circa 1960s) (blue editions). This author sourced a copy of Burg's article from Dr Peter Schenk in Germany and copied it to Johnson in confidence; Johnson immediately released it to the media as his own discovery. *Der Landser* translates as 'The Squaddie'. The controversial magazine finally ceased publication in 2013

'Invasion Met Fire ...' *Evening Star* (Woodbridge), 8 June 1992

'Nazi Landing Attempt ...' *EADT*, 8 June 1992

Ipswich/crematorium – author interview with Derek Johnson, 23 March 1992; BBC *Breakfast News*, 24 April 1992

'Near Ipswich ...' *Sunday Sport*, 12 April 1992

Viz – undated issue, 1992

'attempted to invade ...' Anglia TV news, 17 June 1992

John Gummer – *EADT*, 27 May 1992

Jamie Cann – *EADT*, 7 July 1992

'openess' the so-called Waldegrave Initiative on early PRO releases was announced on 25 June 1992

'Veil lifted ...' *Daily Telegraph*, 7 July 1992

'relentless campaign' *EADT*, 8 July 1992

opening of HO files at PRO – the author was present on the day on behalf of Anglia TV news

'raided in an official ...' Anglia TV news, 7 July 1992

'Secret File Deepens ...' *EADT*, 8 July 1992

'I think there ...' Cann quoted on Anglia TV, 7 July 1992

'There is no ...' MoD Army Historical Branch report ('summary of events'), sent by Cranborne to Cann under cover of a letter dated 17 July 1992 reference D/US of S/RMC 543. Cann also met with Cranborne. In May 2015, the AHB confirmed that the summary was the work of a single author

'The truth is ...' *Daily Telegraph*, 20 July 1992

There is no ...' Gummer interviewed on Anglia TV, July 1992

The Times/thirty-year rule – *The Times*, 15 August 1992

'It's like UFOs ...' *EADT*, 30 July 1992

internet – see for example the highly derivative work of the late Ronald Ashford, archived at www.shford.fslife.co.uk/ShingleSt/index.html?detail=overview

1994 – my first book on the subject was *Shingle Street: Flame, Chemical & Psychological Warfare in 1940, and the Nazi Invasion That Never Was* (CD41, 1994). A revised edition appeared in 2001, under the title *The Bodies on the Beach: Sealion, Shingle Street and the Buring Sea Myth of 1940*. A condensed version of the 1940 story also forms Chapter 6 of *Myths & Legends of the Second World War*, published by Sutton in 2003. The novel *Shingle Street* (2002) is also my work

Peter Haining – Haining (2004). This author threatened legal action but Haining passed away not long after his book was published 'firefight' Anglia TV news, 8 July 2016. The claim was made by Ronald Ashford, who admits that he was never present in the village during the Second World War, yet still informed this author that he somehow 'saw it all'

accepted historical narrative – e.g. The Battle of Shingle Street (BBC Radio 4, January 2005); Gillies (2006); Rankin (2008); *The One Show* (BBC1, 24 October 2014)

'Like all good …' *Reynolds News*, 16 May 1954

'There was little …' *Reynolds News*, 16 May 1954

'The burning-sea …' White (1955), p.22

ACKNOWLEDGEMENTS

The author owes a particular debt of thanks to Christopher Elliott, Ronald Harris, Edwin Horlington, Hadrian Jeffs, Bernard Kimpton, Phillip Knightley, Michael Lucock, Robin Prior, Winston G. Ramsey, Dr Peter Schenk, Dr L.O. Standaert and Nigel West. Thanks are also due to the following historians: Correlli Barnett, Michael Bowyer, David Collyer, R. Douglas Brown, Max Hastings, F.H. Hinsley, Ian V. Hogg, Robert Jackson, Gordon Kinsey, Norman Longmate, James Lucas, Wing Commander John MacBean, Roger Morgan, David Rolf, James Rusbridger, Norman Scarfe, Neil R. Storey, Andy Thomas, Major T.I.J. Toler and Dennis Turner. And to the following journalists: Lindsay Brooke (Anglia TV), Christy Campbell (*The Sunday Telegraph*), Russell Cook (*EADT*), Henry Creagh (*EADT*), Jeremy Hands (Anglia TV), Lisa Hempelé (BBC TV), Malcolm Pheby (*EADT*) and David Weisbloom (*EADT*).

From The History Press, the author wishes to thank Katie Beard, Jo de Vries, Andrew Latimer and Michael Leventhal.

All National Archives (TNA) material is Crown Copyright and is reproduced with the permission of the Controller of Her Majesty's Stationery Office. All quotes from newspaper and television sources are reprinted with the kind permission of the editors concerned. All reasonable effort has been made to trace the copyright holders of material quoted in the text. Both the author and publisher welcome the opportunity to rectify any omissions brought to their attention.

Thanks are also due to the following museum staff: L. Ball (Commonwealth War Graves Commission), Terry Charman and Angela Wootton (Imperial War Museum), Commander P.R. Compton-Hall (RN Submarine Museum), P.J.V. Elliott and C. Richards (RAF Museum), I.D. Goode (Ministry of Defence

Whitehall Library), E. Harris (The Barnes Wallis Trust), Anita Hollier (BP Archive), Gunhild Muschenheim (Goethe Institute), Dr John Rhodes (Royal Engineers Museum) and Martin Sawyer and Jo Bandy (MoD Army Historical Branch).

And more generally to the Imperial War Museum, The National Archives, HM General Register Office, The British Library, Cambridge University Library, PA News Library, Norfolk County Libraries, Colchester Public Library, MoD Army Historical Branch, Bundesarchiv (Koblenz), Le Centre de Recherches et d'Études Historiques de la Seconde Guerre Mondiale (Brussels), Plaistow Press Ltd and Barnwell's Printers (Aylsham). Thanks also to Terry Burchell for his work on several of the illustrations.

Thanks also to the following writers and members of the public who took the time and trouble to contribute: Tom Abram, David Alexander, Stuart Bacon (Suffolk Underwater Studies Unit), Dr J.H. Bamberg, Terry Banham, Pat Barnes, K. Bathwest, W.A. Birkbeck, Francoise Le Boulanger, Peter Brackley, Major J.D. Braisby (Royal Artillery Museum), Andrew Burk, John Rux Burton, Winifred and Frank Buxton, Jamie Cann MP, Bruce Carter, Richard Challis, Nick Champion, Peter Constable, Len Cook, Peter Dachert, Percy Darvell, Christina Di Prima, Frank Dickinson, Jack Driscoll, Clive Dunn, G.H. Evans, Julian Foynes, Chief Superintendent P.A. Gell (Suffolk Constabulary), E.H. Gommo, Daphne Machin Goodall, Nicholas Green, Mr Grout, Sidney Gurton, George Ffoulkes, Hollis Fowler, William Hall, Olga Hardardottir (SIPRI), George Hearse, Beverley Hodgkinson, Regina Hoffman, J.H.D. Hooper, Doris Howes, Laura Humphreys, K. van Isacker, K.T. Hudson, Kenneth Jarmin, Peg and Eric Johnson, Tobin Jones, Rudiger Koschnitzki (Deutsches Institut für Filmkunde), E.C. Leslie, Peter Luther, R.J. Mabb, Agnes Mann, Mrs Marilyn Miles, Christiane Maubant (musées du Havre), D.J. Maxted, Eric Missant, Julian Morel, Frank North, Percy Nunn, T.H. Pimble, Reg Pollintine, Mrs P. Pulford, Herbert Reinecker, J. Rhodes (Royal Engineers Museum), Christopher Richford, G.W. Robertson, C.D. Robinson, Mr Seed, Edward Sharpin, L.R. Sidwell, Bill and Joy Sparks, T.E.A. Spong, J.V. Steward, Don Tate, Alberic De Tollenaere, T.H. Waterhouse, Alfred Weidenmann, Bryan Webb, D.V. Wells, Pamela Wilby, A.G. Williams and Ron Winton.

INDEX

185

Hankey, Lord Maurice
    as civil servant 14, 21, 129
    and MI5/MI6 review 21, 23
    as politician 19, 21, 27
    and PWD 19, 22, 26, 29, 31, 32, 33, 37,
        57, 80, 111
    and submarines 15, 17, 80
    and WW1 experiments 14, 15, 25, 122–3
Harris, Air Marshal Sir Arthur 32–3
Harwich 16, 127
Hastings 36, 115, 118
Higgins, Jack 100, 136
Hitler, Adolf
    death of 110
    and Operation Sealion 30, 33, 34–5, 48,
        55, 60, 72
    and peace offers 34
    and propaganda 41, 106
Hollesley 123–9, 130, 132, 134, 137, 139,
    149, 178
Home Guard 29, 30, 36–7, 41, 54, 59, 85,
    144–6
hospital trains 10, 91–3, 108–9, 116, 136
Huskinson, Air Commodore Patrick 129–
    30, 133
Hythe 9, 29, 54, 59, 66, 118, 120

Immingham 52
Imperial War Museum 111, 112
Ipswich 53, 58, 122, 127, 137, 138, 139, 140
Isle of Wight 33, 55, 102, 113, 114, 117, 167
Ivanhoe, HMS 52, 53

Kelly, Sir David 39–40, 57, 80, 82, 83, 113
Kennedy, Joseph 72, 86, 90, 96, 171
Kimpton, Bernard 37, 103
Klemmer, Harvey 96–7
Knox, Colonel Frank 74, 88

Landser, Der 115, 137
Langstone 49
Le Havre 62, 64, 117
League of Nations 18
Lend-Lease 72, 73
Lewis, Alun 128
Liddell, Guy 34, 54, 84, 97
Lifeboat Inn 122, 124, 129, 131, 137, 139, 141
Lindemann, Professor Frederick 27
Lisbon 39, 42, 58, 60, 76, 84, 93, 96, 165
Littlestone-on-Sea 10, 67, 110, 117, 118, 120,
    140
Livens, Colonel F.H. 29, 31, 36
Livens Projector 29, 32
Lloyd, Sir Geoffrey
    and flame warfare 21, 22, 26, 27, 28, 29,
        31, 33, 39, 134
    as Minister of Information 110, 112
    press conferences 104–5, 107, 110–11
Lody, Karl 64
London 7, 18, 20, 28, 36, 39, 42, 49, 53, 54,
    55, 57, 58, 60, 61, 62, 64, 65, 72, 76,
    79, 83, 85, 86, 90, 92, 96, 97, 99, 107,
    135, 138, 144, 145
Lucid, Operation 11, 43–9
Lucid II, Operation 48
Luftwaffe
    airmen 9, 16, 17, 40, 66, 67, 68, 119
    and Battle of Britain 59, 62, 72, 92, 93,
        97
    and Blitz 53, 61, 90
    and Eagle Day 38
    and Operation Sealion 28, 33, 34
    and propaganda 35, 63
    and PWD 31, 38, 39, 105

Manstein, Erich von 35
Martlesham Heath 126

If you enjoyed this book, you may also be interested in…

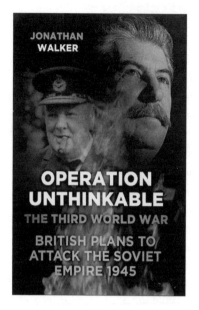

Operation Unthinkable

JONATHAN WALKER

978 0 7524 8718 2

As the war in Europe entered its final months, the world teetered on the edge of a Third World War. While Soviet forces hammered their way into Berlin, Churchill ordered British military planners to prepare the top-secret Operation Unthinkable – the plan for an Allied attack on the Soviet Union on 1 July 1945. Using US, British and Polish forces, the invasion would reclaim Eastern Europe.

The controversial plan called for the use of Nazi troops, and there was the spectre of the atomic bomb. Would yet another army make the fatal mistake of heading East? In *Operation Unthinkable* Jonathan Walker presents a haunting study of the war that nearly was. He outlines the motivations behind Churchill's plan, the logistics of launching a vast assault against an enemy who had bested Hitler, potential sabotage by Polish communists, and he speculates whether the Allies would have succeeded had the operation gone forward.

Well supported by a wide range of primary sources from the Churchill Archives Centre, Sikorski Institute, National Archives and Imperial War Museum, this is a fascinating insight into the upheaval as the Second World War drew to a close and former alliances were shattered. Operation Unthinkable became the blueprint for the Cold War.